SLAVE TRADE AND ABOLITION

Women in Africa and the Diaspora

STANLIE JAMES AND AILI MARI TRIPP

Founding Editors

SLAVE TRADE AND ABOLITION

Gender, Commerce, and Economic Transition
in Luanda

Vanessa S. Oliveira

THE UNIVERSITY OF WISCONSIN PRESS

The University of Wisconsin Press
728 State Street, Suite 443
Madison, Wisconsin 53706
uwpress.wisc.edu

Gray's Inn House, 127 Clerkenwell Road
London ECIR 5DB, United Kingdom
eurospanbookstore.com

Printed in the United States of America
This book may be available in a digital edition.

Library of Congress Cataloging-in-Publication Data

Names: Oliveira, Vanessa S., 1980- author.
Title: Slave trade and abolition : gender, commerce, and economic
transition in Luanda / Vanessa S. Oliveira.
Other titles: Women in Africa and the diaspora.
Description: Madison, Wisconsin : The University of Wisconsin Press, [2021] |
Series: Women in Africa and the diaspora | Includes bibliographical
references and index.
Identifiers: LCCN 2020020428 | ISBN 9780299325800 (cloth)
Subjects: LCSH: Slave traders—Angola—Luanda (Luanda)—History—19th
century. | Slave trade—Angola—Luanda (Luanda)—History—19th century. |
Women—Angola—Luanda (Luanda)—History—19th century. |
Luanda (Luanda, Angola)—Economic conditions—19th century. |
Luanda (Luanda, Angola)—History—19th century.
Classification: LCC HT1419.A5 O45 2021 | DDC 306.3/6209673209034—dc23
LC record available at https://lccn.loc.gov/2020020428

ISBN 9780299325848 (paperback)

To my parents,
VIRGÍNIA *and* VALMIR,

my husband,
ISAAC,

and our children,
MATTHEW *and* SOPHIA

Contents

Illustrations

FIGURES

MAPS

TABLES

Acknowledgments

The research that gave rise to this book was made possible by financial support from several institutions, including the Harriet Tubman Institute for Research on Africa and its Diasporas, the Social Sciences and Humanities Research Council of Canada, the Royal Military College of Canada, and the Caluste Gulbenkian Foundation in Lisbon.

I have had the good fortune of being trained by distinguished scholars in the fields of African history and the African diaspora. First and foremost, I owe a tremendous debt of gratitude to my mentors José C. Curto and Paul E. Lovejoy for their continuous intellectual stimulation and support and their commitment to my training as an Africanist scholar. Between 2016 and 2018, I held a Social Sciences and Humanities Research Council of Canada postdoctoral fellowship at the University of Toronto, which afforded me the time to revise the manuscript. I wish to thank Stephen Rockel for the exchange of ideas and his support for this project.

I am fortunate to have been able to count on the encouragement of many friends and colleagues. Tracy Lopes, Karlee Sapoznik, Gilberto Fernandes, Jeff Gunn, Katrina Keefer, Mariana Candido, Yacine Daddi Addoun, Feisal Farah, Leidy Alpizar, Nielson Bezerra, Bruno Véras, and Estevam Thompson made this journey much more enjoyable. A special thanks to Maria Cristina Fernandes, who kindly created the maps used in this book. Jelmer Vos, Moacir Maia, Solange Rocha, and Faustino Kusaka were crucial in helping me plan my trip to Luanda. The Telos family hosted me in their home in Luanda, and since then they have become my Bakongo family. Flora Telo offered me support and friendship that have lasted to this day. I am also grateful for the assistance of Simão Souindoula (in memoriam), Bruno Kambundo, João Lorenço, and Alexandra Aparício. In Lisbon, Carlos Almeida, Elza, and Amandio have always made my stay pleasant. In Brazil, Ton Ferreira, Marcos Santana, Edna

Nascimento, and Frank Rolin have proved that the distance is not able to break the bonds of friendship forged since we were undergraduate students. My colleagues in the Department of History at the Royal Military College of Canada have been a source of encouragement and intellectual motivation. I am blessed to work with such an incredible group of people.

We historians benefit enormously from the work done by the archivists and librarians who organize the material we use in our research. In Lisbon, I thank the personnel of the Arquivo Nacional da Torre do Tombo, Arquivo Histórico Ultramarino, and Biblioteca Nacional de Lisboa for their assistance. In Luanda, I want to express my gratitude to the librarians and archivists at the Arquivo Nacional de Angola and the Biblioteca Municipal de Luanda.

Mariana P. Candido, Tracy Lopes, Kathleen Sheldon, Joseph Miller (in memoriam), Suzanne Schwarz, Michele Johnson, Linda Heywood, and Stephen Rockel read earlier drafts of the manuscript and offered valuable criticisms. Roquinaldo Ferreira and Daniel Domingos da Silva shared materials and ideas about slavery and the slave trade in Angola. Maureen Garvie did an exceptional job in editing the manuscript.

Finally, I am grateful to my parents, Valmir and Virgínia, and my siblings, Valéria and Valdison, who have been a constant source of encouragement, care, and love. Most of all, I am deeply indebted to my husband, Isaac Choi, and our children, Matthew and Sophia. This book would not have been possible without their support and love.

SLAVE TRADE AND ABOLITION

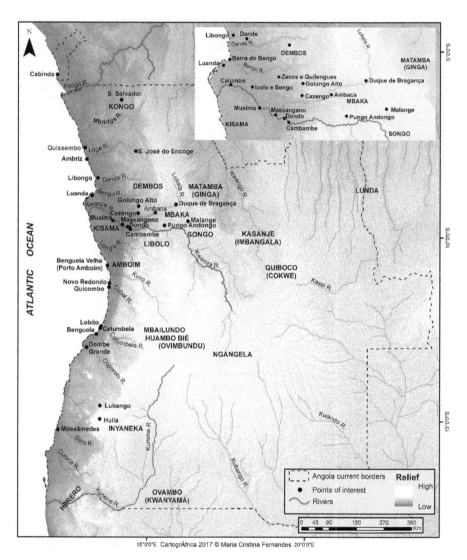

Map I.1. Mid-nineteenth-century Angola. Map by Maria Cristina Fernandes based on the author's data.

Introduction

THE PORTUGUESE TERRITORY of Angola was the place of departure for approximately 1.4 million enslaved Africans between 1801 and 1867. Of this total number, about 535,000 embarked from Luanda, continuing a pattern that made the city the most important Atlantic slaving port in the period of the transatlantic slave trade.[1] Although Luanda shared commonalities with other Atlantic slaving ports in Africa, it also presented some unique features. Luanda had been part of the Portuguese colony of Angola since the sixteenth century, while other West African ports remained under African sovereignty until the nineteenth century.[2] Portuguese officials in Angola, unlike those on other parts of the African coast, were directly involved in the process of the capture and enslavement of Africans through raids and warfare.[3] Local merchants thus faced competition from the Portuguese traders who had established themselves in the colony since the early days of conquest.

The study of port cities has become an integrated part of Africanist historiography. Most studies have focused on the development of West African ports during the era of the transatlantic slave trade.[4] More recently, some scholars have also focused on the development of legitimate commerce in tropical commodities after the abolition of slave exports.[5] In the case of Angola, scholars have explored the dynamics of the slave trade in the ports of Luanda, Benguela, and to a lesser extent the northern ports of Ambriz and Loango.[6] The transition from slave trading to legitimate commerce, however, has received less attention.[7] In particular, what is still missing is an examination of the strategies used by slave traders in face of the economic change operating after the suppression of slave exports.

This book examines how the merchant community of Luanda adapted to the transformations that affected the South Atlantic in the century of the abolition of the slave trade. It pays particular attention to the interactions between foreign and local peoples in the spheres of marriage, trade, and slave ownership. In terms of periodization, this study concentrates on the era beginning in 1808, the date that marks the transfer of the Portuguese royal family to Brazil, and ending in 1867, when the last known illegal shipment of captives departed from West Central Africa.

This study addresses a number of critical questions: How did Luanda-based merchants tap into the new opportunities generated by the British abolition of the Portuguese slave trade north of the equator in 1815? How did local women benefit from the expansion of the trade in captives? How did the merchant community fare after the suppression of the slave trade in 1836? Were slavers able to survive the transition from slave trading to legitimate commerce? What did happen with the enslaved Africans retained in Luanda after the ban on slave exports? In answering these questions, this study advances our knowledge of how global and local processes of change affected the opportunities of Luanda merchants and their ability to adapt to economic and social transformations in the eras of slave trading and abolition. It argues that the merchant community of Luanda was indeed able to adjust to the changes that affected the South Atlantic through the nineteenth century. Many large-scale merchants survived the official suppression of slave exports to become the main investors in the new trade in legitimate commerce. Although colonial authorities believed that the alternative trade in tropical commodities had the potential to replace the slave trade, initially the two trades proved to be complementary rather than mutually exclusive.

Slave Trade, Foreign Merchants, and Luso-African Community

Since the late 1960s, historians have recognized the importance of West Central Africa, particularly Angola, in the transatlantic slave trade.[8] However, they have only more recently begun to appreciate the gendered character of this enterprise. The slave trade led to a great deal of interaction between local and foreign peoples on the western coast of Africa. While many of the locals became victims of the trade, others benefited from it. For male African elites, the selling of enslaved people allowed access to imported goods such as textiles, gunpowder, firearms, tobacco, and alcohol, which increased elites' control over dependents and gave them the capacity to enslave more people for sale.[9] The development of the Atlantic slave trade was also beneficial for some local women, especially those in the emerging coastal slaving entrepôts. Immigrant traders adventuring everywhere along the African coast generally relied on local intermediaries to supply the knowledge of indigenous languages and cultures that allowed these men to establish commercial networks to facilitate the exchange of imported items for African commodities such as gold, pepper, ivory, wax, and slaves, among other items. Many of these cultural brokers were women known variously as *signares* (Senegal), *nharas* (Guinea-Bissau), and *senoras* (Sierra Leone), with whom immigrant men established commercial and, sometimes, intimate relationships. While some of these relationships were casual, others ended in marriage, whether celebrated according to Christian or to African traditions.[10]

In Luanda, local women became indispensable to their immigrant husbands and partners, acting as commercial agents and translators and providing the necessities and comforts of a household. The city's development into a prime slave port depended crucially on the assistance that free and enslaved women provided to incoming males: they integrated immigrant men into local trade networks; they provided domestic services and health care; and they also gave birth to mixed offspring known as Luso-Africans, many of whom would themselves acquire the skills to become intermediaries and cultural brokers.[11]

As in other West African ports, the mixing of European and local populations in Luanda gave rise to new identities and affiliations.[12] This study understands the intermingling of cultures that took place in the coastal enclaves of Angola as a bilateral process created by both Portuguese (including Brazilians) and West Central Africans.[13] In the Portuguese enclaves, many immigrant men married local women, resorted to the assistance of African healers to cure illness and obtain wealth, and presumably learned some local languages.[14] In turn, African populations living in areas under Portuguese control professed Christianity; adopted Portuguese names, clothes, and civil law; and spoke both Portuguese and African languages.[15] In this context, the affiliation to Portuguese culture, alongside skin color and wealth, determined how colonial authorities classified people and even protected individuals from enslavement.[16] As a Portuguese enclave on the coast of West Central Africa, Luanda neither replicated European society nor corresponded to the communities in the Angolan interior. Society in Luanda developed as a result of Portuguese colonialism and Atlantic trade, but Africans (free and enslaved) also shaped the city's life and the making of the Atlantic world.[17]

As was the case for other Europeans in West Africa, Portuguese control over its overseas territories depended on the cooperation of local elites.[18] In Angola, the Portuguese administration relied on the assistance of an elite composed of Luso-Africans and immigrants.[19] The colonial state rewarded elite males with titles of noble orders as well as positions in the local administration and in the militia, thus reducing the need for European personnel in the West Central African settlements.[20] Meanwhile, the Portuguese relied on *degredados* (exiled criminals) and African allies to fight dissidents and extend the conquest. Some *sobas* (African rulers) signed vassalage treaties in exchange for Portuguese protection against other rival groups. In doing so, African allies agreed to pay taxes and tributes; to supply troops, slaves, and food; and to open their territories to Portuguese traders and militia.[21]

By the nineteenth century, the merchant community of Luanda was composed of foreign and Luso-African traders. While some were independent traders, others were agents of firms based in both Portugal and Brazil.[22] This commercial community controlled the export of captives to the Americas, the advancement of credit in the colony, and the supply of food to urban markets and slave ships. Some among them held positions in the Portuguese militias and administration, which theoretically should have prevented their participation in local trade.[23]

Sources

This study relies on the extensive archival and published documentation relating to Angola available in Portuguese archives and the archives of Angola. In Portugal, my research was centered on the Arquivo Histórico Ultramarino (AHU), the Archivo Nacional da Torre do Tombo (ANTT), and the Biblioteca Nacional de Lisboa (BNL). In the AHU, I consulted the extensive documentation of the Correspondência dos Governadores (Correspondence of the Governors of Angola), which contains official reports on the state of the colony, commercial lawsuits, censuses, and reports of conflicts between the colonial administration and African rulers. The AHU also holds the most complete collection of the weekly gazette published in Luanda from 1845 onward, the *Boletim Oficial de Angola* (*BOA*), which provides a wealth of information on the businesses of Luanda merchants and everyday life in the city.

In the ANTT, I consulted the Feitos Findos collection, which contains entitlements of heirs documents that provide information on relationships of African and Luso-African women with the foreign men who moved to Angola in search of wealth or in the service of the colonial administration and the army. At the BNL, I consulted the collection of official letters sent to Portugal from governors of Angola detailing the situation in the colony. These official sources help in understanding metropolitan policies and their often limited application in colonial contexts. Also at the BNL, I was able to consult issues of the newspaper *A Civilização da África Portuguesa* (*CAP*), which was founded in Luanda in 1866 and circulated in other Portuguese colonies in Africa.

Angola has among the most voluminous holdings of documents in sub-Saharan Africa for the colonial period prior to the twentieth century. Three Angolan archives were fundamental for my research: the Arquivo Nacional de Angola (ANA), the Biblioteca Municipal de Luanda (BML), and the Bispado de Luanda (BL). In the BML, I collected a variety of documents that provide

information on local trade, such as commercial books that recorded the trans-
actions of the Terreiro Público (Luanda's public market) and the municipal
slaughterhouse, registers of property taxes, license applications from street
vendors and shopkeepers, registers of land concessions, and correspondence
exchanged between the Câmara Municipal (Municipal Council) and the governors of Angola. These sources allowed me to identify local businesses and
reconstruct the profiles of producers and traders of foodstuffs as well as those
of shopkeepers and street vendors.

In the Arquivo Nacional de Angola, my focus was on its *códices* (codex)
and *avulsos* (loose documents) collections. The registers found in these primary collections, together with the materials available in the BML, helped
me trace the trajectories of merchants in Luanda. Drawing upon registers of
sales and purchases of property, debts and mortgages, dowries, and contracts
of marriage, I was able to examine the ways through which men and women
accumulated property in the colonial capital. I relied on passports of individuals traveling throughout the interior, as well as permissions issued to owners of
coasting vessels in transit between the capital and ports in the north and south
of the colony, to trace the engagement of women in legitimate commerce. This
archive also holds slave registers produced during the mid-nineteenth century,
which contain data on names, sexes, places of origin, ages, body marks, and
occupations of slaves as well as the names and the places of residence of slave
owners. Meanwhile, the reports of the Junta Protetora de Escravos e Libertos
(Board for the Protection of Enslaved and Freed Africans) illuminated the
experiences of the enslaved in their fight against their mistreatment by masters
and mistresses alike. The Bispado de Luanda is the central institution in Angola
for documentation generated by the Catholic Church. There I was able to
examine marriage petitions submitted to the Juízo Eclesiástico (Ecclesiastical
Board) of Luanda by men and women wishing to marry according to the rituals
of the Catholic Church.

Accounts written by foreign men who passed through or settled in Angola
during the nineteenth century supplemented the information available to me
in the quantitative and qualitative materials collected in the Portuguese and
Angolan archives. Together, these sources helped me understand the continuities and the changes taking place in Luanda through the nineteenth century.
Silences were equally valuable in my analysis of the primary sources at hand.[24]
Most foreign observers were silent about women or disregarded their participation in realms other than agriculture and household chores. Colonial officials,
explorers, and religious men were informed by the ethnocentrism, patriarchal
structure, and religious beliefs of their own societies, in which women were
seen as subordinate to men and Africans were seen as inferior to Europeans.[25]

The prior experiences of these observers shaped their representations of African populations.

With the exception of some travel accounts written in Italian and French, the primary sources this study draws upon were originally written in Portuguese. Therefore, the translations of citations used throughout the book, as well as the definitions in the glossary, are entirely my responsibility.

Chapter Outlines

The first chapter of this study examines the origins and development of Luanda as the capital of the Portuguese colony of Angola and a slaving port. It explores the growth of the city into the premier center of the transatlantic slave trade and sets the stage by describing Luanda's landscape and population at the opening of the nineteenth century.

The second chapter explores the transatlantic encounters between local women and foreign merchants in the context of expansion of the slave trade in Luanda. Through both Catholic and African marriages, immigrant men were able to access the personal and commercial resources necessary to participate successfully in the Luanda node of the Atlantic trade in slaves. This chapter also highlights the participation of Luanda's women in the man's world of slave trading. In following the trajectories of three women in particular, Dona Ana Joaquina dos Santos Silva, Dona Ana Ifigênia Nogueira da Rocha, and Dona Ana Ubertali de Miranda, the chapter shows the personal and commercial connections involved in the careers of women slave dealers.

The third chapter explores the production and trade of the foodstuffs that fed the residents of the capital city and provisioned slave ships. This chapter demonstrates that although women made up an important proportion of agricultural producers, most of the suppliers of the Terreiro Público were male. The majority of these men participated in the local militia and owned land and considerable numbers of slaves, allowing them to dominate the provision of food to urban markets.

The fourth chapter analyzes how merchants adapted their commercial strategies after the 1836 suppression of the slave trade in the Portuguese territories in Africa. The presence of warships in the main ports drove Luanda merchants to move their activities to remote locations on the coast, from where they continued to ship captives illegally. The dispersal of the slave trade compromised the efficiency of the British and Portuguese authorities responsible for patrolling the coast of West Central Africa. Meanwhile, officials in Luanda faced the difficult task of enforcing the law at the same time that the colonial state depended on the support provided by the local elite, including slave traders.

The fifth chapter examines the strategies of the Luanda merchant community facing the need to develop legitimate commerce. This chapter demonstrates that many of Luanda's large-scale slave traders had little difficulty in moving into the new commerce. At first, the two trades were in fact complementary, and several slave traders began dealing in tropical commodities while still smuggling slaves. This chapter also highlights the importance of African labor and expertise for the development of the new trade.

The sixth chapter analyzes interactions between masters and the enslaved in the context of expanding local use of slave labor in the era of legitimate commerce. With the termination of the slave trade after the withdrawal of Brazil in 1850, Luanda merchants expanded their internal uses of slave labor in urban occupations as well as in the production of foodstuffs and other items of legitimate commerce. In spite of their dependence on the labor of enslaved Africans, owners did not hesitate to inflict severe punishment on their human property.

A note on spelling: the names of people and places often present several variations in spelling in the historical documentation (e.g., Thereza, Tereza, Theresa, Teresa). To minimize confusion, I have chosen to use the modern spellings in the Portuguese language.

CHAPTER ONE

Luanda and the Transatlantic Slave Trade

EUROPEANS FIRST ARRIVED in West Central Africa in the late fifteenth century to explore the trade potential of local populations. Although they did not find precious metals, they developed a lucrative trade in human beings that reoriented the structure of African societies. For nearly four centuries, the Portuguese traded with local suppliers, exchanging imported goods for enslaved laborers. The slave trade introduced new cultural elements, consumption patterns, and relationships among West Central African populations and turned Luanda, the capital of the Portuguese colony of Angola and the first European city in Africa, into the single most important center of the Atlantic slave trade.

Between 1514 and 1867, an estimated 12.5 million enslaved Africans forcibly left the African continent destined for the Americas. In nearly four centuries of Atlantic slave trading, captives departed from six major coastal regions of sub-Saharan Africa: Upper Guinea, the Gold Coast, the Bight of Benin, the Bight of Biafra, West Central Africa, and Southeast Africa. West Central Africa was the largest supplier of captives throughout most of the slave-trading era, exporting about 5.6 million enslaved Africans, or 45 percent of the total.[1] The Portuguese were the largest slave carriers, shipping about 5.8 million captives, or nearly half of the total traffic, out of Africa. Their trade was conducted mainly from Brazil rather than the metropole, with slaving voyages often departing from the ports of Recife, Salvador, and Rio de Janeiro to acquire captives south of the Congo River and in the Bight of Benin.[2] In West Central Africa, most slaves departed from the Portuguese ports of Luanda and Benguela and the African-controlled ports of Ambriz, Cabinda, Molembo, and Loango. Luanda, however, was by far the single most important port in the transatlantic slave trade, shipping about 2.9 million captives between the mid-sixteenth century and 1867.[3] By the nineteenth century, Luanda was a cosmopolitan port, attracting merchants from different parts of the Atlantic world seeking quick enrichment through the slave trade. The 1815 banning of Portuguese slave exports north of the equator contributed to increased demand for captives in the South Atlantic, creating new opportunities for Luanda-based merchants. This chapter examines the development of Luanda as a slaving port and the impact of the ban.

The Rise of Luanda as a Slaving Port

The arrival in 1483 of the Portuguese explorer Diogo Cão and his men in the Sonyo province of the Kingdom of Kongo marked the beginning of interactions between West Central Africans and Europeans. The expedition, organized by the Portuguese king João II, was intended to explore the African coast and its trade potential. The first interactions were amicable, with exchange of presents between the Portuguese monarch and the *mani Kongo* (king of Kongo), Nzinga a Nkuwu. The *mani Kongo* accepted Catholic baptism, adopting the name João I.[4] After his death in 1506, his son Nzinga Mvemba rose to power as Afonso I. The new king too was interested in cooperation with the Portuguese, especially in the introduction of European technical expertise in his kingdom.[5] Nevertheless, the Portuguese would soon turn their attention to the newly found lands of Brazil and trade with the Orient.

Although the Portuguese found neither gold nor spices in Kongo, a trade in slaves soon developed at the port of Mpinda, located near the mouth of the Congo River. Kongo became the main supplier of captives to the sugar mills on the island of São Tomé and, to a lesser extent, to Portugal in exchange for European cloth and metalware. The centralized kingdom organized raids to take captives in the neighboring states of the Mbundu to the south.[6] A lack of captives for sale in Kongo itself, the export taxes imposed by the Portuguese kings, and the growing demand for slaves in the recently established captaincies in Brazil led traders to seek new suppliers elsewhere. They turned to the Mbundu state of Ndongo, established between the Dande and Kwanza Rivers and ruled by the Ngola. In 1560 the Portuguese sent an official embassy to Ndongo, and soon thereafter slave traders previously operating in Kongo were acquiring enslaved Africans directly in local markets, bypassing the *mani Kongo's* monopoly of the trade.[7]

Despite opposition from the king of Kongo and established traders from São Tomé, the Portuguese, with support of the Crown and the Jesuits, decided to conquer the land of the Ngola. The advocates of conquest exaggerated the potential wealth of the land, extolling the existence of copper and silver mines and reserves of salt.[8] On 19 September 1571, the Portuguese colonizer Paulo Dias de Novais received a charter of donation that made him hereditary overlord and governor for life of a royal colony between the Dande and the Kwanza Rivers and as far inland as he could possess.[9] Dias de Novais, in turn, was bound to populate and defend the new possession. In 1575 the Portuguese captain-governor founded the city of São Paulo da Assunção de Luanda, which became the administrative and military center of the Portuguese conquest in West Central Africa and the base for expansion into the interior.

In their attempts at conquest, known as the Angolan wars, the Portuguese faced more than a century of resistance from local rulers.[10] In the process, the Portuguese enslaved Mbundu populations, whom they sent to the agricultural properties owned by the Jesuits or sold in the transatlantic slave trade.[11] The resistance organized by the rulers of Ndongo, as well as the diseases of the land, jeopardized the progress of the Portuguese *conquistadores*. Dias de Novais died in May 1589 before he could gain full control of the captaincy. He was unable to establish settlers and promote the development of agriculture, as his men were more interested in trading in slaves than in working the land.[12] In face of the success of Mbundu forces against the Portuguese, the Crown took over all the rights and responsibilities in Angola in the hope of reaching the silver mines. Although the Portuguese were able to reach Cambambe, the supposed site of the mines, they found no precious metals of any sort.[13] Nevertheless, their efforts were not in vain, as the captives they acquired in Ndongo satisfied the demand for labor in the island of São Tomé and in the Spanish and Portuguese colonies in the Americas for the next three centuries.[14]

With the advance of the conquest in West Central Africa and the increase in slave trade activities, the Portuguese built a series of *presídios* (fortresses) inland. Some local *sobas* (rulers) seeking protection against internal enemies signed vassalage treaties with the Portuguese, in which they agreed to provide men, facilitate trade, and pay tributes.[15] In spite of these advances into the interior, the Portuguese presence was largely limited to coastal enclaves and the few *presídios* established inland.

In the seventeenth century, the Portuguese continued to face resistance from Ndongo rulers, including Ngola Mbande and his successor and sister, Njinga.[16] Meanwhile, an external enemy also challenged Portuguese dominance in West Central Africa: the Dutch seized Luanda in 1641 after establishing control of Pernambuco in northeastern Brazil and the Mina fort on the Gold Coast.[17] They aimed to control the areas that supplied captives to sugarcane plantations in Brazil. The Portuguese settlers and traders established in the colonial capital fled to Massangano, a town southeast of Luanda. The Dutch invasion disrupted the slave trade, as the Portuguese could now only acquire captives illegally. In 1648 Salvador Correia de Sá e Benevides led an expeditionary force from Rio de Janeiro, recapturing Luanda from the Dutch, and the Portuguese settlers were able to resume their slave-trading operations.[18] In 1654 Njinga finally negotiated a peace agreement with the Portuguese, its terms including the ransom of her younger sister Kambu, the access of Portuguese traders to the territory under her control, and her reconversion to Christianity.[19]

The discovery of gold and diamonds in southeastern Brazil in 1695 increased the need for enslaved laborers in the South American colony, with Angola becoming the main supplier of slaves for the mining districts.[20] That trade increased through the eighteenth century, but competition increased as well. British and French traders, who had predominantly purchased slaves in West Africa to supply their possessions in the Caribbean, now extended their activities to the coast of West Central Africa. They threatened Portuguese dominance over the slave trade, offering goods of superior quality, including cloth, arms, and gunpowder at lower prices, in exchange for slaves in the African-controlled ports of Cabinda, Molembo, Ambriz, and Loango in the north of the colony.[21] As foreign interlopers threatened their monopoly of trade and control of the territory, Portuguese attention shifted from the interior to the coast.

Additionally, from the early eighteenth century, Luanda-based merchants faced internal competition from the southern port of Benguela.[22] Previously, slaves acquired in Benguela had been shipped through the port of Luanda, where export taxes were collected. Benguela attracted slavers' attention particularly because enslaved Africans were cheaper there than in Luanda and its administration was lax compared to that of the colonial capital. Furthermore, ships coming from Portugal, Brazil, and Asia usually stopped in this southern port before heading to Luanda and the other ports near the mouth of the Congo River.[23] By 1770 Brazilian-born slavers held a dominant position at Benguela and a share of the trade at Luanda. Joseph C. Miller has suggested, based on the origin of ships arriving in the ports of Angola, that nearly all of Benguela's commercial correspondents and about half of Luanda's were residents of Rio de Janeiro.[24] Their success was determined in part by the lower cost of the Brazilian alcoholic drink known in Angola as *geribita* as well as by their role as transporters of most of the captives exported to South America.[25] José C. Curto has estimated that from 1710 to the end of the legal slave trade in 1830, one-quarter of the slaves exported from Luanda were purchased with *geribita*, demonstrating the significance of this commodity in West Central Africa.[26] Moreover, Brazilian traders could count on the assistance of the governors of Angola, who had links with the Portuguese colony in South America.[27]

An Era of New Opportunities South of the Equator

The early nineteenth century brought new opportunities for merchants based in Luanda. Foreign competition had declined in Angola by the first decade of the century, when British and French interlopers left the African-controlled ports near the mouth of the Congo River. The French colony of Saint-Domingue, the major producer of sugar in the Americas, was the principal destination of enslaved Africans shipped by the French. With the slave revolution of 1791–1804, France lost Saint-Domingue, significantly decreasing the need for slave labor.[28] Meanwhile, in 1807 Britain made it illegal for British subjects to participate in the traffic of enslaved Africans and encouraged other nations to do the same.[29] As a result, by the early nineteenth century, Portuguese and Brazilian-born traders were able to control the shipment of captives from West Central Africa.

Events in the metropole also echoed in the overseas territories. In 1808 the Portuguese court, followed by most of the nobility and merchant elite, moved to Rio de Janeiro to escape Napoleon's armies during the Peninsular War. Upon his arrival, the prince of Portugal, Dom João VI, quickly opened Brazilian

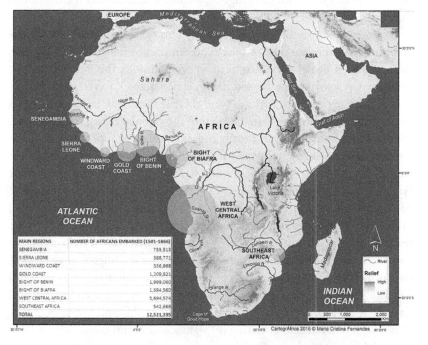

Map 1.1. Main areas of slave embarkation, 1501–1866. Map by Maria Cristina Fernandes based on "Voyages: The Trans-Atlantic Slave Trade Database," accessed January 2020, www.slavevoyages.org/.

ports to international trade, a measure that directly benefited the British, who had assisted the transfer of the Portuguese court.[30] The opening of the ports to international trade contributed to the spread of British capital in Brazilian markets: not only did they purchase Brazilian products at lower prices, but they also provided credit to Portuguese merchants newly arrived in Rio who were connected to the slave trade in Angola.[31] Despite the campaign for the abolition of the slave trade, British merchants continued to supply goods to slave traders of other nationalities and to deal in slave-produced commodities, such as West Indian sugar, American cotton, and West African palm oil.[32] The establishment of the Portuguese royal family in Rio de Janeiro contributed to increased demand for captives from Angola. The labor force necessary to attend the newly arrived merchants and administrative personnel originated in West Central Africa. Curto has argued that the number of enslaved women in Luanda dropped in the first decades of the nineteenth century due to the increased demand for slaves to perform domestic work in the capital of Brazil.[33]

Slaves were not only required in the noble households of Rio de Janeiro. The end of the gold boom in the late eighteenth century led the Portuguese secretary of state, the marquis de Pombal, to promote the development of Brazilian agriculture. Therefore, the demand for captives in the Brazilian market also increased to meet the needs of sugarcane planters in the Northeast, rice and cotton producers in the northern provinces of Maranhão and Pará, and in the coffee estates in the southeastern captaincies of São Paulo and Rio de Janeiro.[34]

In 1815 a treaty between Britain and Portugal limited the export of captives by Portuguese vessels to south of the equator. Some slave traders, however, evaded the law, continuing their activities illegally in the North Atlantic. For instance, slave traders established in Bahia in northeastern Brazil applied for licenses to purchase captives in the ports of West Central Africa, but they headed to the Bight of Benin, where they had formerly acquired captives.[35] Others, however, sought new sources of supply in the South Atlantic, including in Angola.[36] The limitation of slave exports to the South Atlantic led to an increase in the number of captives exported from Angola, opening new opportunities to Luanda-based merchants. From 1816 to 1820, the total number of captives departing from Luanda reached about 92,500, an increase of about 39 percent over the previous half decade (1811–15), when about 66,600 enslaved Africans left the region (see table 1.1). In the next decade, the number of captives fell but remained higher than in the period prior to 1815.

Brazil alone was the destination of about 85.7 percent of all captives (1.2 out of 1.4 million) shipped from West Central Africa between the early and

Table 1.1. Estimated number of enslaved Africans shipped from Angola, 1801–1830

Years	Total, all ports	Luanda
1801–5	188,275	80,635
1806–10	151,701	71,477
1811–15	149,639	66,668
1816–20	256,255	92,558
1821–25	180,725	79,811
1826–30	255,802	74,396
Total	1,182,397	465,545

Source: Daniel B. Domingues da Silva, "The Transatlantic Slave Trade from Angola: A Port-by-Port Estimate of Slaves Embarked, 1701–1867," *International Journal of African Historical Studies* 46, no. 1 (2013): 121–22.

mid-nineteenth centuries. The majority of captives shipped to Brazil disembarked in Rio de Janeiro (southeastern Brazil), while Bahia and Pernambuco represented the second and third major destinations, respectively (see table 1.2). The northern captaincies of Maranhão and Pará (Amazônia) also received captives from West Central Africa, although in smaller numbers.[37]

The Organization of the Slave Trade from Luanda

By the nineteenth century, the merchant community of Luanda was made up of Portuguese nationals and Brazilian-born and Luso-African traders, all deeply attached to the slave trade. According to Miller, merchants in colonial Angola fell into two categories: *de efeitos próprios* (independent merchants) and *negociantes comissários* (commission agents). While the independent merchants operated on their own account, commission agents worked on behalf of Brazilian and Portuguese financial backers, who retained the ownership of goods sent to Africa and of captives shipped to the Americas.[38] Although they were established in Luanda, merchants Francisco António Flores, António Severino de Avelar, Guilherme José da Silva Correia, and António Augusto de Oliveira Botelho were all agents of firms based in Rio de Janeiro.[39]

Independent merchants often started their own trading companies in Luanda either alone or in partnership with other investors. Only a few slave dealers possessed enough capital to operate independently. The Portuguese Augusto Guedes Coutinho Garrido established one of Angola's most profitable commercial firms dealing in slaves with the locally born merchant José Maria Matozo de Andrade Câmara. Garrido came from a respectable gentry family of central

Table 1.2. Major regions of disembarkation of captives in Brazil, 1801–1855

Year	Amazônia	Bahia	Pernambuco	Southeastern Brazil	Other Brazil	Total
1801–5	10,245	14,793	20,852	64,946	0	110,836
1806–10	3,269	8,617	7,933	74,473	0	94,292
1811–15	390	7,107	22,729	94,599	0	124,825
1816–20	10,730	36,391	38,754	96,762	0	182,637
1821–25	4,581	30,469	29,028	102,700	0	166,778
1826–30	3,834	55,735	25,469	155,983	452	241,473
1831–35	554	645	5,550	14,634	0	21,383
1836–40	517	5,280	12,286	130,637	0	148,720
1841–45	0	1,640	8,241	65,302	0	75,183
1846–50	0	2,757	2,073	32,651	0	37,481
1851–55	0	720	0	2,001	0	2,721
Total	34,120	164,154	172,915	834,688	452	1,206,329

Source: David Eltis et al., "Voyages: The Trans-Atlantic Slave Trade Database," accessed January 2020, www.slavevoyages.org/.

Portugal and probably entered Angola as an administrative official.[40] Câmara was born in Angola into a Portuguese family whose arrival in the colony dated back to the eighteenth century. The men of the Matozo family served in the local militia and became wealthy through their participation in the traffic in captives. Câmara's father, Inocêncio Matozo da Câmara, was also a notable slave trader.[41] Together Câmara and Garrido entered the pantheon of the most successful merchants based in Luanda.

There existed a third category that cannot be ignored: the petty traders, who exported a few captives at a time. These part-time slave dealers made their living predominantly as tavern keepers or small-scale food suppliers.[42] Some foreign-born petty traders moved to Angola on their own, attracted by the possibilities of quick enrichment. In 1819 Desidério José Marques da Rocha decided to leave Pernambuco in northeastern Brazil and "test the waters" on the other side of the Atlantic Ocean. Convinced by stories of success he heard from a certain José Calafinho, Rocha headed to Angola, bringing with him gold, cash, and two trunks of blue *chitas* (textiles). Rocha intended to purchase slaves in Luanda to sell in southeastern Brazil. However, he died in Angola, succumbing to the diseases of the land.[43] A short lifespan was a major characteristic of the foreign men who settled in the colony, notorious for its unhealthy environment.[44] Those who survived, however, could lay the foundations of a prosperous career in the slave trade.

Independent merchants and commission agents sold trade goods on credit to Luso-African and African licensed itinerant traders, known as *sertanejos* or *aviados*, who in turn headed caravans to *feiras* (official markets) in the interior to exchange those commodities for captives.[45] Among these *sertanejos* were Tomé Francisco, Luiz Aras, and Felipe da Costa Palermo, all of whom requested licenses in 1784 from the Câmara Municipal (Municipal Council) of Luanda to deal in slaves.[46] Merchants provided assortments of trade goods known as *banzo*, composed mainly of textiles, *geribita*, firearms, beads, salt, and other imports equivalent to the value of a male captive in the prime of life, known as a *peça*.[47] The imported articles that became available with the trade generated new needs and consumption patterns among the populations of Angola, signaling prestige and privilege.[48] After acquiring the commodities, traders prepared to depart in caravans to the *sertão* (interior), which included recruiting *carregadores* (porters) to transport the imported wares and acquiring provisions to feed them. Slaving activities in the interior of Angola were for the most part concentrated in the *feiras* (inland market), which is why *sertanejos* were also known as *feirantes*. The main slave markets were located in Dondo, Ambaca, Pungo Andongo, Encoge, Libolo, and Kasanje.[49]

From the time of departure until the return to Luanda, a caravan could take anywhere from months to years to complete its objective. Sometimes *sertanejos* had to stop at several marketplaces until a full *libambo* (coffle) was secured, which might be from twenty to one hundred captives.[50] The Kingdoms of Kasanje and Matamba dominated trade in the hinterland of Luanda, exercising the role of intermediaries in the supply of enslaved Africans. The *feira* of Kasanje was the most important marketplace in the interior where captives destined for Luanda were sold.[51] This dependence would change in the nineteenth century, when *sertanejos* tapped into sources of slaves in regions closer to the coast and under greater influence of the colonial government, based in Luanda.[52] *Sertanejos* often had to rely on the assistance of bush traders, known as *pombeiros*, who took imported wares on credit and returned with small lots of captives from even more remote locations in the interior to complete the *libambo*.[53] Many *pombeiros* were effectively enslaved Africans themselves, working on behalf of masters residing in Luanda.[54] Free *pombeiros* often risked being illegally enslaved while trading in the interior.[55] Once the coffle of enslaved Africans was completed, the *sertanejo* led the caravan in the long march back to Luanda.

While the ownership of the trade goods rested with merchants in Luanda, the ownership of the captives rested with the *sertanejos* until the coffle reached the coast. A contemporary observer described this process: "When the *feirantes* return to the capital, they sell the captives and pay what they owe to the *arma-dores* (merchants who supplied the imported goods on credit), who then offer them a new assortment of *fazendas* (trading goods) to engage in another commercial venture."[56] Itinerant traders were therefore constantly in debt to merchants in Luanda. To increase their profit margins, traders sometimes resorted to a strategy known as *reviro*, which was the sale of enslaved Africans to another merchant who paid more per *peça* than the original supplier of the *banzo*. This practice was the subject of many complaints from both local merchants and colonial authorities.[57]

In colonial Angola, unlike in other parts of the African continent, Portuguese officials were directly involved in the process of capture and enslavement of people through raids and warfare.[58] Commanders of *presídios* were often connected to merchant families in Luanda, who sought these positions for the advantages they offered in the acquisition of captives.[59] Foreigners and colonial authorities made frequent note of the excesses committed by these mid-level colonial officials in the interior. One late eighteenth-century observer, for example, highlighted that commanders would often "divert soldiers from their military duties, using them on their behalf in the interior, which leaves the outpost with no troops and no respect."[60]

Even traders from Brazil and Portugal traveled into the Angola interior to purchase captives, becoming *sertanejos*. Since the early seventeenth century, several laws had prohibited white merchants from traveling into the interior, at the risk of losing their assets, paying fines, and being arrested. However, Luanda authorities were never able to enforce these laws, and white men continuously ventured into the *sertões*.[61] Sometimes even criminal exiles and former sailors became *sertanejos*. In 1758, the Portuguese Crown finally eliminated the prohibition, resulting in an increase in itinerant trade throughout the interior.[62] Roquinaldo A. Ferreira has argued that the spread of local and foreign *sertanejos* throughout the hinterland of Luanda significantly increased enslavement in the regions of Angola under Portuguese control. Itinerant traders sold imported goods on credit to Africans; when they were unable to settle their debts, they, their relations, or their subjects were enslaved and sent to coastal urban centers for shipment to Brazil.[63] The expansion of itinerant trade thus resulted not only in higher instances of indebtedness among Africans but also in the escalation of enslavement.

Urban Life in Nineteenth-Century Luanda: Landscape and Population

In the years after its foundation, Luanda became a place of interaction for people coming from different parts of the Atlantic world.[64] From the first Portuguese who arrived to conquer and colonize the land of the Ngola to subsequent settlers, exiles, missionaries, traders, and military and administrative personnel, these foreigners were mainly males who shaped the socioeconomic fabric of the colony alongside local men and women. Almost all engaged in local trade, in spite of the existence of laws that forbade administrative and military men from taking part in commercial activities.[65]

In the early nineteenth century, the capital of Angola was divided into a *cidade alta* and *cidade baixa* (upper town and lower town), which comprised, respectively, the *freguesias* (parishes) of Nossa Senhora da Sé, the cathedral seat of the bishop, and Nossa Senhora dos Remédios, an ordinary parish church (see figure 1.1). The Freguesia da Sé was the administrative center where the governor and military and ecclesiastical authorities resided in close proximity to public buildings like the Câmara Municipal, the jail, the Santa Casa de Misericórdia (Holy House of Mercy) and its hospital, and the Church of Nossa Senhora da Conceição (Our Lady of the Conception). The Freguesia de Nossa Senhora dos Remédios, in the *baixa*, represented the commercial district established around the shipping, sheltered in an extensive bay.[66] Located here were the slaughterhouse and the *quitandas* (outdoor markets) of Coqueiros,

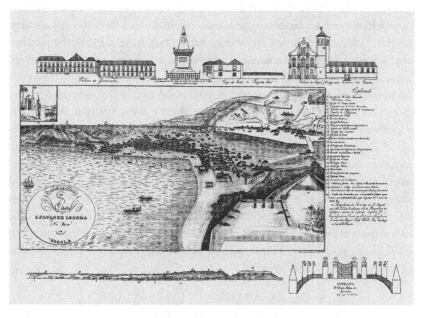

Figure 1.1. View of Luanda's upper and lower towns, 1825. Source: Perspectiva da cidade de S. Paulo de Loanda no reino de Angola / A. L. P. da Cunha; fecit Bour. Paris: Langloumé, 1825. Biblioteca Nacional de Portugal, cota: cc-1698-a.

Feira Grande, Venda dos Pratos, and Feira do Bungo, as well as the Terreiro Público (Public Market) and most of the taverns and shops. The lower town also accommodated the *armazéns* (warehouses) and *sobrados* (Portuguese-style houses) of the wealthier merchants, the cemetery, the *quintais* (barracoons) crowded with slaves waiting to be shipped across the Atlantic Ocean, and *cubatas* (straw-roofed round houses) where poor Africans and some of the enslaved resided.[67]

In 1802 the population of Luanda was 6,925 inhabitants: 4,093 free and 2,832 enslaved. Portuguese authorities classified inhabitants into three groups: 710 *brancos* (whites), 1,060 *pardos* (of mixed Portuguese and African origin), and 3,932 *pretos* (blacks). Although most inhabitants were men (3,785), women comprised the majority of the enslaved (1,471), evidencing their importance in the labor force underpinning this colonial society.[68] For the following forty years or so, the population of Luanda experienced an absolute decline due in large part to intense Brazilian demand for enslaved laborers.[69] The higher number of males exported in the Atlantic market as well as the preference for women in the internal market resulted in Luanda becoming a female-dominated society.[70]

Black Africans, free and enslaved, composed the majority of the population at any time during the nineteenth century. Although they were mostly of Mbundu origin, the captives who arrived in the city came from a multitude of locations. A great number of the captives awaited embarkation in the baracoons located in the *baixa*, while others remained in town. The urban population depended heavily on slave labor to carry out artisan crafts, transportation, and domestic work. Slaves were artisans in craft workshops, domestic servants in the *sobrados*, and field workers in the agricultural properties of the rural suburbs and nearby interior.[71] Free Africans also migrated to Luanda, likely seeking better opportunities in a port that was also the administrative center of the colony.[72] Those who lived in the Portuguese enclaves, spoke Portuguese, and professed Christianity could be perceived as whites or mixed race and were, theoretically, protected against enslavement.[73]

The white inhabitants represented a minority of the population and were mainly males of Portuguese origin, whether born in the metropole, in the Atlantic islands, or in Brazil. While some were merchants engaged in the slave trade, others occupied positions in the administration and the militias of the capital or in the *presídios* of the interior. Merchants commonly filled positions in the colonial administration, including the Municipal Council and the Fazenda Real (Royal Treasury), which might have assisted in the advancement of their careers.[74] Some white men arrived as *degredados* (exiles) of the Portuguese Inquisition and the royal judiciary to "pay" for their crimes overseas. Soon after arriving in Angola, many *degredados* went to the interior, where they were required to enlist in the army. In the absence of administrative officials, they also filled positions within the Portuguese administration. Others, however, remained within the urban confines of the capital.[75] Some of those in temporary exile who survived the disease environment chose to stay once their terms of banishment ended, finding possibilities of enrichment as farmers or merchants.[76] As well, Luanda often received temporary contingents of white males who arrived in the ships that anchored off the bay. Ship captains and their crews remained in town until the completion of the cargo, which could take from one to several months.[77]

Before the late nineteenth century, white women, unlike men, rarely ventured to settle in Luanda, with the exception of exiles or a few wives and daughters who accompanied their husbands and fathers. Indeed, few women seem to have followed Dona Guiomar Anacleta de Carvalho Fonseca e Camões, who arrived in Angola in 1772 with her husband, Governor Dom António de Lencastre (1772–79), and their daughter, Dona Francisca Felizarda de Lencastre.[78] In 1802, in a population of 3,140 women, only 334 of them were white.[79] Fears around an often-lethal epidemiological environment may have contributed to the decision of married men to leave their wives and children behind.[80] Moreover, by moving to Luanda alone, men had the chance to experience the sexual pleasures of the tropics, which had long permeated the European imagination.[81] Travelers and explorers commonly described overseas possessions as places of sexual freedom, portraying immigrant men as victims incapable of resisting the advances of "hypersexualized" African women.[82] In the late eighteenth century, the Brazilian-born military officer Elias Alexandre da Silva Corrêa, then serving in Angola, attributed the "weakness" of European men there to the heat and to the "fire of sensuality" of African women.[83]

With few white women available, immigrant men entered relationships with women of African and Luso-African backgrounds. The offspring of white men and free local women were known as whites or *pardos* (mixed European and African origin).[84] They adopted Christianity, learned both Portuguese and Kimbundu, and dressed in European fashion. The men occupied middle-level administrative and military positions or followed their immigrant fathers into careers in trade. It was not uncommon for wealthy families to send their sons to schools in Brazil and universities in Portugal.[85] Eduardo Matozo Gago da Câmara, son of Inocêncio Matozo Câmara, attended law school at the University of Coimbra in Portugal. After graduation, he moved to Lisbon, where he married and established a law office.[86] His elder brother, José Maria Matozo de Andrade Câmara, remained in Angola, where he became a successful slave trader like his father.[87] The daughters of the Luso-African elite were taught by

European tutors to sew, embroider, play the piano, and read and write in Portuguese and sometimes even other European languages, such as Italian and French.[88] Their parents arranged their marriages with *homens de bem* (men of good reputation), preferably of Portuguese origin. Some of these women became merchants themselves, supplying local markets with staples and at times engaging in slave trading either alone or as commercial partners of their foreign husbands. In Angola, they became known as *donas*, a term that originated in the title granted to noble and royal women in the Iberian Peninsula and was subsequently adopted in the overseas territories to designate women of high socioeconomic status living in accordance with Portuguese norms of respectability.[89]

Immigrants living everywhere on the western coast of Africa became intimate with local trade and cultures.[90] The interactions between indigenous populations and foreigners living in the Portuguese enclaves of Angola gave rise to a Luso-African society characterized by bilateral transformations.[91] In this process, newcomers learned local languages, married local women, took part in African rituals, consulted with healers, and engaged in local trade. Africans living in the Portuguese enclaves adopted Christianity, Portuguese naming practices, civil law, clothes, architecture, and language.[92] Linda M. Heywood has argued that, because of the demographic weight of the Mbundu population and the tendency of Bantu cultures to change over time by absorbing external elements, African components were more dominant than European in the Luso-African society that emerged in Angola.[93]

One example of the prevalence of African elements was the endurance of Kimbundu as the *língua geral* (common language) of Luanda. In the late eighteenth century, Silva Corrêa indicated that while local women were talkative within the household, where they spoke Kimbundu, they remained silent in public, revealing that they spoke little or no Portuguese. The Brazilian-born officer also noted that local males "speak Portuguese, but are elegant in Ambundo [Kimbundu]," meaning that they had better command of the Mbundu language.[94] Most Luso-Africans were descendants of Kimbundu-speaking women, who initiated them into Mbundu society and culture from an early age at the same time that they mastered the Portuguese culture of their foreign fathers. Jan Vansina has attributed the failure of the Portuguese language in the Luso-African context of Luanda to the scarcity of European brides, the lack of schools for boys and the provision for the education of girls, and the low number of white residents.[95]

Contemporaneous observers often criticized the assimilation of local customs by whites, whether nonnative or locally born. The Brazilian-born José Pinto de Azeredo, who worked as a physician and taught medical students in late eighteenth-century Luanda, condemned the use of *milongos* (medicines) that local healers prescribed to both *filhos do país* (children born in Angola) and Europeans, asserting that "many benign diseases become deadly through the hand of these tricksters."[96] Silva Corrêa also noted that whites participated in "heathen" religious rituals led by Africans.[97] Kalle Kananoja has explored documentation from the Portuguese Inquisition regarding the case of João Pereira da Cunha, a military commander in Angola who faced charges of witchcraft and idolatry. Cunha had apparently sought the assistance of an African healer to cure an illness and achieve economic success.[98] Meanwhile, many Africans who had converted to Christianity continued to practice indigenous religious rituals and adore their idols at home.[99] This mixing of cultural elements was a feature of other West African ports as well. Danish men on the Gold Coast used fetishes to swear in African workers, a practice that was against the Christian religion.[100] In Senegambia, *lançados* and *tangomaos* (Portuguese-speaking adventurers and merchants) wore African garments and protective amulets, underwent circumcision and scarification, sought treatment from African healers, and participated in African rituals of divination.[101] In Cacheu, Guinea region, baptized Christians were accused of witchcraft, superstition, and idol worship.[102] In Angola, religious and administrative authorities often attributed the persistence of "African superstitions" to the shortage of priests and lack of funding for the few churches.[103] In the end, however, neither Africans nor Europeans fully converted to each other's culture; instead, they adopted some elements while also keeping their own cultural expressions.

Donas, Foreign Merchants, and the Expansion of the Slave Trade in the South Atlantic

THE TRADE IN ENSLAVED AFRICANS depended on interactions between local and foreign peoples, mainly Portuguese- and Brazilian-born men who sojourned or eventually settled in Angola. While many of the locals became victims of this interaction through raids and kidnapping, others profited from it. Lacking knowledge of African cultures and trade networks, immigrant traders relied on local intermediaries, who acted as translators, cultural brokers, and commercial partners. Women of mixed origin were especially sought as wives and commercial partners, providing the established households, access to local trade networks, and health care that were essential for the survival and success of nonnative men in Angola. Local wives also took advantage of the connections and capital brought in by their foreign husbands to advance their careers in trade. This chapter explores marriage practices and the trajectory of three women merchants in the context of slave trade expansion in West Central Africa.

For Want of a Woman

Scholars have highlighted the cosmopolitan character of the merchant communities in ports along the western coast of Africa.[1] The merchants and commercial agents who established themselves in Angola came from different parts of the Portuguese Empire, such as Portugal, Brazil, the Azores, Madeira, Cabo Verde, Goa, and São Tomé.[2] They, as well as the Portuguese administrative and military personnel sent to the colony, were often young males of marriageable age who found very few white women with whom they could establish families locally. As was the case in other ports along the western coast of Africa, in Luanda the sexual imbalance among new arrivals and the needs of everyday life soon facilitated the emergence of relationships between incoming males and local African and Luso-African women.[3]

Almost from the very beginning of the Portuguese military occupation of West Central Africa, the Portuguese Crown attempted to establish a white population in Angola by periodically sending convicted prostitutes, orphans, and other single women to Luanda and, to a lesser extent, to Benguela. These efforts, however, were unsuccessful.[4] Unlike French policies in Saint-Louis in Senegal that prohibited cohabitation with African women, Portuguese policies in Angola encouraged relationships between immigrant men and local women as a way to attract and keep foreign males in a territory known worldwide as the end of the road to degradation.[5] Among the instructions that the former governor of Angola, Francisco Inocêncio de Sousa Coutinho (1764–72), sent in 1772 to his successor, Dom António de Lencastre (1772–79), was a recommendation to favor those immigrant males who married into the local population: "There is a need to establish males so that through marriages the population can be increased, otherwise this kingdom will fall in decay, as there will be no one to serve. Your Excellency must favor the newly married with white or almost white women, giving them all support you can."[6]

Although Coutinho's recommendation was that his successor support men who married "white or almost white women," meaning Portuguese or Luso-Africans, foreigners also had sexual encounters and entered long-term relationships—usually without official marriage—with black African women, both free and enslaved. However, the colonial state did not recognize these arrangements, known throughout the Portuguese Empire as *amasiamentos*.[7] The private of the Portuguese army Joaquim de Santana, for example, had two *amásias* (concubines) in Luanda, the free black women Joana Cristóvão and Marta Agostinho. From these relationships were born two sons: in November 1815, Joana gave birth to Luís, and in May 1816, Marta gave birth to Joaquim.[8] Domingos Fançony, an exile of Neapolitan origin, arrived in Luanda in March 1821, when he was about twenty-five years old. Although he died officially single, through his time in Angola he entered into relationships with at least three black women: the enslaved Maria João and the free blacks Joaquina Francisca and Luzia Isabel. Through these relationships, he fathered six children: Teresa, Manuel, José, Francisca, Angélica, and Domingas.[9]

As Mariana P. Candido has highlighted, women in West Central Africa have not constituted a homogeneous or unified group. Divisions existed among women who were herders and farmers, elites and commoners, young and old.[10] The experiences of women living in urban areas under Portuguese control and in Mbundu communities were also quite different. Everywhere in western Africa, indigenous women were sources of wealth as providers of work and children.[11] Women carried out agricultural work and household chores and contributed to the increase of kinship groups; meanwhile, they remained subject to the authority of husbands and elders in their communities. Men were often in charge of warfare, hunting, fishing, clearing of fields, and building of houses.[12]

The Mbundu were matrilineal, meaning that the transmission of the family's line and goods was through the female line. They practiced polygamy, allowing men to have as many wives as they could afford.[13] The husband divided his time among his wives, who could live in the same compound or separately. Wives depended upon collective land, where they grew crops for subsistence, and they could market their excess production. If a woman did not meet her obligations, the husband could return her to her parents, receiving back whatever amount he had paid for the bridewealth.[14] Although a woman usually did not have a say in the agreement that led to her marriage, she could leave it at any time and be reintegrated into her lineage.[15]

Contemporary observers, probably unaware of the sexual division of labor among the Mbundu, often pointed to the "burden" of indigenous women exploited by their "lazy" husbands. The Portuguese jurist António Gil, for instance, stated, "There is no one more unhappy and more dignified than the women, maybe more even than the slaves. They [women] work with a hoe to support their children and husband."[16] Carlos José Caldeira, another Portuguese, claimed, "The men are very lazy. When they are off from working in porterage, they spend the days lying near the house, smoking a pipe or having fun and getting drunk in *batuques* [festivities] or dances."[17] The "exploitation" of indigenous women described in these accounts contributed to propagate the image of the Mbundu as "uncivilized" and the belief in the superiority of Portuguese culture.

Women born from Luso-African families in the Portuguese enclaves were often classified as *brancas* or *pardas* and as Portuguese subjects.[18] They received Portuguese names and Christian baptism, dressed in European fashion, and were literate and trained in domestic and fine arts.[19] Raised in households where slaves did the domestic work, they grew up to become slaveholders themselves. Owning slaves freed Luso-African women from performing household chores, contributing to the enhancement of their prestige.[20] In spite of receiving training in Portuguese culture from a young age, many of these women maintained ties with Mbundu culture, becoming fluent in Kimbundu, consulting with local healers, and even engaging in indigenous religious practices.[21]

In Luanda, most Luso-African women entered marriages arranged by their parents with men of Portuguese origin.[22] By the nineteenth century, these women could draw on many generations of experience with Portuguese language and culture and on a Luso-African community with deep historical roots in Luanda and in the wide Atlantic world. As Portuguese subjects, they amassed wealth through rights of inheritance as wives and daughters as well as through their participation in trade. They exercised power over both free dependents and the enslaved that they possessed. Their economic success and social prestige presumably gave them a degree of independence relative to the men in their lives, particularly their husbands.

Marriage Practices and the Requirements of Trade and Everyday Life

Foreign merchants required a basic infrastructure to establish themselves in Luanda, including accommodation, health care, and slaves to prepare food, do the laundry, and transport themselves and their merchandise—to list but a few daily needs. At the same time, they also needed translators and assistants to connect them with *sertanejos* and suppliers of slaves and commodities in the interior. Many immigrant traders were able to obtain these daily and commercial requirements by entering into relationships with local women, the daughters of Luso-African and African families, who opened the doors of their houses and local market networks to their new partners. Portuguese traders had been entering marriages with women on the western coast of Africa since the late fifteenth century and were probably the pioneers of this practice.[23] Even men who were already married in Europe or in the Americas did not hesitate to enter into casual or long-term liaisons with African women.[24]

For indigenous communities along the western coast of Africa, the exchange of women was a means to consolidate relationships between foreigners and local elites. Marriage within this particular context was an economic, social, and political affair that allowed different groups of people to be connected.[25] In the nineteenth century, marriage was a strategy to consolidate commercial and political alliances both in Portugal and in its overseas territories.[26] The practice was also a common one in other European societies, where well-to-do families, including royalty, married off their offspring to maintain or expand their economic and social status.[27] The history of marriage between European men and local women in Luanda was part of a process that occurred throughout the Atlantic world during and after the era of the Atlantic slave trade.[28]

In spite of the efforts of the Portuguese administration to encourage people to marry, Catholic marriages in Luanda were far from commonplace; the elites who professed Christianity were among the few who drew upon this sacrament.[29] In his study of the interior administrative outpost of Ambaca, Jan Vansina has concluded that Catholic marriages were difficult to arrange because they required the payment of a dowry.[30] His observation could well apply to the colonial capital, where Portuguese and Luso-African parents also provided dowries to daughters soon to be married; the custom of providing dowries, common in Portugal and other European countries, had been transferred to their colonial possessions.[31] The possibility of a dowry served to raise the status of single women, attracting potential suitors. Dowries varied according to the wealth of the donors, usually the parents of the bride. They could include rural and urban property, jewelry, money, and slaves, among other assets. Usually, the dowry provided to the bride represented an advance payment of her *legítima*, a portion of the inheritance that she was entitled to as a daughter.[32] The Ordenações Filipinas, the legal code used in Portugal and its domains, granted women the sole ownership of assets they acquired as a dowry. Parents also resorted to the *escritura de dote* (register of dowry) to guarantee that the assets they provided to daughters would not become part of the couple's estate.[33] In Saint-Louis, Eurafrican families also provided their daughters with dowries; unlike Portuguese law, however, French law gave husbands primary control over the use of these assets to support their economic ventures.[34]

Nevertheless, there were other reasons why men and women in Luanda did not officialize their unions. Applying for a marriage petition and requesting documents from parishes abroad cost money and took time. Couples who wished to enter into matrimony had to file a marriage petition with the Junta Eclesiástica (Ecclesiastical Board), pay a fee, and present a guarantor, who would take responsibility for depositing the documents that the board requested, including baptismal registers, banns of marriage, proof of marital status, and (in the case of a widow or widower) burial records. On 4 January 1834, the secretary of the government of Angola, Manuel António Jorge de Carvalho e Sousa, from Vila Real in northern Portugal, filed a petition to marry the locally born Dona Apolinária Matozo de Andrade e Câmara. The board requested that Sousa provide a register of his baptism within a year so that the couple could marry. Sousa paid the fee of 60,000 *réis* and presented the landowner António de Mesquita as his guarantor.[35] Such obstacles probably prevented some couples of more modest means from formalizing their relationships.

In contradistinction to the wishes of the colonial administration, the majority of couples in Luanda, irrespective of social status and skin color, were in common-law unions.[36] The Luso-African Dona Maria da Costa Pinheiro and Portuguese Sergeant-Major Sérgio da Silva Rego, for example, were in a common-law relationship in spite of their Catholicism and their membership in the local elite. On 20 April 1816, a son, José, was born from their union.[37] In 1817, the free black Africans Francisco Jerónimo and Ana Jorge were also in a common-law relationship.[38]

Some white men also married African women in the style of the country. The Mbundu celebrated matrimony through a ceremony known as *lambamento*. The Portuguese bureaucracy, however, did not recognize such unions. In the late eighteenth century, the Brazilian-born officer Silva Corrêa left descriptions of this Mbundu matrimonial practice. In a demonstration of his bias, he claimed that African families "offered female virginity to anyone willing to pay" in what he considered to be an "auction." "Catholics are the least scrupulous buyers," he claimed, "competing in auctions for women."[39] What Silva Corrêa labeled an "auction" was in fact the bridewealth or payment made to seal marriage contracts among Mbundu families.[40] The bridewealth was often paid in *fazendas* (imported trade goods), including *missangas* (beads), textiles, and *aguardente* (sugarcane brandy), among other items.[41]

Silva Corrêa added that after the "auction," the woman passed through a process of purification, remaining in a dark room for forty days. During this time, she washed her body every day with special herbs to become *afulada* (lighter skinned), while her relatives celebrated with food, music, and dancing in the next room. Following the period of seclusion, husband and wife shared a bed for the first time. If the husband concluded that his wife was a virgin, he would congratulate her parents, who could then celebrate with musket shots and dances. If he concluded to the contrary, he was entitled to break the agreement and receive reimbursement from her parents, or he could remain married and receive an *opanda*, a payment from the man who had dishonored his wife.[42]

Gil described a case of a husband who accused his wife of not being a virgin. The woman maintained that it was in fact her husband who had sex with her prior to their marriage, promising to marry her as soon as he was able to pay for the bridewealth. However, the man claimed that she was already not a virgin when they first slept together. The woman had no other choice than to resort to the *juramento de indua*, a Mbundu ceremony used in cases of dispute. A local *ganga* (healer) prepared a beverage infused with the bark of a tree. The beverage was subsequently divided into two equal amounts, each consumed by the litigants. The innocent was the first person to expel the beverage, while the other litigant felt "the pain of death." To prepare the antidote, the *ganga* charged an amount corresponding to the price of a young captive, or from 20,000 to 40,000 *réis*. Unfortunately, Gil offered no information on the final verdict in this particular case.[43] Other African societies used similar ceremonies involving beverages to settle disputes. The Ga of the Gold Coast used a beverage they called *adom*. The practice was not restricted to Africans, as Danish men also used *adom* to settle disputes with local peoples.[44]

Marriages in the style of the country were also common between Ovimbundu women and men of Portuguese origin in Benguela and its hinterland. The Portuguese António Francisco Ferreira da Silva Porto and the Hungarian Lazslo Magyar, for instance, each married women related to the *sobas* (African rulers) of Bié in the mid-nineteenth century. Through these relationships, both men gained access to local resources and trade networks.[45] We have no evidence of how European men who married according to local practices viewed their unions with African women in Angola. Pernille Ipsen work's reveals that Danish men at Christiansburg in the Gold Coast did not regard their *cassare* unions with Ga women as marriages in a Christian sense.[46] Similarly, Carina Ray claims that while Gold Coasters referred to liaisons between European men and African women as marriages, British officers saw them as illegitimate or temporary sexual relationships.[47] Marriages in the style of the country typically ended with the death or permanent departure of the immigrant husband to Europe, allowing African women the freedom to remarry and European men to enter a legal marriage in their home country.[48]

Children born from parents officially married according to the Catholic Church rituals were considered *filhos legítimos* (legitimate children), while offspring of couples living in common-law unions were known as *filhos naturais* (children born in the state of nature).[49] As for inheritance, the Ordenações Filipinas granted all children, independent of sex, an equal share of their parents' assets through the *legítima*.[50] Even children born out of wedlock were entitled to a share of the inheritance, as long as they were not the product of an adulterous or sacrilegious relationship. Fathers could also acknowledge and make provisions for *filhos naturais* in their wills.[51] Colonial officials often classified the children born from biracial unions as whites or *pardos*. These offspring adopted markers of European culture to distinguish themselves from other Africans in Luanda: their names, clothes, language, and religious practices identified them as Luso-Africans, like other Eurafrican groups in places such as Osu, Saint-Louis, Gorée, Bissau, and Cacheu.[52] Luso-Africans in Luanda moved between African and European cultures, mixing elements from both in their daily lives. They lived in a city where Kimbundu was spoken everywhere and the African population was demographically predominant. Their mothers were Africans or of mixed origin and maintained ties with the Mbundu culture of the region. Luso-Africans' knowledge of both African and European cultures gave them advantages in functioning as commercial intermediaries, and some served in middle-level positions in the colonial administration and militias.

Through Catholic or Mbundu matrimonial arrangements, incoming males accessed established households that provided accommodation, food, and care during illness as well as connections to trade networks that increased their participation in local commerce. As was the case in other ports in West Africa, the services that wives and slaves offered could make the difference between life and death.[53] One anonymous nineteenth-century observer wrote, commenting on the poor conditions of the hospital in Luanda, "Happy is the man who can receive treatment at home and to whom God has given a wife and daughters to take care of him."[54] Indeed, without such care, malaria, diarrhea, yellow fever, and other tropical diseases could quickly kill the Portuguese stationed in the colony.[55] The development of Luanda as the premier Atlantic slaving port depended on the assistance that free and enslaved women offered to incoming merchants.

While foreign males entering into marriage in Luanda gained the companionship of a spouse or partner and connections from her family members, local families, by marrying their daughters to nonnative men, secured access to imported goods and an export market for African commodities, extending their businesses across the Atlantic. The women who entered into these marriages were thus able to access both worlds, enhancing their prestige and becoming intermediaries between foreign traders on the coast and African suppliers inland. They could also sell in local shops and taverns the imported goods their husbands and partners supplied.[56] Even though these marriages were arrangements of convenience, the personal and economic strategies involved in Catholic and Mbundu marriages did not exclude the possibility of affection and sexual attraction between the men and women in these alliances.

The connections that foreign husbands provided, as well as their fortunes, assisted in the advancement of the careers of merchant women. From the early days of Portuguese interactions with West Central Africans, women married to settlers became known as *donas*, reflecting their affiliation to Portuguese culture and their respectable positions in colonial society. The first *donas* emerged from the alliances between Kongo rulers and Europeans, resulting in the conversion of the royal and noble families of the kingdom to Christianity, beginning in the late fifteenth century. In the process, Kongo royalty adopted Portuguese names and noble titles, including Dom and Dona.[57] A similar practice was used in seventeenth-century Matamba when, following the conversion of Njinga to the Christian faith, she became known as Dona Ana de Sousa.[58] Late in that century, the title was already being adopted by women of high status who were affiliated to Portuguese culture in Angola.[59]

Spouses and Business Partners

Following the 1815 ban on slave exports north of the equator, slave traders established in Luanda increased their fleet to meet the growing demand in West Central Africa for captives. They invested in faster ships, such as *bergantins* and schooners, and in larger vessels like *galeras*, intensifying their participation in slaving. Merchants who had acquired wealth through participation in local trade took advantage of the boom in slave exports. António José Brochado, a supplier of manioc flour to the market of Luanda, purchased a ship on 10 February 1825, initiating his participation in the slave trade.[60] Some new investors acquired ships in partnership with other traders. On 25 February 1829, the former outcast Arsénio Pompílio Pompeu do Carpo purchased a ship with António Homem de Vasconcelos.[61] José da Silva Maia Ferreira, a well-known Luanda slave trader, acquired five ships on his own between 1832 and 1833.[62]

Luanda women merchants also benefited from the expansion of the slave trade in West Central Africa. Entering the trade required a great investment in capital as well as access to suppliers and commercial networks that connected the interior to the African coast. Although some local women were familiar with these networks, most did not possess the capital to enter the slave trade. Nevertheless, extant records confirm that some women were able to enter the Atlantic market either alone or as partners of immigrant merchants. Luso-African women were particularly successful in applying the capital they had inherited from deceased parents and husbands, as well as the profits of their own work supplying local markets, to investing in the transatlantic slave trade.

Dona Ana Joaquina dos Santos Silva, also known as the "Queen of Bengo" and "Baroness of Luanda," although far from the only woman slave trader based in Luanda, was certainly the best known. She was born in Luanda in 1789, the only daughter of a Portuguese military officer, Joaquim de Santana Nobre dos Santos, and the Luso-African Dona Teresa de Jesus.[63] Dona Ana Joaquina was first married to Portuguese major João Rodrigues Martins, with whom she had her only daughter, Dona Tereza Luíza de Jesus.[64] The daughter's name was likely a tribute to Dona Ana Joaquina's mother. Tereza was born on 4 December 1815 and baptized some three weeks later in the Church of Nossa Senhora dos Remédios, in the commercial area of the lower town. The child's godparents were the military officer Joaquim Ribeiro de Brito and Nossa Senhora do Carmo (Our Lady of Mount Carmel).[65] Besides his military position, Brito was also a trader, supplying beans and cattle to urban markets.[66] Martins, Dona Ana Joaquina's husband, also invested in livestock; at one point, he owned two hundred head of cattle, illustrating that he had accumulated some wealth in Angola through his military position as well as his marriage to a local woman.[67] The baptism of a child was an occasion to reinforce or establish networks between parents and godparents. That Martins chose a military officer and merchant as his daughter's godfather suggests that he was trying to expand his commercial network.[68]

The couple lived in an imposing Portuguese-style palace located in Bungo, in the commercial district of the lower part of town, which they acquired on 5 May 1824 (see figure 2.1).[69] A replica of the original building stands today as a monument to Dona Ana Joaquina's success. The amount they paid for the *sobrado* (1.600$000 or um conto e seiscentos mil *réis*) would have been enough to purchase 228 slaves (in the 1820s, a male slave cost 70,000 *réis*).[70]

Figure 2.1. Tribunal Provincial de Luanda (Provincial Court of Justice), formerly Dona Ana Joaquina's palace, Luanda, 2019. Photo by author.

In the early nineteenth century, Dona Ana Joaquina was already success-ful in local trade. She owned agricultural land in the interior where her slaves produced maize, manioc flour, and beans for subsistence and to provision slave ships and urban markets.[71] She initiated her investments in the traffic in human beings at a time when the slave trade was expanding. She could count on capi-tal from her own business as well as connections and financial support from her husband. Although the date of her father's death is unknown, it is likely that at this point she had already inherited whatever he had been able to amass throughout his life, which was certainly considerable, as he was a military offi-cer and cattle merchant.

Between 1824 and 1832, Dona Ana Joaquina purchased four ships to export captives across the Atlantic Ocean: *Boa união*, *Felina*, *Nazareth*, and *Minerva*.[72] Throughout her career, the Queen of Bengo owned (or partly owned) at least ten ships sailing between destinations all around the Atlantic world, includ-ing Luanda, Benguela, Lisbon, São Tomé, Montevideo, Rio de Janeiro, Per-nambuco, Bahia, and the Congo River. The vessels shipped captives and goods belonging to her and to other local merchants.[73] In 1827, for instance, Dona Ana Joaquina sent 449 captives to Pernambuco aboard the *Boa união*.[74] In 1835 her ship *Pérola* crossed the Atlantic with 490 captives destined for southeast-ern Brazil.[75]

Following the death of her first husband at an unknown date, Dona Ana Joaquina married Joaquim Ferreira dos Santos Silva, a Brazilian merchant.[76]

In 1839 Silva was a candidate for the position of *deputado* (member) of the Portuguese Cortes (the Parliament) alongside other prominent members of the local elite, demonstrating his growing prestige in Luanda.[77] Then, in the early 1840s, Dona Ana Joaquina became a widow for the second time. On 14 July 1847, António Alves da Costa Júnior, from Minho, in northern Portugal, filed a marriage petition with the Ecclesiastical Board in Luanda to marry Dona Ana Joaquina, becoming her third husband.[78]

Dona Ana Joaquina signed official documents and wrote letters herself, evidencing that she had received some kind of formal education, probably from a tutor in Luanda.[79] As a merchant, she exploited an extensive commercial network that extended as far as the Lunda Empire east of Angola. Through the nineteenth century, she extended her business across the Atlantic Ocean in places such as Brazil, Portugal, Uruguay, and São Tomé. Her fame attracted the attention of several foreigners who spent time in Angola. In the early 1830s, the Italian Tito Omboni wrote in his book *Viaggi nell'Africa Occidentale* that although she resided in Luanda, Dona Ana Joaquina "is obeyed by the most distant tribes. No one dares oppose her will."[80] In her house in Luanda and in her many agricultural properties in the interior, she hosted important figures such as the governors of Angola and other Europeans visiting the colony. Another foreign observer described her as a woman whose reputation "was well merited in consequence of her amiable manners, and the great hospitality which she displayed to those who were so fortunate as to be her guests."[81]

Dona Ana Ifigênia Nogueira da Rocha is another example of a Luandan woman slave trader. Although active as a merchant in the same period as Dona Ana Joaquina, her career has been largely ignored. Until 1816, colonial officials referred to Dona Ana Ifigênia in the extant documentation as a widow, without reference to the identity of her first husband.[82] A land and slave owner in the early nineteenth century, she had already become the largest supplier of beans in Luanda, providing this staple item to the local market and slave ships.[83] The growing demand for captives from West Central Africa after the 1815 treaty between Britain and Portugal encouraged her to invest in the transatlantic slave trade. In 1817 she owned a ship, the *Nossa Senhora da Conceição e Senhor dos Passos*, dedicated to the transportation of captives across the Atlantic Ocean. In November 1817, her ship crossed the Atlantic headed to Bahia with 453 captives aboard.[84]

By 1819 Dona Ana Ifigênia had entered into her second marriage, this time to a ship captain and landowner named Félix José dos Santos.[85] In the early nineteenth century, Santos made several trips to northeastern and southeastern Brazil as captain of the *Caçador* and the *Santo António Protetor*, ships that belonged to the Luanda-based merchants João Gomes Vale and António de

Queirós Monteiro Regadas, respectively.[86] Santos also owned land in the district of Dande, where he, like his wife, produced beans to supply the market of Luanda.[87] After their marriage, the couple expanded their investments in urban real estate, land, and ships. Dona Ana Ifigênia and Santos acquired four *arimos* (agricultural properties) in the interior and three *musseques* (country estates) and three *casas terreas* (a one-story house) in Luanda.[88]

Between 1820 and 1827, they intensified their activities in the slave trade (see table 2.1). Over seven years, the couple organized fifteen trips exporting 7,158 enslaved Africans. Their investments were not limited to Angola; they also purchased captives in Mozambique for sale in the Americas.[89] Some of these commercial ventures were made on their own accounts, while others were carried out in partnerships with other merchants. Commercial partnership was an efficient way of reducing risks, allowing merchants to invest less capital in a single voyage than if they were shipping all their human property on one ship. Slavers preferred to distribute captives throughout several voyages, as waiting to accumulate enough slaves to fill an entire vessel was expensive and could be lethal to their cargo.[90]

Another woman merchant caught the attention of a foreigner who sojourned in Luanda a decade later. On 10 October 1841, Gustav Tams arrived on the Angolan coast with a commercial expedition led by José Ribeiro dos Santos, the Portuguese general consul in Altona, Germany, where Tams served as a medical doctor.[91] Tams left us numerous insights into local trade based upon observations he made during a period of four and a half months. In Luanda, the German doctor observed a number of women of interest to him. Among them was Dona Ana Francisca Ubertali de Miranda, whom he described as a woman "born in the interior, and brought as a slave to Loanda, where she now lives in great style, and carries on a prosperous trade in slaves."[92] The German doctor, however, presented no evidence for his claim that she had been born into slavery in the interior.[93] As revealed by her obituary published in the local gazette the *Boletim Oficial de Angola* (*BOA*), Dona Ana Ubertali had in fact been born in Luanda in 1793, the daughter of Félix Francisco Forte and an unknown woman.[94]

As was common to other Luso-African women, Dona Ana Ubertali married more than once—in her case, no fewer than four times. Her first husband was Carlos Ubertali, an Italian medical doctor who went to Angola as a *degredado* as punishment for political crimes. In the 1820s, Carlos Ubertali became the *almoxarife* (superintendent) of the Armazéns Nacionais (Military Arsenal). By the 1830s, he owned numerous slaves, land, and a large amount of gunpowder, which was deposited in the Fortress of Penedo in the capital.[95] His position as superintendent of the Military Arsenal may have facilitated his access to

Table 2.1. Enslaved Africans shipped by the couple Dona Ana Ifigênia Nogueira da Rocha and Félix José dos Santos

Name of vessel	Owner of vessel	Year	Place of slave purchase	Destination	Enslaved Africans
Bergantim NS da Conceição e Sr dos Passos	Félix José dos Santos	1823	Luanda	Rio de Janeiro	450
Schooner Lucrécia	Félix José dos Santos	1824	Ambriz	Rio de Janeiro	300
Galera Mercantil	Félix José dos Santos	1824	Luanda	Rio de Janeiro	430
Bergantim NS da Conceição e Sr dos Passos	Félix José dos Santos	1824	Luanda	Rio de Janeiro	407
Galera Mercantil	Félix José dos Santos	1825	Luanda	Rio de Janeiro	730
Schooner Lucrécia	Félix José dos Santos and Francisco de Borges Barbosa	1825	Luanda	Rio de Janeiro	340
Galera Mercantil	Félix José dos Santos	1826	Luanda	Rio de Janeiro	730
Bergantim NS da Conceição e Sr dos Passos	Félix José dos Santos	1826	Ambriz	Rio de Janeiro	417
Bergantim Mariana	Félix José dos Santos	1826	Quilimane	Rio de Janeiro	523
Schooner Lucrécia	Félix José dos Santos and Manoel Ribeiro da Silva	1826	Luanda	Rio de Janeiro	319
Bergantim Mariana	Félix José dos Santos	1826	Cabinda	Rio de Janeiro	520
Bergantim Mariana	Félix José dos Santos	1827	Quilimane	Rio de Janeiro	556
Bergantim NS da Conceição e Sr dos Passos	Félix José dos Santos	1827	Luanda	Rio de Janeiro	478
Bergantim Mariana	Félix José dos Santos	1828	Mozambique	Rio de Janeiro	400
Bergantim Mariana	Félix José dos Santos	1829	Lourenço Marques	Rio de Janeiro	558

Source: David Eltis et al., "Voyages: The Trans-Atlantic Slave Trade Database," accessed January 2020, www.slavevoyages.org/.

gunpowder, a highly valued item in the interior markets. Later during that decade, the Italian Tito Omboni noted during his visit to Angola that Ubertali was experimenting with coffee and cotton and had found diamonds.[96] Ubertali died a wealthy man at an unspecified date, and Dona Ana Ubertali inherited his fortune. She remarried three times and was widowed twice more. After the death of her third husband, whose identity remains unknown, she then entered into matrimony with her last husband, the Portuguese lieutenant colonel Luiz António de Miranda, and took his name.[97]

According to Tams, a significant part of her wealth came from the traffic in slaves in the city.[98] Although Dona Ana Ubertali was known predominantly as a slave trader, she also invested in agricultural land and urban real estate and advanced credit to small-scale traders. She owned slaves, cattle, *fazendas*, urban real estate, agricultural land, sailing vessels, furniture, and silver, gold, and iron bars.[99] Among her properties was a house in Bungo, the same district of the lower town where Dona Ana Joaquina had her luxurious palace.[100] In 1846 the street where Dona Ana Ubertali's *sobrado* was located was named Miranda Street in honor of her last husband, illustrating his prestige in the Angolan capital.[101]

Like Dona Ana Joaquina, Dona Ana Ubertali signed official documents herself, demonstrating that she had received some instruction, probably from private tutors, as was common for the daughters of the Luanda elite. Her marriages with well-positioned European men such as Dr. Ubertali and Lieutenant Colonel Miranda may well have contributed to her wealth and opened up commercial opportunities. Meanwhile, her husbands benefited from her knowledge of local trade networks and cultures.

The trajectories of these three women merchants have some aspects in common. Their Portuguese names indicate that they were born from unions between immigrant men and local African or Luso-African women. Like their mothers, they married immigrant men who may have facilitated their access to imported goods and foreign markets; in the process, they also assisted in developing the fortunes of their husbands in Angola by providing a household and access to local trade networks. In association with their husbands, these three women prospered in the internal market and found new opportunities in slave trading after 1815. Their local influence and mastery of Mbundu and Portuguese cultures contributed to their successful careers as merchants.

The strategy shared by these women merchants seems to have been the common path followed by many traders in Angola: they initially invested in the local market and, after acquiring enough capital, ventured into the transatlantic slave trade. Other women merchants too were involved in activities connected to the traffic, although the number of women who sent ships across the Atlantic Ocean is much smaller than that of men. In the southern port of Benguela, women acted as *sertanejas* (itinerant traders) as well as suppliers of slaves to coastal merchants.[102] Other wives assisted male merchants by acting as both cultural brokers and associates. Since only the names of the husbands appear in official records, the women's stories remain untold. These women merchants belonged to the group of individuals who benefited from the slave trade, although they also had to live with the risks and violence it produced.[103] They were particularly well situated to take advantage of the Atlantic slave trade, as were the *mulatresses* of Christiansborg and the *nharas* and *signares* and *senhoras* of the Senegambia region. They too contributed to the development of European trade and colonialism, to the great detriment to the lives of less privileged Africans.

CHAPTER THREE

Feeding the Residents of Luanda and Provisioning Slave Ships

I N MOST PORTS along the western coast of Africa, urban dwellers depended on the populations of the hinterland to produce their food. Men and women of African, Luso-African, and European origins owned land in the interior, where indigenous people, free and enslaved, tended the land to produce staples for subsistence and to supply slave ships and urban markets. Large quantities of beans, maize, and manioc flour grown on the banks of the Kwanza, Dande, and Bengo Rivers arrived in the city on a daily basis on the back of porters or on board boats—except in times of famine, caused by droughts and floods. This chapter examines the origin of crops and the profile of suppliers provisioning the city of Luanda and slave ships during the early nineteenth century.

From *Arimos* to Urban Markets

Stanley B. Alpern considered the introduction of new crops from the tropical Americas as the main, albeit indirect, contribution of early European inter-action with western Africa. The reasons for the adoption of new food sources in Africa were many, including the subsistence needs of European settlers and the supplies required by the crews and slave cargos on ships dispatched to the New World.[1] Meanwhile, cultivation of new crops contributed to the accel-eration of population growth, even if that cultivation was at the expense of nutrients.[2] Cassava, maize, and beans were the most important of these crops for the populations of West Central Africa. In Angola, the production and trade of foodstuffs involved several agents in an intricate commercial network. From the agricultural properties located on the riverbanks to the tables of Luanda's residents, food staples passed through many hands: free and enslaved field workers, merchants, boatmen, and retail sellers. Both men and women were present at every stage of this provisioning chain.

In 1799 the Brazilian-born physician José Pinto de Azeredo published his analysis of diseases found throughout Angola.[3] In line with the humoral pathology of his day, he investigated the environment and living conditions of the population, including the eating habits that might counter the unhealthy miasmas of the damp coastal plain. According to Azeredo, fish were the most common source of protein for Luanda's residents because of their abundance in the cold offshore current and consequent affordability. The *nacionais* (local Mbundu people) also ate *infunge*, a thick porridge made from manioc flour, rice, or *fuba* (maize meal) and seasoned with palm oil, spices, and *ginguba* (peanuts).[4]

Silva Corrêa also paid particular attention to local cuisine in his *História de Angola*. The Brazilian-born officer noted that manioc flour, beans, and maize were the main staples of Luanda residents. He pointed out that the consumption of beef, pork, and goat meat was a privilege of the upper classes, who could afford their high prices. The wealthy also consumed luxuries imported from overseas, such as wine, olive oil, beer, cheese, tea, butter, and pastries, found in shops and taverns throughout the city.[5] In times of famine, canned items became the main source of nutrients for those who could afford them.[6] Since slaves prepared the meals in wealthier households, they likely introduced African flavors to the cuisine, as was the case in Gorée and Saint-Louis.[7] Slaves could also be trained to prepare meals in the European style that appealed to the taste of their masters.[8]

The plainer local foodstuffs that fed the majority population of Luanda came from agricultural properties known as *arimos*, located in the suburbs and in the immediate interior. Based on decades of experience in Angola in the seventeenth century, António de Oliveira de Cadornega stated that the verb *arimar* derived from the Kimbundu verb *kurima*, meaning "to plant or to cultivate."[9] Cadornega highlighted the existence of *arimos* in the Luanda rural suburbs of Bem-Bem and Sequeli and on the islands of Cazengo and Desterro, where the wealthy residents had their *quintas* (country estates).[10] By the nineteenth century, the rural suburbs of Luanda had expanded to include the neighborhoods of Nossa Senhora do Rosário, Nossa Senhora de Nazaré, Alto das Cruzes, and Maianga.[11] Most *arimos*, however, were found along the banks of the Kwanza, Bengo, and Dande Rivers, producing vegetables, fruits, beans, cassava, maize, millet, and livestock, all of which fed the producers and their families, slaves, and dependents, while the surplus was sold in the various markets of the town (see map 3.1).[12]

Foreign observers usually commented on the good quality of land along the rivers, at the same time attributing the low productivity to the idleness of indigenous populations. Silva Corrêa remarked that the limited variety and low productivity of fruit and vegetables resulted from the "laziness of the

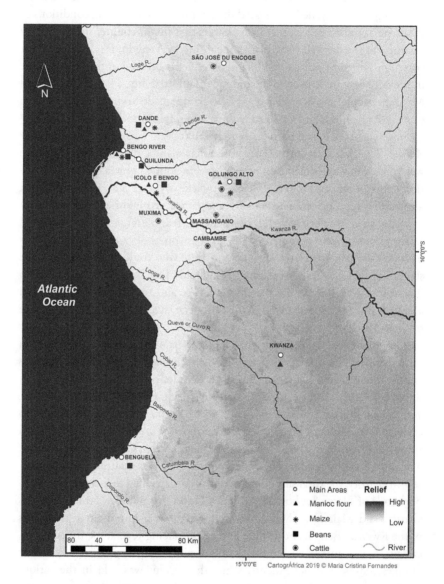

Map 3.1. Main areas of foodstuff production in Angola, 1815–1828. Map by Maria Cristina Fernandes based on the author's data.

inhabitants" as well as from the droughts and river floods that frequently brought famine in the wake of feasts.[13] Another observer stated a similar opinion, asserting that "the land is productive" while adding that "the deep lethargy in which the local population live through their natural indolence makes scarce the basic staples that the inhabitants need for their subsistence."[14] Views such as these illustrate the paternalism of the colonial enterprise: metropolitan authorities perceived indigenous populations as unable to "progress" without Portuguese tutelage. Well into the twentieth century, the Portuguese state continuously resorted to the "laziness" of Africans as a justification for the use of compulsory labor.[15]

In fact, environmental conditions and the pressures of the transatlantic slave trade were the real reasons for the periodic cycles of low agricultural productivity. Instances of extended droughts lasting from one to three years occurred at least once every decade, destroying crops and killing livestock. After the droughts ended, rainfall caused rivers to flood, destroying agricultural fields. These environmental issues made the population more vulnerable to malnutrition and consequently to diseases, particularly smallpox epidemics.[16] Moreover, raiding bands destroyed farmland and captured able young cultivators to sell to Atlantic slavers, further contributing to the shortage of food.[17] During periods of famine, provisions came from São Tomé e Príncipe and as far away as Portugal and Brazil.[18] In 1817, when Luanda experienced another of its many famines, beans from Rio de Janeiro and Pernambuco temporarily relieved the hunger of the town's population.[19]

In 1772 Governor Francisco Inocêncio de Sousa Coutinho left a memorandum for his successor, Dom António de Lencastre, highlighting that agriculture was the sector "without which no government can succeed in war or in peace, no trade can be done, no navigation can be sustained, and no troops can be mobilized."[20] In this context, perhaps Coutinho's most important legacy was the construction in 1765 of a regulated public market in Luanda, the Terreiro Público. During the earlier eighteenth century, Luanda had experienced severe droughts, which were followed by poor harvests and sicknesses, interrupting the regular supply of basic provisions. In addition, some traders were able to monopolize the supply of agricultural produce and control prices. The creation of the Terreiro Público was an attempt to guarantee regular and affordable food supplies to residents and to slave ships.[21]

The supply of foodstuffs to urban markets involved three principal phases: production, transportation, and retail distribution. Small-scale farmers, with the support of family members and a few slaves, cultivated the land in the *arimos* and orchards located within the town.[22] Slave labor, however, predominated in the fields of the interior. In the Bengo region, the majority of the enslaved tending the land were women, following a common pattern in African communities in which women were responsible for agricultural work.[23] Most owners of inland agricultural properties resided in the urban area, away from the diseases to which they believed Africans were immune. In the absence of masters, African and white *muculuntos* (overseers) were responsible for managing the *arimos*.[24] Some overseers were white *degredados* with experience in agriculture. The exile Manuel José Rodrigues, born in Braga, northern Portugal, was an overseer in the district of Icolo e Bengo, dying there from typhoid fever in 1851.[25]

Both free and enslaved carriers and boatmen transported crops to Luanda from the *arimos* established along the riverbanks. Most foodstuffs were carried on small ships and flat-bottomed, locally built riverboats called *dongos*, although the use of enslaved porters was also common.[26] While some large-scale producers owned riverboats, others had to pay freight to shipowners or managers of enslaved porters to deliver their produce to the market. Food staples entered the Terreiro Público in sacks and were weighed in *exeques* (approximately 60 kilograms, or about 132 pounds). The market administration taxed every *exeque* of produce, and the Municipal Council retained the sum thus raised.[27]

Not all producers had the infrastructure and capital necessary to trade on their own accounts. Small-scale farmers were unlikely to be able to pay the costs of transportation and the taxes imposed by the Terreiro Público; they often chose instead to supply large-scale producers and foodstuff traders. Wealthy individuals owning land, slaves, and riverboats were able to trade independently.

Households in Luanda relied on outdoor markets, grocery stores, taverns, and street vendors to supply on a retail basis the food they required for sustenance. Retail sellers acquired the produce they offered from the Terreiro. Both men and women owned shops and taverns in Luanda, where they offered a variety of items, including alcoholic beverages, groceries, staples, and meat. In 1827 Dona Pruciana owned and operated a tavern where she sold spirits and pork meat.[28] João Cipriano dos Santos also offered alcoholic beverages and food in his tavern.[29] Most retail establishments were owned by Luso-Africans, but some free blacks too owned taverns and small shops in town. In 1827 the black woman Josefa owned a tavern in the *baixa* (lower part of town).[30] Other black women, probably unable to pay for the license required from shop and tavern keepers, traded items directly from their houses, in contravention of municipal bylaws. This was the case with Maria Raposo, who was fined 1,000 *réis* in July 1831 for selling *fazendas* (imported trade goods) in her house without a license.[31]

The retail trade of the streets and outdoor markets represented one of the few employment opportunities open to poor free and enslaved women, who were generally excluded from specialized trades.[32] Faced with limited occupational prospects, poor African women entered the retail trade as *quitandeiras*, as street vendors were known in Angola. Luanda had four *quitandas* (outdoor markets): Mercado dos Coqueiros, Quitanda Grande, Venda dos Pratos, and Feira do Bungo, all located in the *baixa*.[33] All kinds of *fazendas secas e molhadas* (wet and dry goods) could be found in these markets for sale, either from the baskets of ambulant *quitandeiras* or in their stalls. Masters commonly employed enslaved women in retail trade or rented them out for this purpose. Both free and enslaved *quitandeiras* had to carry licenses issued by the Municipal Council. Nevertheless, many poor black women peddled in the town streets without proper documentation, taking the risk of being caught and fined by municipal inspectors. The black woman Rosa, for example, was fined 2,000 *réis* for selling goods in the streets without a license on 30 December 1820.[34]

Beans

Common beans (*Phaseolus vulgaris*) were reported in the Kingdom of Kongo as early as the seventeenth century, and by the eighteenth century *vulgaris* was established in West Africa.[35] Bean supplies rose seasonally in Angola with the beginning of the rains in October and peaked from January through March.[36] Besides being one of the main staples that fed Luanda's inhabitants, alongside manioc flour and maize, beans provided essential protein for captives waiting in the *quintais* for embarkation and during the Middle Passage.[37] On 5 January 1815, the master of the Portuguese ship *Ave Maria* purchased twenty *exeques* of beans in the Luanda public market.[38] The ship belonged to Manuel Ribeiro Coelho and transported captives from Angola to Bahia and to Pernambuco in northeastern Brazil. On 12 March 1816, the *Ave Maria* left on a voyage under Captain João Crisóstomo, transporting 579 captives to the port of Salvador, in Bahia, on a passage that took thirty-six days to complete.[39]

A scribe was in charge of recording all produce brought to the public market and sold there.[40] This responsibility generated a series of transaction books recording the names of suppliers and buyers, the origin and volume of crops, and the dates of arrival and sale. Between January 1815 and December 1817, the Terreiro received 11,889 *exeques* of beans, mainly from the district of Dande and to a lesser extent from Golungo, Bengo, Icolo, Quilunda, and the interior of Benguela (see map 3.1 and table 3.1). Following droughts in 1817, the public market also received supplies from Rio de Janeiro and Pernambuco in Brazil.[41]

Most beans were grown on private land with the labor of enslaved Africans. On 11 January 1816, Maria Lopes Paim supplied the Terreiro with seventeen *exeques* of beans produced in her *arimo*, Mussengo-amumba, in the district of Dande.[42] *Carregadores*, as porters were known in Angola, transported 4,680

Table 3.1. Suppliers of beans, 1815–1817

	Number of suppliers	*Number of* exeques	*Percentage*
Men	325	10,663	89.7
Women	34	1,099	9.2
Convents	2	127	1.1
Total	361	11,889	

Source: BML, códice 041, registo de entradas e saídas de feijão.

exeques, or 39 percent, of the beans entering the market during this period; the remainder reached the Terreiro on riverboats. Men supplied 10,663 *exeques*, or 89.7 percent, of the beans. Most men supplying beans were members of the local civilian militia, ranging from colonels to privates. Among them were Colonel José Francisco Pacheco, Sergeant Francisco Militão Matozo, and Lieutenant Joaquim Teixeira Mendonça.[43] In spite of the laws that forbade their participation in trade, administrative and military personnel commonly engaged in commercial activities, including trade in foodstuffs and in slaves.[44] Their positions in the militia may have facilitated their access to land and slaves, allowing them to produce foodstuffs to supply slave ships and urban markets.[45] Among these men, Sergeant António Gonçalves de Carvalho was the largest supplier. He produced beans in his *arimos* located in the districts of Dande and Icolo and also purchased them from small peasants, such as a man named Manuel Silvestre.[46] It was common for large-scale producers to cultivate crops on their land and to handle produce from small peasants as well, which they purchased or sold for a commission. Private Joaquim Ribeiro de Brito supplied the Terreiro with beans that he purchased from two African women, Inácia António and Engrácia Domingos.[47] Inácia and Engrácia were small-scale producers who likely did not possess the means to supply the market directly, paying the costs of transportation and taxes. Even men in prestigious positions supplemented their incomes by participating in local commerce whenever they found an opportunity. On 2 January 1816, Chief Surgeon Joaquim José Ferreira de Campos supplied the Terreiro with twenty-four *exeques* of beans he had purchased from the orphans of Euzébio Francisco de Carvalho.[48] On 27 April 1816, Chief Surgeon Joaquim Nogueira da Silva delivered five *exeques* of beans to the Terreiro.[49]

Religious institutions and clerics also engaged in foodstuff supply. It was not uncommon for religious men to own land and slaves that could be employed in agricultural production. Some individuals upon their deaths left land and other goods to religious institutions, contributing to their property holdings.[50] The convents of Our Lady of Carmo and São José were listed among the food suppliers; however, together these institutions supplied only about 1 percent, of the beans sold in the market. Father Joaquim de Santana e Faria, Father Joaquim Nunes Garcez do Espírito Santo, Father Manuel António, and Father Manuel Pinto de Barros were listed among the bean suppliers.[51]

Free black men engaged in foodstuff supply as well. Most were small-scale peasants supplying between one and ten *exeques* produced in private plots of land by family members and possibly some slaves. The black man Miguel Pedro, for example, supplied seven *exeques* of beans to the Terreiro on 18 January 1816, his only appearance in the public market's register.[52] It is likely that his family produced beans for subsistence, and that year they had a surplus, which he marketed. A few among this group produced beans on a large scale, as was the case of Agostinho João Manuel. On 18 January 1817, he delivered to the market sixty-eight *exeques* of produce cultivated in his own *arimo*, located in the district of Icolo.[53] Agostinho likely owned slaves, who tended to the land in his *arimo*. Other Africans, however, seem to have produced beans in association, possibly on communal land. On 30 November 1817, a group of black Africans delivered 330 *exeques* of beans overland. The Terreiro scribe labeled the men under the category of *diversos pretos* (several blacks).

Women also supplied foodstuffs, but only about 9.2 percent of the beans the market received between January 1815 and December 1817 were brought by women. Most were *donas* of Luso-African origin who owned land and slaves that they used to produce foodstuffs to feed their households and supply urban markets. Dona Máxima Leonor Botelho de Vasconcelos, for example, was the daughter of Commander Alexandre José Botelho de Vasconcelos, who became the governor of Benguela in 1796.[54] Vasconcelos was himself a landowner, crop producer, and trader, supplying manioc flour to Luanda's public market.[55] Dona Máxima followed in her father's footsteps, investing in crop production and cattle. She supplied the Terreiro with beans cultivated with the labor of enslaved Africans in her *arimos*, located in the district of Dande.[56] The largest female bean supplier was Dona Ana Ifigênia Nogueira da Rocha; she alone delivered 46 percent of the beans supplied by women. The beans originated in her own *arimo* in the district of Dande and from the land of five peasants, from whom she purchased produce.[57] Her prominence as a food supplier appears even more significant when we consider that these sales did not represent the totality of her produce, part of which she used for subsistence and part to supply her own slave ships, which transported slaves to Brazil.

Some female small-scale farmers also supplied beans to the Terreiro; however, they usually delivered fewer than ten *exeques*. On 10 January 1816, Maria de Franca supplied nine *exeques* of beans to the Luanda market. She appeared in the Terreiro records only once, which suggests that she was a one-time sup-plier.[58] Most of these women were *pretas livres* (free blacks), who probably grew beans on collective land to feed their families and marketed the surplus. For instance, on 4 March 1816, the black woman Luíza Domingos supplied the pub-lic market with seven *exeques* of beans.[59] Here again, this was her only delivery; given the small amount recorded, we can assume that she did not usually supply beans to large markets, although she may have sold small quantities informally. Some women cultivated beans to supply large-scale merchants. On 5 July 1817, the black woman Engrácia Domingos sold seven *exeques* of beans to Lieutenant Joaquim Ribeiro de Brito, which he then supplied to the Terreiro.[60] It is likely that she simply did not have the capital required to market her own produce in Luanda. Together, black men and women provided about 32 percent of the beans entering the market during this period.

Manioc Flour

Manioc comes from the cassava plant, a leafy shrub native to tropical America, typically growing about five to twelve feet high and sometimes reaching as high as eighteen feet. Its bulbous central root can be processed, dried, and eaten as a staple carbohydrate in human diets, and its leaves are a nutritious supple-ment. The cassava plant tolerates poor soils and pests that destroy other crops, and it is exceptionally resistant to drought—all qualities that made it a crop well suited to tropical Africa, particularly the sandy, dry soils of Angola.[61] The roots, buried in the ground, could also survive the raids carried out by ban-dit groups intent on capturing people for the slave trade; these bandits also destroyed fields and harvests of grain crops.[62]

The Portuguese had brought cassava from Brazil during the sixteenth cen-tury, and its roots subsequently gained favor in West Central Africa.[63] By the eighteenth century, cassava leaves, roots, and processed derivatives had all become major components of the diet of local populations in Portuguese Angola.[64] However, at the same time that cassava supported local populations through drought years, it provided insufficient nutrients, leaving those depen-dent on it weakened and consequently more vulnerable to diseases.[65]

Despite the abundance of cassava in Angola, local production of manioc flour struck visitors as "primitive," given that the process was entirely manual. Silva Corrêa noted that in Angola, unlike in Brazil, the roots were not peeled prior to grinding, resulting in a flour that was dark and bitter. Nevertheless, this shortcut made the process of preparation cheaper, and the end product was even preferred, according to the Brazilian-born military officer, for "being healthier and providing more nutrients to black Africans."[66] This dark common flour was not the only type available in Angola. Silva Corrêa described three types of manioc flour: the expensive and rare "white flour," which producers and their families made to feed themselves or supplied by special order to others; a "mediocre flour," which was cheaper and therefore more accessible to customers; and an "inferior flour," which fed Africans, the enslaved in particular. He also noted that captains of slave ships purchased the inferior flour in the Terreiro Público to feed their crews and captives.

Between January 1826 and November 1827, the Luanda public market received 9,910 *exeques* of manioc flour, which came mainly from the districts of Bengo, Dande, and Golungo and, to a lesser extent, from Kwanza and Icolo (see map 3.1 and table 3.2). Manioc flour from Brazil and São Tomé e Príncipe also arrived in the city public market during periods of drought to relieve the hunger of residents. In March 1827, the ship *Santo António* arrived in Luanda carrying seventy *exeques* of flour from Bahia.[67] In October 1827, the *Sam Sebastião Africano* supplied the public market with 250 *exeques* of manioc flour from the island of São Tomé e Príncipe.[68] The local population, captains of sailing vessels, and the Fazenda Real (Royal Treasury) were the main purchasers of this produce. Between March and December 1827, the captain of the ship *Amazona*, which transported captives from Angola to southeastern Brazil, purchased 302 *exeques* of manioc flour. That year, the ship disembarked 491 slaves in Rio de Janeiro and another 467 the following year.[69] The Royal Treasury acquired manioc flour particularly to feed the military personnel stationed in the city.[70]

Again, the great majority of suppliers of manioc flour were men, including priests, military personnel, and individuals of modest means. Together they supplied about 93.8 percent of the manioc flour entering the market in this period. Vicar Francisco Pereira de Contreiras, Priest António Francisco das Necessidades, and Priest José do Rosário were some of the religious men among the suppliers.[71] As they did with beans, large-scale producers cultivated cassava in their *arimos* and handled manioc flour from small farmers. António José Brochado supplied the Terreiro with 147 *exeques* of manioc flour—79 *exeques* from his property and the remaining 68 originating from small-scale farmers such as Luiz Xavier da Costa and Isabel Antónia.[72]

Table 3.2. Suppliers of manioc flour, 1826–1827

	Number of suppliers	Number of exeques	Percentage
Men	417	9,298	93.8
Women	20	612	6.2
Total	437	9,910	

Source: BML, códice 055, registo de entradas e saídas de farinha, vol. 1.

Some foodstuff suppliers were also prominent slave traders, producing crops to supply their slave ships and urban markets. One of the better-known merchants who prospered through both the foodstuff trade and the commerce in human beings was Inocêncio Matozo de Andrade. Matozo de Andrade owned slaves and *arimos* in the district of Dande, where he produced manioc flour for his own household and to supply the Luanda market and slave ships. On 10 July 1827, he sold the captain of the *Amazona* thirty *exeques* of manioc flour.[73] The head of the Matozo family also purchased manioc flour from small farmers like Victor Amádio.[74] Matozo de Andrade kept part of the manioc flour he produced or purchased to feed the captives transported to Brazil in his slave ship, the *S. Marcos*.[75]

Women too were participants in the manioc flour trade, albeit in significantly smaller numbers than men, supplying about 6.2 percent of the produce during this period. The majority were *donas* who owned land and the labor necessary to produce staples. Among them was Dona Ana Joaquina dos Santos Silva, who produced manioc flour with slave labor in her *arimos* in the districts of Dande and Bengo. While she retained part of her produce to feed her many slaves, a significant amount supplied her slave ships. These alone should have consumed a great part of the flour originating from her agricultural properties. Eventually, she also supplied some produce to the Terreiro, likely when she could count on a surplus. On 10 July 1826, she supplied the Luanda market with 15.5 *exeques* of flour, a relatively small amount and the only amount she delivered that year.[76] In 1827, however, she appeared in the records of the Terreiro four times, delivering 90 *exeques* in total.[77]

Blacks also produced manioc flour to supply the Terreiro, whether individually or in association. Together they provided 34.5 percent of the manioc flour entering the market between January 1826 and November 1827. Most blacks were men and sporadic suppliers; for a few, the production of manioc flour seemed to be their main activity. Lourenço Miguel made a single appearance in the register on 22 October 1827, when he supplied eight *exeques* of manioc flour.[78] João Francisco Quicanguela was a recurrent supplier; between January and November of the same year, he supplied the Terreiro six times with a total of thirty-three *exeques*.[79] This was still a small amount compared to the volume of flour that most Luso-Africans and nonnatives supplied.

Among black African suppliers, only seven were women: Ana Alves, Grácia Luísa, Luíza Antónia, Margarida João Paulo, Maria Francisca, Maria Lourenço, and Grácia António. These women were small-scale and occasional suppliers, delivering small amounts of between two and eighteen *exeques*. In spite of being small-scale producers, they did not sell their manioc flour to large-scale merchants but supplied the Luanda market directly. Maria Francisca, for example, herself supplied the Terreiro with two *exeques* of the manioc flour that she produced in the district of Golungo.[80]

Maize

Maize was probably the first New World crop to cross the Atlantic, although exactly when it reached western Africa and who brought it remain open to debate.[81] Maize had greater requirements to flourish than cassava: better-watered areas and greater input of labor, especially for the clearing of new fields.[82] Alongside manioc and beans, maize became one of the main crops consumed in West Central Africa. Farmers produced both *milho-painço* (millet, a crop native to Africa) and *milho americano* (maize) in the environs of Angola. In the second half of the seventeenth century, Cadornega noted that both maize and millet were being cultivated in the rural suburb of Bem-Bem in Luanda.[83] Africans grilled maize on the cob or boiled it in water; they also appreciated maize flour, called *fuba*, in spite of it being more expensive than manioc flour. Each slaving ship anchored in the bay of Luanda acquired four sacks of maize to feed the chickens the ship carried for officers to dine on and to mix with beans to feed enslaved Africans.[84] Luanda's public market probably received both millet and maize, given that Africans favored the former, while European and Brazilian palates were more inclined toward the latter.

The provision of maize to the Terreiro is better documented for the second half of the nineteenth century.[85] Only sparse records exist for the previous period, providing limited information regarding the volume, origins, and suppliers of this produce. The few registers include thirty-two entries made between November 1827 and February 1828 (see table 3.3). In spite of their limitations, these registers allow us to pinpoint the main areas of maize production, and they suggest the profile of suppliers.

Most of the maize in these records came from the district of Dande, in the valley of the river of the same name. Some also came from Golungo, Icolo, and Bengo, nearer Luanda (map 3.1). As with suppliers of manioc flour and beans,

Table 3.3. Suppliers of maize, November 1827–February 1828

	Number of suppliers	*Number of exeques*	*Percentage*
Men	30	133	94.3
Women	1	3	2.2
Convents	1	5	3.5
Total	32	141	

Source: BML, códice 034, registos diversos incompleto.

most suppliers in the maize registers were men, including priests and military personnel. Together these men accounted for thirty out of the thirty-three suppliers listed in the records. They delivered 133 of the 141 *exeques* of maize listed in the sparse records. Priest Francisco Pereira de Castro, for example, supplied three *exeques* of maize to the public market in February 1828.[86] Black Africans also supplied maize to the market. A black man named Manuel Bernardo supplied forty-two *exeques* on 31 January 1828.[87] The Convent of Carmo, also among the suppliers of manioc flour, supplied five *exeques* of maize to the Terreiro during this period.[88] The main consumers were the local population, the Royal Treasury, and slave ships. On 4 February 1828, the Royal Treasury purchased one *exeque* of maize, probably to feed the military.[89]

Only two women were listed in the records. One of them was Dona Ana Joaquina do Amaral, then a single woman and the owner of agricultural properties dedicated to the production of maize in the Dande and Bengo valleys. On 31 January 1828, she delivered three *exeques* of maize to the Luanda market.[90] A second woman mentioned in the registers was Dona Maria João, a small-scale farmer who produced maize to supply larger traders. On 4 February 1828, she sold one *exeque* of her maize to a man named António da Silva, who delivered it to the public market.[91]

Beef: The Meal of the Privileged

The prevalence of the disease-carrying tsetse fly, which flourished in lightly wooded, less populated areas, limited the presence of cattle in Angola. Given the scarcity of large livestock among West Central Africans, owning cattle became a sign of prestige and economic power restricted to rulers who accumulated herds through tribute paid by the populations subject to them. In the Kwango region, the Lunda, Cokwe, and Imbangala used cattle as gifts to Portuguese authorities and European traders and as payment for bridewealth, but they rarely ate beef. Among the Lunda, chiefs enhanced their prestige by wearing belts made of cattle tails.[92] The sacrifice of cattle was also common for occasions such as the inauguration or death of an African ruler. According to Portuguese cleric José Sousa de Amado in the mid-nineteenth century in the Kingdom of Kasanje, the death of the ruler was celebrated with both animal and human sacrifices. Amado noted that during the funeral, a man and a woman, most likely enslaved, were buried with the ruler. Three months after the ruler's burial, a man and an ox were sacrificed in honor of the deceased. He also noted that the first year of governance of a new ruler was marked with a feast in which a man, an ox, a castrated sheep, a dog, a rooster, and a pigeon were sacrificed and eaten by the attendees.[93] Nutrition, then, was not the only purpose for raising cattle. Africans who raised cattle and sheep did so to supply white customers, but they rarely killed or consumed these animals themselves, except upon occasions of community celebrations or during funerals.[94]

Most of the cattle supplying the beef requirements of Luanda's well-to-do inhabitants were raised in interior areas along the Kwanza, such as Massangano, Muxima, and Cambambe, as well as in higher areas around São José do Encoge and Golungo (see map 3.1).[95] Barns for cattle, pigs, goats, and sheep were found throughout the lower and upper parts of the town, even though they were forbidden by Luanda's municipal bylaws. Dona Maria Apolinária, for example, owned a pigsty in Pelourinho Square, in the center of the *cidade baixa*.[96] The cattle for consumption in Luanda were processed in the slaughterhouse located on Bressane Square, in the *cidade alta*.[97]

The slaughterhouse also received swine, mainly from the district of Bengo. Pigs wandering freely through the streets eventually also mixed with others brought in from elsewhere to produce the pork that fed inhabitants.[98] Once the meat was processed in the slaughterhouse, tavern keepers purchased it to sell in their establishments. While beef was expensive and its consumption was restricted to the elite, pork and goat meat were more affordable. Chicken was appreciated by most of the urban population because it was cheap.[99]

As they did with manioc flour, beans, and maize, men again made up the great majority of beef suppliers. They included a wide range of civilians, military personnel, and priests. Two particular institutions appear in the registers of the municipal slaughterhouse as suppliers of beef: the Convent of Carmo and the Trem Real, or the quartermaster (supply) corps of the military. A disproportionately large number of the traders who were engaged in supplying cattle were also slave dealers. António de Queirós Monteiro Regadas was both a cattle supplier and an owner of the slave vessel *Santo António Protetor*, which transported captives to Pernambuco and the Amazon region in northeastern and northern Brazil, respectively.[100] Family relations of António de Queirós Monteiro Regadas also engaged in both the cattle business and slave trading. Luís de Queirós Monteiro Regadas, for example, acted as captain on voyages of the *Santo António Protetor* and owned captives carried to Pernambuco aboard the same vessel.[101] Alongside his two brothers, Francisco de Queirós Monteiro Regadas was a prominent supplier of cattle to Luanda's slaughterhouse.[102] Other merchants who traded in both slaves and cattle included José Manuel Vieira da Silva, who in addition to being a military officer was owner and captain of the slave vessel *Bom Jesus Triunfo*, which transported captive labor to Pernambuco,[103] and Isidoro Alves, who exported enslaved Africans to Rio de Janeiro on his vessel, *São José Diligente Vulcano*.[104] The business of supplying cattle to the Luanda consumer market required a greater investment than the production of crops, limiting this trade to wealthy merchants, for the most part men, who also invested in the transatlantic slave trade. Investment in multiple businesses allowed Luanda slave traders to diversify their activities and thus mitigate the risks associated with putting all their capital into slave voyages.

While women of modest means were able to supply crops to the Terreiro, they did not provide cattle. The women who were involved in supplying beef to the slaughterhouse of Luanda were all wealthy *donas*.[105] Among them, two stand out: Dona Maria Bonina Tavares and Dona Máxima Leonor Botelho de Vasconcelos. Dona Maria Bonina Tavares owned captives and land and invested in the production of crops and cattle raising. In the early nineteenth century, she invested in cultivating cassava and maize on her *arimos* in the districts of Bengo and Dande; both crops were destined for the Terreiro Público.[106] She was also a regular supplier of beef to the Luanda slaughterhouse: between February and April 1825, she supplied thirty head of cattle to feed the Luanda elite.[107] Supplying beef, manioc flour, and maize to urban markets, as well as owning slaves, made Dona Maria Bonina a wealthy woman.[108]

Dona Máxima Leonor Botelho de Vasconcelos also produced maize and beans and raised cattle to supply Luanda's public market and slaughterhouse.[109] Her *arimos* were located in the districts of Icolo, Bengo, and Calumbo, while she resided in Luanda with her children and slaves.[110] A widow, Dona Máxima enjoyed a certain prestige in the interior. She was the only woman—alongside seven male residents of the district of Calumbo, five military officers, nine *sobas* (local rulers), and Chief Lieutenant Manuel Félix Batista—who was invited on 28 October 1838 to swear in the Political Constitution of the Portuguese Monarchy, which consolidated Portugal's republic.[111] Undoubtedly, her father's position as former governor of Benguela, as well as her own successful career as a trader, contributed to Dona Máxima's influential position in Luanda and its hinterland. As a wealthy woman, she was able to stand side by side with men and enjoy the respectful attention of political authorities. Nevertheless, because of her gender, she was never able to occupy one of the administrative positions usual for men of high status, even those who originated as exiled criminals.[112]

Women merchants thus acted alongside men in supplying foodstuffs to urban markets, although in smaller numbers than their male counterparts. Wealthy *donas* produced and sold foodstuffs that they shipped to the public market, sometimes in their own vessels. Although some women became merchants and acquired wealth through their participation in this trade, they did so within a gendered social structure. In the foodstuff trade, as in the trade in slaves, the majority of suppliers were men, although most of the producers and farmers were probably women. While some wealthy *donas* were able to compete with men, small-scale farmers could supply urban markets only through the patronage of big traders, most of whom were Luso-African and immigrant men.

CHAPTER FOUR

Selling People Illegally

As the suppression of the transatlantic slave trade reached into the southern hemisphere in 1836, members of Luanda's merchant community faced the uncertain prospect of replacing slaving—the only business many of them had ever known—with the production of tropical commodities. With warships patrolling the main ports, Luanda-based merchants moved ongoing slaving out of the sight of official surveillance to smaller, remote locations under African control. From these remote ports, they continued exporting captives well into the 1860s, as well as benefiting from prestigious positions within the colonial state. This chapter explores the impact of abolition on the Luanda merchant community and the conduct of the slave trade during the period of illegality.

The Abolition of the Slave Trade in the South Atlantic

The first half of the nineteenth century was marked by political events that greatly affected the Portuguese empire. In 1820 a liberal revolution broke out in Portugal, and the country was given a constitution. In the next year, King João VI, then living in Rio de Janeiro with the royal family, was obliged to return to Lisbon to take his place in the new government and to swear to uphold the constitution.[1] In 1822 Brazil became independent from Portugal, and the following year a rebellious group in Benguela attempted to join the newly independent country. The Luanda government sent reinforcements to the southern port, crushing the rebellion, known as Confederação Brasílica.[2] Brazil's independence should have impacted its commercial activities in Angola, as Portugal forbade foreign nations from trading in its African territories. Also, this action could have benefited metropolitan merchants, who would now monopolize the slave trade. Nevertheless, Portuguese authorities in Lisbon and Angola did nothing to restrain Brazilian merchants. Authorities in Lisbon allowed Brazilian merchants to continue carrying on their trade in Angola as a way to maintain the economic viability of the colony and to keep the Brazilian market open for Portuguese wine. As José C. Curto notes, after Brazilian independence, *geribita* continued to be one of the most important items of exchange in the slave trade, while the newly independent country was also the premier consumer for Portuguese wine.[3] Rio de Janeiro continued to be the main destination of slaves who embarked from Luanda until the end of shipments from its port in the mid-1840s.

For several years, Portugal refused to recognize the independence of its former colony in South America. Britain, on the other hand, in exchange for recognition of Brazilian independence, negotiated a treaty with Brazil. Concluded in 1826, the treaty established that Brazil was to gradually reduce slave imports and outlaw the slave trade from Africa as of March 1830. Although the treaty's effectiveness is arguable, slave departures from Luanda did experience a momentary decline. Between 1816 and 1820, about 92,500 captives embarked from the port of Luanda, while in the five succeeding years preceding the treaty (1821–25), this number fell slightly to about 79,800 (see table 4.1). Uncertainty regarding the treaty may have induced slave traders to reduce the numbers of slaves sent to Brazil. In the period 1826–30, the number of captives exported fell to 74,396, but between 1831 and 1835 the trade experienced a drastic decrease, with only 54,637 captives exported from Luanda. Two facts may account for this decline: the impending ban brought with it fears of economic ruin to slavers established in Luanda, and some Brazilian merchants had started leaving Angola

Table 4.1. Estimated number of enslaved Africans shipped from Luanda, 1816–1850

Years	Luanda
1816–20	92,558
1821–25	79,811
1826–30	74,396
1831–35	54,637
1836–40	137,906
1841–45	29,947
1846–50	44,839
Total	514,094

Source: Daniel B. Domingues da Silva, "The Transatlantic Slave Trade from Angola: A Port-by-Port Estimate of Slaves Embarked, 1701–1867," *International Journal of African Historical Studies* 46, no. 1 (2013): 121–22.

as early as the 1820s.[4] Meanwhile, Brazilian merchants were no longer under the authority of Portuguese navigation laws and often refused to call at Luanda. Instead, they traded in the northern ports to avoid Portuguese customs in the capital, with the resultant drop in the number of slaves exported from Luanda.[5]

On 10 December 1836, the Portuguese government banned the export of captives from all of its overseas territories in Africa.[6] Slavers thus increased their activities before Angolan ports were closed to their business. While between 1831 and 1835 the number of captives exported from Luanda was 54,637, in the period 1836–40, this number rose drastically, with 137,906 captives shipped illegally. After the passing of the 1836 ban, Portuguese authorities sent warships to patrol the coast of West Central Africa and created the Tribunal das Presas (Court of Prizes) to prosecute smugglers.[7] African suppliers and the trade community in Angola reacted with alarm, resulting in the dismissal of Governor António Manuel de Noronha (1839–39) after he made efforts to enforce the law.[8] In 1839 Great Britain passed the Palmerston Act, establishing that any ship sailing under a Portuguese flag and suspected of transporting slaves was subject to seizure and judgment by the Court of the British Admiralty.[9] Shortly thereafter, Portuguese and Royal Navy cruisers began patrolling the western coast of Central Africa south of the equator in search of illegal slave cargoes. Vessels from France, the United States, and Brazil joined British and Portuguese patrols in repressing slave trade activities along the Angolan coast.[10] According to Ferreira, by the late 1840s, French patrols were even more active than the British in this particular region. And during the 1850s, it was the United States that was especially active in combating slave traders along the littoral of Angola.[11] Slavers, however, found a way around the Palmerston Act, using alternative flags of those countries not bound by treaties, such as Brazil and the United States.[12]

In 1842 Great Britain and Portugal agreed on the establishment of the Anglo-Portuguese Court of the Mixed Commission at Luanda to prosecute vessels engaged in slaving apprehended by the anti–slave trade squadrons of both nations.[13] The Office of the Mixed Commission was established on 14 September 1844, while other commissions had been operating in the Atlantic world for more than two decades in places such as Sierra Leone, Brazil, Cuba, and Suriname.[14] The Luanda court was composed of six officials—two commissioners, two arbitrators, and two secretaries—of nationalities equally distributed between Great Britain and Portugal.[15] Between 1844 and 1870, this institution proceeded against thirty-three ships suspected of slave trading. A total of 137 slaves were found in six of these vessels, considered *boa presas* (good prizes). The Tribunal das Presas, established by the Portuguese to enforce the 1836 ban on slave trading, emancipated another two thousand to three thousand Africans.[16] The captives rescued from slave ships were automatically placed under the category of *liberto* (liberated African) and required to serve an apprenticeship of seven years under the charge of the Junta de Superintendência dos Negros Libertos (Board of Superintendence of the Liberated Negroes), created in late 1845.

Yet the number of Africans liberated by the Mixed Commission in Luanda was certainly small when compared with the total slave exports from Angola during this period. What explains such a small number? A letter sent by the governor of Angola, Pedro Alexandrino da Cunha (1845–48), on 25 October 1845 to the Portuguese minister of overseas affairs sheds some light on the issue. In the letter, the highest authority in Portuguese Angola denounced the "abusive practice" of British and Portuguese cruisers "freeing" people found on vessels captured for involvement in the illegal slave trade. He cited the case of the vessel *Audaz*, which after seizure was taken to São Tomé e Príncipe, where the cargo was disembarked clandestinely. According to Cunha, when the *Audaz* arrived in Luanda, only the shipmaster and a few seamen were on board; the Mixed Commission promptly released the vessel in August 1845.[17] Further, some of the individuals nominated for positions on the Mixed Commission had themselves been engaged in illegal slave trading, while British authorities cultivated friendships with local merchants, including slave traders. In one example of this intriguing alliance between slave traders and British officials, Dona Ana Ubertali nominated José Teodoro de Oliveira and Guilherme Cypriano Demony as executors of her will.[18] Demony was no other than the British secretary of the Mixed Commission in 1845.[19] The corruption within the Mixed Commission and the parallel activities of the Tribunal das Presas may explain the low number of slaves liberated by the former during twenty-six years of operation in Angola, turning it into one of the less productive courts of its kind.

In any case, the creation of the Prize Court and the Anglo-Portuguese Mixed Commission offices, as well as the presence of warships from several nations, prevented slavers from exporting captives directly through Angola's government-regulated ports. As a result, the number of captives exported from Luanda dropped substantially. Between 1836 and 1845, the number of captives departing the Angolan capital declined by 78 percent, from 137,906 to 29,947. By the mid-1840s, slave exports from Luanda were virtually nonexistent. Merchants established in the former single most important Atlantic slaving port managed to continue exporting captives only clandestinely, from smaller locations away from the capital.

Dispersing the Slave Trade

By the 1840s, Ambriz, Cabinda, and the Congo River had replaced Luanda as the primary export center of the slave trade (see map 4.1). These locations

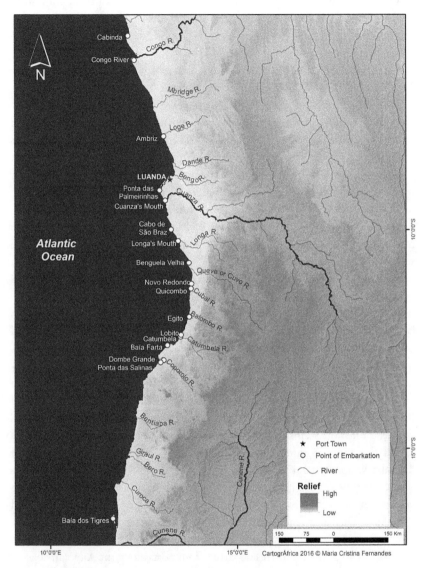

Map 4.1. Main ports of illegal slave departures in West Central Africa, 1840–1867.
Map by Maria Cristina Fernandes based on the author's data.

stood outside the area of Portuguese surveillance and so were more suitable for the covert embarkation of captives.[20] In fact, trading from these ports was far from a novelty to slavers: due to high duties charged in Luanda for commodities imported from Brazil, as well as the protectionism that benefited Portugal-based investors, Brazilian traders and Luso-Africans residing in the city had been embarking captives from the northern ports since the early nineteenth century.[21]

The traffic to the south of Luanda was as lively as that to the north. Places like Ponta das Palmeirinhas, the mouths of the Kwanza and Longo Rivers, Cabo de São Braz, Benguela Velha, Novo Redondo, Egito, Catumbela, Quicombo, Dombe Grande, Lobito, Ponta das Salinas, Moçâmedes, Baia Farta, and Baia dos Tigres housed the *feitorias* of traders who operated in slaves as well as in legitimate goods. The dispersal of so many places of embarkation made it difficult for the naval patrols to combat slavers; at the same time, it shows that the repression of illegal shipments was quite effective in Luanda.[22] The dispersal of slave shipments was a tactic adopted elsewhere on the west coast of Africa. In order to evade the attentions of the British navy, slavers based in Ouidah moved their activities to other ports to the east and west, to which slaves were sent by canoe along the coastal lagoon.[23]

Ferreira has highlighted how the dispersal of shipping activities after 1836 generated a food crisis in Luanda, since the incoming slave ships had also brought a significant part of the staples that sustained the local urban population.[24] During the periods of ecological crises that recurrently encroached upon the production of crops, only the staples arriving in Luanda aboard ships from Brazil, São Tomé e Príncipe, and Portugal relieved the hunger of the population. On 3 October 1845, for example, Pedro Alexandrino da Cunha, then governor of Angola, requested that the governor of São Tomé e Príncipe send manioc flour and firewood aboard vessels bound for Luanda to relieve the pressing need for those items in the city.[25]

On the opposite side of the Atlantic, Brazil remained the main place of disembarkation for captives shipped from West Central Africa, as had been the case during the era of legal slave trading (see table 4.2). Approximately 264,100 enslaved Africans forcibly left West Central Africa for Brazil between 1836 and 1855 alone. The Caribbean, particularly Cuba, was the second main destination, receiving 57,159 slaves in that same period, while 2,371 ended up in North America. Almost all of these captives departed from ports along the Angolan coast.[26]

The higher risks associated with the illegality of the trade forced most small-scale slave traders out of business, leaving only large-scale merchants whose commercial firms controlled the advance of *fazendas* (imported trade goods) to sources of captives in the *sertão*.[27] Merchants established in Brazil were now responsible for financing and organizing a large portion of the illegal

Table 4.2. Main destination of enslaved Africans illegally shipped from West Central Africa to the Americas, 1836–1865

Period	Mainland North America	Caribbean	Brazil	Total
1836–40	—	6,483	148,720	155,203
1841–45	490	2,563	75,183	78,236
1846–50	—	2,005	37,481	39,486
1851–55	—	9,443	2,721	12,164
1856–60	1,881	26,813	—	28,694
1861–65	—	9,852	—	9,852
Total per country	2,371	57,159	264,105	323,635

Source: David Eltis et al., "Voyages: The Trans-Atlantic Slave Trade Database," accessed January 2020, www.slavevoyages.org/.

slave trade in Angola.[28] Some of the slave traders residing in Luanda who engaged in illegal slaving were in fact commercial agents of firms based in Rio de Janeiro; among them were Francisco António Flores, António Severino de Avelar, Guilherme José da Silva Correia, and António Augusto de Oliveira Botelho. Luanda merchants were also involved in illicit slaving activities; their numbers included Francisco Barboza Rodrigues, Arsénio Pompílio Pompeu do Carpo, Augusto Guedes Coutinho Garrido, José Maria Matozo de Andrade Câmara, António Félix Machado, Dona Ana Ubertali, and Dona Ana Joaquina dos Santos Silva.[29] These merchants, all part of the local elite, owned *feitorias* on bays between the Congo River and Ambriz and in ports to the south, where they traded in tropical commodities and captives. Dona Ana Joaquina dos Santos Silva owned *feitorias* in various locations in the interior of the colony, including in Ambriz, Benguela, and Moçâmedes, from where she dealt in slaves and tropical commodities.[30] Câmara and Garrido owned *feitorias* in Moçâmedes and in Cabo Lombo, locations from where illegal shipments of captives departed for Brazil.[31] Dona Ana Ubertali was also the proprietor of a *feitoria* in Moçâmedes in partnership with Bernardino José Brochado.[32]

One foreign observer visiting Luanda in the mid-nineteenth century, probably of Portuguese origin, recorded his suspicions that the warehouses established in the northern and southern ports supposedly to deal with legitimate goods had in fact been set up for the purpose of dealing in captives: "It is on the banks of the Zaire River that the traffic in slaves is most active, and many commercial warehouses, not to say all of them, are no more than cloaks for or depend on this type of trade, which the conventions proposed by a humane England and accepted by an ingenuous Portugal turned into the most profitable of the whole coast."[33] It is clear that a number of traders established ware-houses away from Luanda to escape prosecution. It is also probable that some were active in trading both tropical commodities and captives simultaneously.

The Conduct of the Illegal Slave Trade

The organization of the illegal slave trade did not differ greatly from that of the legal trade. One important difference, however, was the method of embarka-tion. To circumvent the risks involved in the illegal operations, traders embarked captives at night from secluded shores onto small launches. These launches then had to cut through the surf to reach the slave ships, which were anchored at sea. In 1841 the German physician Gustav Tams met with Arsénio do Carpo to treat him for a liver ailment. On that occasion, Tams's patient described how he operated within the context of illegality, which the doctor recorded:

> A rapid mode of travelling was indispensable for Mr. Arsénio, for he was often
> obliged to take very long journeys on horseback during the night, when his per-
> sonal presence was suddenly required at the places where his slaves were embarked.
> Considerable and repeated losses had induced him to adopt the plan of embark-
> ing the slaves during the night at a distance from Loanda. One morning, when
> I paid him a professional visit on account of a chronic disorder of the liver . . .
> he told me that, although he was so ill, he had ridden sixteen leagues during the
> preceding night, in order to be present at the embarkation of his slaves to the
> south of the river Dande.[34]

Another contemporary observer claimed that Dona Ana Joaquina dos San-tos Silva had ordered the construction of a tunnel connecting the palace where she lived in Launda's *baixa* to the beach, through which she exported captives illicitly.[35] Although such a scheme sounds improbable, it provides support for rumors of her continuing activities as a slave trader in town. Dona Ana Joa-quina dos Santos Silva undoubtedly engaged in illegal slaving, but she did so from her *feitorias* located away from Luanda. For instance, on 11 July 1846, her ship *Maria Segunda* left Angola with 490 captives aboard, headed for Bahia.[36] On 2 November 1846, the *Maria Segunda* again crossed the Atlantic, carrying another 490 captives, destined for disembarkation also in Bahia.[37] In 1850 Brazil-ian authorities captured her vessel, the *Oriente*, near Rio de Janeiro with a cargo of 200 captives, who had embarked from Novo Redondo and Quicombo. The cargo was intended for delivery to an agent in Rio, Joaquim Pinto da Fonseca, whose brother, Manuel Pinto da Fonseca, was established in Luanda.[38]

Dona Ana Joaquina was certainly not the only woman merchant who extended her slave-trading activities into the period after 1836. Few women, however, had sufficient capital to invest in the trade, and following the ban on slave exports, that did not change. Between 1843 and 1844, a certain Ana Félix de Angola sent three shipments of captives to Rio de Janeiro. In 1843 her brig *Nossa Senhora da Conceição de Maria* transported 662 captives from Luanda to Campos in the captaincy of Rio de Janeiro.[39] In that same year, Ana Félix shipped 358 captives to Rio de Janeiro aboard the *D. Ana de Portugal.*[40] The following year, she sent 333 captives on the schooner *Lealdade*, which embarked from Ponta Negra, bound for Rio de Janeiro.[41] A woman named Ana Sebastiana was responsible for the shipment of 118 captives to Pernambuco aboard the *União* in October 1847.[42] Other women probably engaged in illegal slaving in association with husbands or foreign partners. However, most women dealing in slaves were likely smaller investors, freighting consignments of a few slaves ranging in number from two to ten.

Slavers tried to transport as many captives as possible on every voyage to compensate for the greater risks of such enterprises. On 4 February 1845, the Brazilian vessel *Albanez* left Luanda in ballast, carrying only a small cargo of wax and having declared that it was bound for Pernambuco. Instead, the ship headed south of the Kwanza River, where a British patrol intercepted it carrying 230 enslaved Africans aboard.[43] Some vessels undertook several shipments of captives before being captured. On 22 May 1845, at 4:00 a.m., the Portuguese cruiser *Relâmpago* came upon a vessel anchored off the bay of Cabo Ledo. The crew tried to escape as soon as the *Relâmpago* began advancing on them with guns firing. While most of the crew escaped by boat, seven men were found aboard the vessel, including Captain Miguel Angelo Moutano, the pilot, José Merello, and the foreman, António Soares. The vessel was fully equipped to transport a large cargo of captives. In the course of the trial, the three members of the captured crew testified that the vessel was the *Cacique* and that it left Cabo Frio in the captaincy of Rio de Janeiro for the coast of Angola to ship captives. The vessel was carrying *pipas* (barrels), bales, and consumables to sustain a human cargo. The men also disclosed that the owner of the vessel was a certain Mirandinha and that a few months before, the *Cacique* had successfully transported enslaved Africans from Angola to Rio de Janeiro.[44]

In 1846 a ship belonging to the Luanda-based merchants Garrido and Câmara was found in Cabo Frio after disembarking with a cargo of 160 captives. The ship had departed from Cabo Lombo, north of the mouth of the Congo River, where Câmara had a farm. The free Cabindas Benito and Fernando Xilumba and the Muxiloandas Joaquim António and José Pedro were responsible for loading the vessel with the stores and equipment necessary for the Middle Passage. They disclosed that the embarkation took place on a Saturday, from noon to 8:00 p.m., under the supervision of Câmara himself.[45]

After finishing their work, the four free men were forcibly taken aboard by the captain, a man named Sampaio, as it weighed anchor for Brazil.[46] The voyage from Cabo Lombo to Cabo Frio took thirty-seven days, after which the captives were delivered to a certain José Pacheco. Subsequently, the vessel was abandoned on a beach, where it was found by a Brazilian warship. Whether the forced removal of the four free Africans to Brazil was an attempt at kidnapping is not known; in any case, it seems likely that Pacheco was unwilling to take part in it, as he sent the four African men back to Angola on the German ship *Argos*. The testimony of the apparently kidnapped Africans was essential to prove the participation of Câmara and Garrido in the illegal slave trade.[47]

During the trial, Câmara and Garrido accused Governor Cunha of blackmailing witnesses to testify against them. They attested that the governor had offered cash and threatened the black Africans who testified against them with incarceration and physical punishments.[48] Câmara's and Garrido's accusations had no effect, as all the evidence pointed to their involvement in the illegal shipment. In the end, both merchants were sentenced to nothing more than payment of bail.[49] Still, given their compromised reputations, they were removed from the administrative board of the Santa Casa de Misericórdia, to which they had been nominated in 1845, and were replaced by two other leading merchants, António José Coelho Vilela and João da Silva Ramos.[50] Garrido had also been nominated as first substitute for the *juiz ordinário* (justice of the peace) of Luanda, a position from which he resigned following the accusations.[51] Yet despite the consequences following the 1846 capture of their vessel, this was not the last illicit shipment Câmara and Garrido organized. In August 1849, Garrido again shipped 415 captives to southeastern Brazil.[52]

Those found guilty could be charged fines and lose their vessel and everything on board. On 8 August 1847, at 5:30 a.m., the *Relâmpago* captured the Brazilian vessel *Itagoahy* near Mussulo, south of Luanda. The vessel had eleven people on board and was equipped to carry captives, with barrels of water, manioc flour, beans, vegetables, dry meat, mats, and lengths of chain. The master, Joaquim José Robeiro, the pilot, Jacinto José Maria, and the captain, Teodoro Casimiro Reis, declared that they had been hired by the owner of the vessel, José António Velho da Silva, to transport a cargo of slaves. The vessel had left Rio de Janeiro on 20 June 1847, fully equipped to carry between two hundred and three hundred captives. The sailor José Alves Pinto, however, offered testimony different from that of his superiors. According to Pinto, the vessel left Rio de Janeiro and headed for São Sebastião in the captaincy of São Paulo. However, three days into the voyage, Pinto declared, they had to change the destination due to poor weather conditions. In Pinto's version of events, the *Itagoahy* ended up on the Angolan coast due to the lack of knowledge of the captain and the pilot. Pinto's version, however, was not credible enough to convince the authorities. On 28 September 1847, the captured vessel, the foodstuffs it carried, and the equipment found on board were all sold at public auction.[53]

"Generous" Slave Traders and the Colonial State

At the same time that Portuguese authorities in Luanda were supposed to enforce antitrafficking legislation, the government depended on the "generosity" of the local elite, including slavers.[54] In 1839 Dona Ana Joaquina dos Santos Silva offered to dispatch her ships *Maria Segunda* and *Conceição de Maria* to Montevideo, Uruguay, to transport a cargo of horses and mules for the army as well as a variety of trade goods.[55] On 16 May 1843, Manuel Francisco Alves de Brito and the Brazilian slave trader Severino de Avelar financed the construction of a road connecting the upper city to the rural suburb of Maianga, in the *baixa*.[56] In May 1849, Arsénio do Carpo purchased typographical equipment for the government to promote the development of the press in Angola.[57] In the same month and year, the slavers Francisco Barboza Rodrigues, Manuel Joaquim de Souza Monteiro, and Augusto Garrido donated foodstuffs to feed the military.[58] As these examples illustrate, the colonial state could not dispense with the assistance provided by the merchant community, many of whom were slave traders. In Guinea-Bissau, where Portuguese control of the territory and local populations was inefficient, the administration was completely dependent on the "benevolence" of local traders.[59]

Given such contributions to the "welfare" of the colony, men involved in illegal slaving were even able to request titles of nobility from the Portuguese Crown. On 13 December 1843, the slave traders António Severino de Avelar and Arsénio do Carpo both applied for knighthoods in the Ordem de Nossa Senhora da Conceição de Vila Viçosa. Governor Lourenço Germack Possolo (1843–45) recognized that "detractors" of Carpo claimed that he was a slave trader, and Possolo stated that he was "not entirely convinced that this information was absolutely false." Still, he did not refrain from highlighting the importance of this merchant to the Portuguese project in Angola: "[He] is the only agent here of the Britannia shipping line, exchanging letters with Lord Aberdeen, who not only writes to him directly, as I have witnessed many times, but his house hosts every official from that nation who arrives here: they make use of his horses and carriages and have great consideration for him. This same Arsénio has always been the man whom previous governors have chosen to promote various projects [in the colony]." It is certainly remarkable that a slaver maintained close connections with British authorities who were responsible for enforcing the suppression of the traffic in captives. As for Avelar, Governor Possolo described this "holder of a self-made fortune" as a close friend of Carpo. The highest-ranking administrator in Angola then acknowledged that "both men have been useful instruments from which this government cannot separate itself," concluding that "it is appropriate to grant them the titles that they are so fond of."[60]

By collaborating with the Portuguese government in Angola, merchants bought their way into positions where they could shield their businesses—including the illegal trade in slaves. It was not uncommon to find slavers occupying important administrative positions. After the dissolution of the Municipal Council of Luanda in 1845, a provisional council was established composed of Francisco José de Sousa Lopes, Bernardino da Silva Guimarães, António da Costa Rodrigues, João Cheldorico de Moura, and Francisco Barboza Rodrigues.[61] Lopes and Barboza Rodrigues were notorious slave traders.[62] Between 1837 and 1853, Carpo similarly occupied a number of positions in the administration, from president of the Municipal Council of Luanda to commander of various inland districts and *presídios*.[63] Even more impressively, Augusto Garrido became secretary of the British and Portuguese Mixed Commission for the suppression of the slave trade in 1851, even though five years earlier he had faced charges for involvement in the illegal trafficking of captives, along with his associate José Maria Matozo de Andrade Câmara.[64] As W. Gervase Clarence-Smith has pointed out, this was certainly "a curious position for one of the greatest slavers of the nineteenth century."[65]

In 1850, a new law enacted in Brazil that made it illegal for captives to be imported finally began to be enforced. This definitive termination of the trade had a deep impact throughout Angola, as Brazil was the main destination of captives who embarked along the coast of this Portuguese colony. Following 1850, many merchants—including slave traders—left Luanda and relocated in Portugal, Brazil, and, to a lesser extent, New York.[66] One of these was the Brazilian José Narciso Correia, who embarked for Rio de Janeiro in January 1850, leaving behind Remígio Luiz dos Santos and Francisco de Paula e Oliveira as his legal agents in the Angolan capital.[67] As happened in other ports on the African coast earlier in the century, some merchants based in Luanda saw their business vanish.[68] In June 1850, the merchant Serafim José de Sousa Machado announced the bankruptcy of his commercial house.[69] João Manuel Lourenço faced a similar loss.[70] Likewise, the commercial firm of the slave trader Francisco Barboza Rodrigues declared bankruptcy in 1851.[71] Even the prosperous Arsénio do Carpo encountered economic setbacks in the early 1850s. Many of his assets, including a *sobrado* and a warehouse, were sold in public auctions to pay his debts to creditors.[72] Still, he was accused of fraudulent bankruptcy and embezzlement.[73] The downfalls of Carpo and Rodrigues demonstrate that the crises generated after the prohibition of slave imports in Brazil ruined even some of the larger merchants. Others sold or mortgaged their properties in order to avoid bankruptcy. In December 1851, Domingos José Pereira announced the sale of his warehouse and slaves.[74] In June 1852, Francisco Pereira dos Santos Vandunem also sold his ship and slaves.[75]

The withdrawal of Brazil from the trade may have been more efficient in reducing illegal slaving activities from Angola than the actual repression by antitrafficking warships. After 1850, only a few traders remained engaged in slaving, supplying captives predominantly to Cuba.[76] Rumors about the continuation of illegal shipments of captives circulated in Luanda. Carlos José Caldeira mentioned that during the few days he stayed in the city in 1853, he heard about two cargoes of captives leaving from the vicinity.[77] The final phase of the illegal slave trade saw slavers using small coasting vessels as a last resort to avoid suppression.[78] Slavers and merchants had used the smaller vessels previously to support the traffic by carrying provisions, equipment, correspondence, and even captives from outlying parts of the coast to Luanda. With the evasions, they reversed direction, carrying captives to outlying ports. The *Oriente*, which belonged to Dona Ana Joaquina dos Santos Silva, for example, was a small vessel of twenty-six tons that she had previously employed in coasting voyages for upward of four years.[79] It may have been easier for slavers and crew to escape capture using smaller ships. This was the case of the thirty-nine-ton *Rival*, which was surprised by the British warship *Sealark* while preparing to embark captives close to Quicombo on 25 December 1850. The crew of the *Rival* was able to avoid capture by running the vessel onshore, where the British had no jurisdiction as per the 1842 Treaty.[80]

The 1836 ban of slave exports and the subsequent repression from British and Portuguese patrols affected the ability of merchants to export slaves from Luanda. Slavers found a solution by dispersing their activities to remote locations and from there continuing to supply the demand for captives in Brazil. Nevertheless, Brazil's withdrawal from the trade in 1850 resulted in the retreat and bankruptcy of merchants whose businesses were directly or indirectly connected to the traffic in captives. Although traders engaged in illegal shipment of Africans to the Americas until the 1860s, they did not refuse outright to invest in the trade in commodities from the *sertões* and in experiments with commercial agriculture. In any case, only wealthy merchants were able to survive the transition by investing in legitimate commerce the capital they had accumulated through slave trading.

CHAPTER FIVE

Meeting the Challenges of the Transition

C OLONIAL AUTHORITIES IN mid-nineteenth-century Lisbon and Angola expected that the trade in tropical commodities would replace slave exports. Nevertheless, the two trades proved to be complementary rather than mutually exclusive. From the 1840s onward, a number of private investors and government-led organizations promoted the growth and trade of coffee, cotton, and sugar, as well as wax and ivory for the external market. The capital that was invested in legitimate commerce originated in the slave trade, with former slavers investing in tropical commodities while some continued the illegal shipment of captives. This chapter examines the strategies used by members of the Luanda merchant community who faced the need to develop legitimate commerce.

Moving into the "New" Trade

From the early nineteenth century, the Angolan administration began to consider commercial agriculture and the development of tropical commodities as viable alternatives to the slave export trade. Luís da Mota Feo e Torres, who governed Angola between 1816 and 1819, had already highlighted the potential of local commodities for trade. According to the governor, the coffee, cotton, and sugarcane grown locally were of good quality, the two latter items even better than the ones produced in Brazil. He also noted the existence of a commerce in beeswax and ivory collected by Africans. However, he remarked that the slave trade "has contributed to ruin all other sectors" of the economy.[1]

Although the trade in slaves had become the most important economic activity in the colony, local populations also traded in other items like ivory and beeswax. These commodities, however, were of trivial importance in comparison with the trade in captives.[2] With the illegality of the slave trade the commerce in tropical commodities gained new impetus to meet demand in northern Europe and in the United States.[3] Alongside ivory and wax, the collection of gum copal and orchil (a source of a deep purple dye) and the production of palm and peanut oils, coffee, and cotton also received new incentives. By the 1840s, Luanda merchants were investing in the trade in tropical commodities and commercial agriculture without having abandoned the illegal shipment of slaves.[4] Indigenous items that had been produced for local consumption for centuries were now transformed into commodities for the export market. The incentives of the government and the capital of private investors, along with African expertise, were essential in the process.

Scholars have analyzed the effects of the economic transition in different contexts in West Africa. The classical work of Anthony Hopkins claimed that the transition from slave exports to legitimate commerce caused a "crisis of adaptation" on the coast of West Africa, undermining the wealth and power of existing elites.[5] In the process, the former slavers and the commercial firms that controlled the slave trade suffered in the era of legitimate commerce from increasing competition from small-scale traders and private investors. Hopkins's argument, however, has been contested by other scholars who argue that in some coastal societies, the existing elites were generally able to dominate the new trade as they had done the old.[6] Although some studies have discussed the transition in Angola, few have examined the strategies that slave traders used to adapt to the changing economy.[7]

Even though Luanda slavers faced financial losses with the end of the trade, they did not disappear from the economic scenario. On the contrary, they were key investors in the new trade and remained central to the advancement of credit in the colony. A closer examination of the responses of the merchant community to the transformation of the Angolan economy after 1836 further illustrates their resiliency as a class. After the era of slave trading, slave dealers continued to benefit from access to capital and from government assistance and prestige in the colonial society.

While most ports in West Africa had experienced this transition earlier in the century, in West Central Africa it took place only after the 1840s with the decline of the illegal slave trade and the rise in investment in the export trade in tropical commodities. Despite the legal abolition of the trade in 1836, transatlantic exports remained at a high level until at least the mid-nineteenth century, when Brazil banned the importation of captives. As happened in other West African ports like Lagos and Saint-Louis, a large portion of the capital invested in legitimate commercial activities in Angola had its origin in the legal and illegal slave trade.[8] The economic structures based on credit that had developed during the slave trade era were extended to the new trade, with coastal merchants continuing to fund most initiatives in the commercial and agrarian sectors.[9] Thus, the system of credit operating during the context of licit commerce did not suffer alterations from that operating during the slave trade era.

With the legal banning of the slave trade, the Angolan administration decreed a number of policies intended to promote the development of commercial agriculture and the exploration of tropical commodities. Among them was the opening in 1837 of the Angolan ports to trade with other nations and the occupation of land classified as *terras baldias* (uncultivated land)—regardless of the African presence in these territories—by merchants willing to invest in agriculture.[10] The Luanda administration asked authorities in Portugal, Brazil, Goa, and São Tomé e Príncipe to send seeds and samples of crops to Angola. On 28 February 1845, Governor Possolo requested that wheat, barley, and rye be sent from Portugal so that they could be experimented with, particularly in the *arimos* that belonged to the state.[11] In December of the same year, Governor Pedro Alexandrino da Cunha requested seeds or plants of piassava palm from Bahia and bamboo from Goa.[12] Cunha was tireless in his efforts to promote the development of the agricultural sector in Angola, as foreign observers who passed by Luanda during the mid-nineteenth century recognized.[13] On 10 October 1845, Governor Cunha informed the Portuguese overseas minister, "I employ all of the time I have in promoting, through all of the methods and means at my disposal, the development of agriculture in this country, the exploration of the rich iron mines, and everything else that constitutes the wealth of its soil, encouraging the inhabitants to take care of their real interests, abandon forbidden speculations in which they risk their capital, and favor other sectors where their interests meet those of the state."[14]

By the mid-1840s, José Joaquim Lopes de Lima had noted that commodities such as ivory, wax, gum copal, and orchil, in addition to minerals like sulfur and saltpeter, had already begun to find places in the export trade of Angola. Meanwhile, the cultivation of coffee, cotton, and sugarcane had also experienced growth, allowing him to anticipate that "within a short time the advantages of the new colonial system started five years ago will be tangible."[15]

In the late 1840s, the Angolan government established an agricultural colony in Moçâmedes, in the southern extremity of Angola, with settlers from Brazil and from the Island of Madeira, in the process depriving the Ndombe and the Kuvale, the original owners, of their land. The government provided the new immigrants with land, seeds, and equipment as well as labor to assist in setting up farms.[16] Several Luanda merchants, including the slave traders Dona Ana Joaquina dos Santos Silva, Arsénio do Carpo, António Félix Machado, and Cândido José dos Santos Guerra, donated capital to the benefit of the new settlers.[17] The new settlers soon began to develop agricultural fields for the production of foodstuffs, sugarcane, and cotton.

Some of the settlers established in Moçâmedes were former farmers who contributed to the transfer of technology from Brazil to Angola, particularly in the construction of sugar mills, the production of sugar cane, and the distillation of *aguardente* (sugar cane brandy).[18] The Brazilian agricultural sector of the mid-nineteenth century became the model for the development of commercial agriculture in Angola. From Brazil came seeds, expertise, and techniques applied in agricultural enterprises funded by the colonial state and private investors. Angola's first gazette, the *Boletim Oficial de Angola*, began publication in 1845 in the context of this economic transition. Its weekly pages disseminated instructions on how to grow and produce crops based on the Brazilian experience.[19] Similarities between the two landscapes, including the climate and the use of slave labor, certainly facilitated such connections.

Luanda merchants created partnerships and companies with government support to promote the economic development of the colony. While some initiatives were successful, others failed due to lack of funds or skilled personnel. In 1835 a group of investors created the Companhia de Agricultura e Indústria de Angola e Benguela to produce sugar, cotton, and other crops. Several of its investors were slave dealers, who quickly abandoned the company to focus on the trade in captives.[20] Also, in 1838 a company for the exploration of petroleum was founded east of Luanda, but it faded after the head of the project, the Swiss doctor Lang, died.[21] In 1839 a group of twenty-seven merchants and Governor António Manuel de Noronha (1839–39) created the Companhia Mineralógica de Angola e Benguela to promote the mining of "all products, with the exception of precious metals." The group acquired machinery from Lisbon to establish an iron mine in Golungo Alto, east from Luanda; however, the mine did not succeed, due to a lack of skilled personnel. One year later, associates unanimously decided to shut down the company.[22]

Luanda merchants, many of them former slavers, continued to control the advancement of credit to small-scale traders. In 1846 a total of thirty-three merchants received authorization from the Royal Treasury to issue credit in Luanda (see table 5.1). The group included recognized slave dealers like Dona Ana Joaquina dos Santos Silva, Dona Ana Francisca Ubertali de Miranda, Augusto Garrido, Francisco António Flores, and Francisco Barboza Rodrigues. Despite the presence of women, men continued to dominate the advancement of credit. Men were better able to accumulate capital, since they represented the majority of traders in the foodstuff supply and in slaving.

It was not uncommon for merchants to take debtors to court to retrieve the capital they had advanced. As one of the largest creditors in Angola, Dona Ana Joaquina dos Santos Silva resorted to judicial authorities several times in order to receive payment from debtors. On 10 February 1849, after a long judicial

Table 5.1. Merchants authorized to issue credit in Luanda, 1846

D. Ana Joaquina dos Santos Silva	José Lourenço Marques
D. Ana Francisca Ubertali de Miranda	José Moreira da Costa Lima
António Lopes da Silva	José de Oliveira Nunes
António José Coelho Vilela	José Vieira da Silva
Apolinário Francisco de Carvalho	Manoel António de Magalhães e Silva
Augusto Garrido	Manoel António Rodrigues
Bernardino Massi	Manoel Francisco Alves de Brito
Cândido José dos Santos Guerra	Manoel Joaquim de Souza Monteiro
D. Delfina de Miranda Britos Vieira	Manoel José Pereira
Francisco António Flores	Manoel do Nascimento e Oliveira
Francisco Barboza Rodrigues	Manoel Pereira dos Santos Vandunes
João José Domingos Pereira	Miguel Lino Ferreira
João de Souza Neto	Pedro de Torres Ribeiro
Joaquim José Monteiro	Remígio Luiz dos Santos
Joaquim Luiz Bastos	Valentim José Pereira
José António Pereira	Victoriano de Faria
José de Carvalho Bastos	

Source: Boletim Oficial de Angola, no. 54, 19 September 1846, 2.

dispute, the judge of the district of Luanda determined that the properties that Idelfonso Inácio de Menezes had presented as collateral in a loan he obtained from Dona Ana Joaquina should go to public auction to pay the debt.[23]

Merchants who had accumulated capital through the slave trade also led most private initiatives during the transition. José Maria Matozo de Andrade Câmara, for example, experimented with cotton and coconut cultivation on his farm in Cabo Lombo, the same locale from where he embarked captives illegally. Câmara counted on support from the government, which sent him an experienced farmer from Goa named Cristóvão José de Mendonça, as well as two Indian assistants, to establish the coconut plantation.[24] In 1852 Governor António Sérgio de Sousa (1851–53) announced in the Boletim Oficial the good results that Câmara had obtained in the extraction and production of coconut derivatives.[25] In 1853 Câmara sent samples of coconut oil and cordage to Lisbon in the hopes of finding a market for the items.[26] Besides this enterprise, Câmara also invested in the production of roof tiles and lime as well as in cattle, all for the internal market.[27] In December 1854, Câmara passed away, leaving some debts. Part of his shares in the Garrido & Câmara company were sold to pay creditors, leading his partner to declare bankruptcy.[28] Garrido, nevertheless, found an interesting solution for his economic recovery. Câmara had been married to Dona Mariana Joaquina de Faria e Câmara. Their only child, a daughter, Maria da Conceição, had died before her third birthday, leaving Dona Mariana as the sole heiress to the couple's estate.[29] The properties she inherited included three *sobrados* and the farms Bemfica and Cabo Lombo, along with numerous slaves.[30] After Câmara's death, his well-to-do widow entered into her second marriage with no other than Augusto Garrido, her deceased husband's longtime associate.[31] Together, the couple acquired many properties in Luanda and in the interior of the colony, including land and urban real estate.[32] They also established the firm Garrido Câmara & Cia, which brought *colonos livres* (free settlers) and *serviçais* (servants) to São Tomé e Príncipe.[33] Under the guise of "free settlers," forced laborers were exported to the islands to work on cocoa and coffee plantations there.[34]

Dona Ana Joaquina dos Santos Silva also invested simultaneously in the illegal slave trade and the trade in tropical commodities. In anticipation of the imminent abolition of the slave trade, between 1826 and 1830 she acquired seven *arimos* in the immediate interior of Luanda, increasing her participation in foodstuff supply and commercial agriculture.[35] She also acquired land in Irajá, in the city of Rio de Janeiro, to invest in the production of coffee.[36] Dona Ana Joaquina was among the pioneers in the production of sugarcane in Angola.[37] In 1846 she had hired a Frenchman, Pedro Regueure, to establish a sugar mill on her property located in the district of Bengo. When Regueure was unable to deliver the expected results, Dona Ana Joaquina hired Manuel J. C. de Farias, a settler from Pernambuco, to finish the mill four years later.[38] Dona Ana Joaquina may well have visited sugar mills in Brazil herself during her trips to that country.[39]

During his stay in Angola in the early 1850s, Francisco Travassos Valdez visited Dona Ana Joaquina's *arimo*, Capele, in the district of Bengo and noted the existence of a sugar mill.[40] The visit of Governor Adrião Acácio da Silveira Pinto (1848–51) to Dona Ana Joaquina's agricultural property during his mid-1850 tour of the district of Icolo e Bengo illustrates the support of the Luanda administration for private investors willing to experiment with commercial agriculture. By then, according to Governor Pinto, "the sugar manufacture was well advanced, and Mr. Farias hopes to be able to manufacture sugar and alcohol later this year."[41] Carlos José Caldeira disclosed that in 1851, Dona Ana Joaquina was able to produce samples of sugarcane and *aguardente*, which were "extremely valuable commodities for the commerce of this country with both its hinterland and its metropole."[42] In contrast to the port of Ouidah, where large-scale enterprises were owned by men, in Angola both women and men owned plantations.[43]

As was also the case in Lagos, the category of trade goods exchanged for tropical commodities remained almost the same as it had been during the slave trade era.[44] *Fazendas* previously used in the interior of Angola to acquire captives, including firearms, gunpowder, *aguardente*, and textiles, were also extended on credit in the trade in legitimate commodities.[45] Cane brandy, for example, was often sent into the *sertão* on consignment for the acquisition of tropical items.[46] Traders such as Dona Ana Joaquina thus were greatly interested in producing *aguardente* to exchange for export goods in the interior and to supply other traders.

Portuguese and Brazilians who arrived in Angola from the early to mid-nineteenth century in search of wealth also invested in the new trade. In 1846 Governor Possolo reported that after nine years of experimentation, the Brazilian João Guilherme Barboza had been able to develop an extensive coffee plantation in Angola.[47] His achievement was met with great enthusiasm from the administration, which granted him land and the title of knight of the order of Nossa Senhora da Conceição de Vila Viçosa.[48] By early 1850, Barboza's production had reached two thousand *arrobas*.[49] Based on his experiment, the Portuguese authorities increased support for the commercial production of coffee, with this cash crop soon cultivated in districts such as Muxima, Massangano, Cambambe, Pungo Andongo, and São José do Encoge, among other places.[50]

The slave trade had required very large investments, a factor that kept women and small-scale producers away. Passports granted to individuals and to coasting vessels during the era of legitimate commerce evidence growing movement of women from the coast into the *sertões* and between northern and southern ports, which indicates their growing participation in trade. On 25 October 1849, the twenty-year-old black African Mariana José traveled to the Dembos *a seus negócios* (on business), accompanied by an enslaved woman of her property named Guilhermina.[51] Constança de Campos, also a black African woman, headed for the same destination on 25 November 1849: she too went away "on business."[52] Indigenous women were traditionally responsible for agricultural work and neighboring trade, and it is likely that they also marketed palm and peanut oils as well as coffee and cotton in small quantities.

Luso-African women who owned land, slaves, and coasting vessels (see table 5.2) particularly benefited from the new alternative trade. They established *feitorias* in northern and southern ports to trade in legitimate items. In the 1860s, Dona Amélia do Carmo Torres Bastos frequently traveled from Luanda to the ports of Moçâmedes and Loango *a seus negócios* aboard one of

Table 5.2. Female owners of coasting vessels, 1861–1869

Owner	Vessel(s)	Destination(s)
D. Amélia do Carmo Torres Bastos	*Lancha Sultana, Caique Amélia*	Moçâmedes, Bengo, Southern Ports, Loango, Northern Ports
D. Amélia Joaquina de Oliveira	*Lancha Clipper, Lancha Cobra, Lancha Serpente*	Novo Redondo, Congo River, Ambriz, Northern Ports
D. Amélia da Silva Regadas Chelderico	*Lancha Tereza*	Bengo
D. Ana de Jesus Rodrigues	*Lancha Minerva*	Novo Redondo, Ambriz, Zaire, Moçâmedes, Southern Ports, Salinas do Sul
D. Ana Vitoria Rodrigues	*Palhabote Nine*	Moçâmedes, Novo Redondo, Salinas, Cuio, Northern Ports
D. Antónia Joana	*Lancha Jovem, Erminda*	Egito
D. Civina Augusta de Lemos	*Lancha Viajante*	Novo Redondo
D. Emília Augusta de Magalhães	*Palhabote Paquete do Sul*	Novo Redondo, Moçâmedes, São Tomé, Zaire, Northern Ports
D. Henriqueta Adelaide de Oliveira	*Cinco de Março*	Northern Ports
D. Izabel Silva Menezes	*Escaler Virgínia*	Northern Ports
D. Maria Aurélia de Oliveira	*Escaler Nereida, Lancha Clipper*	Novo Redondo
D. Maria Luiza Albino Rodrigues	*Lancha Victória, Lancha Justina*	Northern Ports
D. Maria Madalena de Brito	*Palhabote São Luís*	Northern Ports
D. Mariana Joaquina de Faria e Câmara Garrido	*Lancha Quimcolo*	Ambriz
D. Rita Alegre de Faria	*Lancha Fortuna*	Novo Redondo

Source: ANA, Luanda, Avulsos, códices 136, 142, 146, 147, 1412, 1602, 1192, 1736, 3814.

her own vessels, the *Sultana, Esperança*, and *Amélia*.[53] Similarly, Dona Amélia Joaquina de Oliveira traveled on business to the northern ports of Ambriz and the Congo River, as well as to Novo Redondo, south of Luanda.[54] The women who owned vessels and warehouses along the Angolan coast were often *donas* and of Luso-African origin.

African Labor and Expertise

African expertise was essential in the economic transition that overtook West Central Africa following the end of the slave export trade. Africans had experimented with most of the items that became important in the export trade long before they attracted the interest of the colonial administrators and private investors.[55] For centuries, local populations in Angola had extracted and consumed cotton, wax, peanuts, and palm and peanut oils. In the late eighteenth century, Africans extracted ivory from elephants, hippopotamuses, and manatees. While ivory was not of much use locally, the Royal Treasury exported relatively small quantities.[56] Beeswax was used to make candles that were burned in religious services and at funerals.[57] Indigenous peoples had long used cotton to produce textiles, had drawn upon it as currency, and had made *tangas* (pieces of cloth) as well as fishing nets and lamp and candle wicks.[58]

Africans also cultivated and consumed *ginguba* (peanuts) in various forms: fresh, roasted, boiled, or ground with manioc flour, salt, and sugar as well as a flavor enhancer. Indigenous peoples consumed the coconut of the palm tree, fresh or roasted, while they used palm oil to cook with and to anoint the body. During times of war, rubbing the skin with palm oil was believed to help one slip out of the hands of the enemy. Well-to-do residents of Luanda burned groundnut and palm oil in lamps to light their houses.[59] Given that Africans had experimented previously with items that became of interest to export, legitimate commerce depended entirely on the expertise of indigenous populations. Skilled Africans, not Europeans, knew the sources of ivory and wax as well as how to produce oil from peanuts and palms. Some African communities specialized in the collection of specific items for export. The Cokwe, for example, became renowned as hunters of elephants as well as collectors of wax and rubber.[60]

Investors were also completely dependent on African porters to move *fazendas* and tropical commodities into and out of the interior.[61] Unlike slaves, who walked from the interior to the coast, items of legitimate commerce had to be carried on the back of human porters. Coastal merchants and their intermediaries frequently faced difficulties in finding the human power necessary to organize caravans to trek into the *sertões*.[62] Traders established in Luanda counted on the assistance of commanders of the *presídios* and districts to recruit *carregadores* (porters). In exchange, commanders received illegal tributes and bribes in *fazendas* and cattle, which by the mid-nineteenth century amounted to 3,000 *réis* per porter.[63] Some commanders threatened African rulers, sending punitive expeditions to communities that refused to supply porters, sometimes giving rise to insurrections and leading to imprisonment of whole families.[64]

Religious and administrative authorities frequently denounced the unscrupulous practices of commanders in the interior. In 1845 Father António Francisco das Necessidades warned the Portuguese administration that traders often paid bribes to commanders in the districts of Golungo Alto and Ambaca so that they would provide porters.[65] On March 1846, Governor Cunha requested that the commander of the district of Golungo Alto recruit three hundred porters to transport *fazendas* from Luanda to Kasanje to the merchant Manuel Francisco Alves de Brito. The governor advised the commander that he should make sure the porters received fair payment.[66] His concern resulted from the common practice of commanders retaining for themselves the payments designated for porters.[67] Foodstuff producers also required porters to transport crops from *arimos* located in the immediate interior to urban markets. In September 1847, the commander of the district of Dande committed to providing twenty-four porters weekly to Dona Ana Ubertali to transport manioc flour and beans from her *arimos* in the interior to the public market in Luanda.[68] In addition to the risk of not being paid, the Africans who were drafted were also subjected to harsh treatment en route, including malnutrition and even starvation. In the mid-1850s, the Brazilian trader Joaquim Rodrigues Graça noted that porters sent to the interior with *fazendas* belonging to Dona Ana Joaquina dos Santos Silva had starved due to the limited food provided during the trip.[69] Moreover, porters were responsible for any goods they damaged or lost during transportation.[70]

Africans also organized their own caravans, into which European and Luso-African merchants often embedded their commercial operations. Yet this was possible only for a privileged group of African rulers who had the political power to recruit traders and porters and provide services and protection throughout the journey.[71] Ovimbundu and Imbangala *sobas*, for example, organized caravans and consequently required a reliable labor force to carry commodities to the coast.[72] During his trips throughout the hinterland of Luanda in the early 1850s, Valdez witnessed large numbers of Africans porters carrying the commodities that underpinned legitimate commerce, including groundnuts, palm oil, ivory, and wax.[73] In the same decade, Caldeira noted, "Transportation is all made on the backs of porters, who almost always have to move along rough paths, over ridges, up cliffs, and through the bushes."[74]

The government and private investors periodically attempted to find solutions to remedy the shortage of *carregadores*. One initiative came from the merchant community: in 1843, Dona Ana Joaquina dos Santos Silva, Arsénio do Carpo, Francisco Teixeira de Miranda, António Severino de Avelar, Manuel Francisco Alves de Brito, and Francisco António Flores presented a proposal to the government for the creation of a shipping company, the Companhia de Navegação da Costa. The proposal, which included the purchase of a ship in Rio de Janeiro to move cargo along the coast from Moçâmedes to Luanda, counted on the support of Governor José Xavier Bressane Leite (1842–43).[75] The company, however, was short-lived; several, if not all, of the company associates were by then involved in illegal slaving, which may have made the service they provided suspicious. In 1845 Governor Possolo experimented with camels to transport tropical commodities.[76]

The Luanda government offered incentives to Africans who engaged in the production of export items. In 1845, for example, the administration exempted from military service Africans who produced at least 150 kilograms of coffee per annum.[77] By 1855 the government was sparing Africans from working as porters if they cultivated 50 *braças* of land.[78] Although these measures may have contributed to the lack of *carregadores*, they opened up the new trade for indigenous small-scale producers who manufactured palm and peanut oils and coffee with the labor of family members, dependents, and presumably a few slaves. As was the case in Lagos, the majority of Africans who engaged in the new trade in Angola may have done so as brokers or small-scale traders, supplying the large-scale merchants who controlled the export trade.[79]

The Internal Market

In 1850 the population of Luanda reached 12,565 people, an increase of about 7,000 over the 5,605 residing in the city at the end of 1844. As José C. Curto has argued, such an increase could not have stemmed from natural reproduction; instead, it resulted from the accumulation of enslaved Africans who previously would have been exported across the Atlantic Ocean.[80] As was the case in other towns on the west coast of Africa, in Luanda too the enslaved population was absorbed into the domestic market.[81] The expansion of legitimate commerce implied an increase in the domestic demand for slaves employed in the production and transport of tropical commodities. In addition, slaves were also employed on agricultural land to produce foodstuffs needed to feed the growing urban population.

Many economic activities associated with the internal market received extra impetus from the rising number of inhabitants, including the need for more food and housing. During his 1852 visit to Angola, Caldeira noted that the cultivation of cassava, maize, and beans had recently expanded. As a result, he added, the importation of these foodstuffs from São Tomé e Príncipe and

Rio de Janeiro had decreased, with "production in this country [Angola] now close to consumption."[82] This growth in foodstuff production experienced by the mid-nineteenth century was directly connected to the end of the slave export trade. Although the merchant community of Luanda had already engaged simultaneously in slaving and the foodstuff trade, slavers subsequently intensified the use of land to produce crops to meet the demand of the growing population in the capital.[83]

There was a rush for concessions of land after 1836 to establish coffee, cotton, and sugarcane farms to produce commodities for export, but individuals interested in growing foodstuffs to supply urban markets also requested *terras baldias* in the interior and near Luanda. Among the beneficiaries were slave traders, including Dona Ana Joaquina dos Santos Silva, Dona Ana Francisca Ubertali, Ricardo da Silva Rego, José Maria Matozo de Andrade Câmara, Augusto Garrido, Francisco António Flores, Francisco José das Neves, João Bernardino da Costa Carneiro, and João Osmundo Toulson.[84] Although members of the elite requested land for cultivation, the use they made of the concession varied from sale to lease. Dona Margarida Lopes Faião obtained three *braças* of land in the district of Bengo, which she sold to Dona Antónia da Conceição Carneiro for 50,000 *réis* on 31 March 1863.[85] Women also rented out agricultural land as a tactic to avoid losing their rural holdings to the state as abandoned lands. In 1866 the sisters Dona Antónia Pinheiro Falcão, Dona Ana Pinheiro Falcão, and Maria Esperança Pinheiro Falcão leased a plot of land in Carimbolo to Dona Mariana Joaquina Garrido for a period of six years at the rate of 8,000 *réis* monthly.[86] Women were thus as much part of the process of land expropriation as men, accumulating land as speculative investments to increase their wealth.

African women also invested in the production of foodstuffs to supply local markets. For instance, on 7 January 1864, the free black Africans Maria André da Paixão and Felipa Pedro das Dores purchased a *musseque* containing a water dam, a house, three copper pots in which to roast manioc flour, twenty-four slaves, and a cassava plantation.[87] Through this acquisition, Maria and Felipa likely intended to produce manioc flour in partnership to supply local markets. Agricultural produce also played an important role in the access of African small-scale entrepreneurs to the trade of commodities for export. Africans obtained the resources to enter long-distance trade from their own production of manioc flour, tobacco, cotton, hoes, and cattle. They exchanged these items for *fazendas*, which they used to acquire wax and ivory in the interior.[88] The trade in ivory and wax thus led, even if indirectly, to the intensification of agricultural production.

Wealthy women also resorted to partnerships in commercial enterprises, likely in order to reduce the risks involved in them. In 1866 Dona Mariana

Joaquina de Faria e Câmara Garrido purchased half of the farm Quimcolo in Ambriz, north of the capital. There, in partnership with Dona Ana de Jesus Henriques Perdigão, she established a sugar mill dedicated to the production of *aguardente*.[89] Four months later, Dona Mariana Joaquina purchased Dona Ana de Jesus's shares, becoming the sole owner of the Sociedade de Quimcolo. At the time, she hoped to soon be able to export *aguardente* to Portugal.[90] She frequently traveled from the port of Luanda to Ambriz aboard her vessel *Quimcolo* "on business."[91]

Changing Relationships

After the era of the slave trade, Luanda continued to attract immigrant men from Portugal and its overseas territories. Some white males had left Portugal between the 1820s and the 1850s, escaping the civil wars involving constitutionalists and absolutists. Although most Portuguese subjects chose Brazil as their new destination, a smaller number settled in Angola.[92] The new immigrants were poor men with little or no capital seeking quick enrichment and adventure. While some arrived as administrative and military personnel, others became shop and tavernkeepers, attending to the daily needs of inhabitants. A common element in the trajectories of these men was the fact that they often married local women a few years after settling in the colony. As did their predecessors, they too chose Luso-African wives, considering them more "civilized" than indigenous women.[93] By the mid-nineteenth century, they were able to draw on many generations of experience with interracial marriage in the Portuguese overseas territories.

While women from previous generations had become wealthy through relationships with immigrant husbands, by the mid-nineteenth century, Luso-African women in Luanda had achieved wealth through their own participation in the local and international trade. Unlike women in the Gambia region, who had their economic independence threatened by the introduction of cash crops, Luso-African women in Angola invested in the cultivation of cotton, coffee, and sugarcane and benefited from the need for foodstuffs in urban markets.[94] They were able to amass considerable wealth, including slaves, land, urban real estate, and luxury goods, outside of their relationships with foreign men.

Yet in spite of their economic prosperity, Luso-Africans had their identity threatened after the era of the slave trade. During that era, social perceptions, wealth, and family connections were more important in determining one's skin color than actual phenotype.[95] Colonial authorities classified the locally born descendants of Portuguese (and Brazilian) men with local women as both white and Portuguese, regardless of their skin color and birthplace. Nevertheless, the definition of white was questioned in the 1850s, when birthplace became relevant in determining one's classification. The official census indicated that 1,240 white individuals lived in town in 1850: 820 men and 420 women. The unknown author(s) of the *Almanak statístico da província d'Angola e suas dependências para o anno de 1852* questioned this number, stating that Luanda then had but 830 white inhabitants, 670 of whom were men and only 160 of whom were women. The classification purposed by the *Almanak* excluded from the category of whites those individuals of mixed origin born in the colony. Luso-African families who had taken advantage of their wealth to whiten the social and legal complexions of their offspring were no longer classified as white; rather, they were transferred into the category of *pardos*. According to Curto, "The white population of Luanda was thereby bleached to include only those born in Europe."[96] It is likely that the author (or authors) of the *Almanak* was a Portuguese who was dissatisfied with the labeling of people of mixed ancestry as white in Angola. He was therefore attempting to distinguish himself and his compatriots from Luso-Africans. Regardless of the reasons behind the redefinition in the *Almanak*, the new understanding of "whiteness" was quickly adopted by other foreign observers, including Carlos José Caldeira and David Livingstone.[97]

In a similar process, on the Gold Coast after the era of slave trading, Eurafricans faced growing discrimination. As Carina Ray has shown, by the mid-nineteenth century, multiracial Africans were excluded from government posts they had once enjoyed special access to.[98] Furthermore, interracial unions became a source of colonial anxiety with serious consequences for European men's professional prospects. Although interracial sexual relations remained an enduring feature of colonial society well into the twentieth century, such unions became clandestine.[99]

In Luanda, the few white inhabitants of Portuguese and Brazilian origin discriminated against local women married to white men through other arrangements than a Catholic marriage. By the mid-nineteenth century, an instance of this conflict had become public through the pen of Joachim John Monteiro, a British geologist who traveled throughout colonial Angola between the late 1850s and the early 1860s. He described the quarrel:

> [The theater] was once closed for a considerable length of time on account of a difference of opinion amongst the inhabitants as to whether only the few married and single ladies should be admitted, or whether the many ladies living under a diversity of arrangements should be on equal terms with the rest. This very pretty quarrel was highly amusing, and gave rise to the most lively scandal and recrimination between the two contending parties, but the latter and more

numerous and influential section carried the day, and ever since the doors have
been open to all classes of the fair sex, and the boxes on a gala night may be seen
filled with the swells of the place, accompanied by the many black, mulatto, and
white lady examples of the very elastic state of morals in fashion in Angola.[100]

The episode Monteiro described shows that women living in common-law
unions were discriminated against by those married according to the traditions
of the Catholic Church—even though the latter represented a minority. Since
Catholic marriages were limited to the elite, we can assume that the women "living under a diversity of arrangements" were, for the most part, dark-skinned.

As was the case in the Gold Coast, in Angola as well the end of the slave
trade lessened the need for cross-cultural knowledge from cultural brokers.[101]
In the new context, colonial racial discourses gained power, and the identity
of Luso-Africans as white and Portuguese was increasingly questioned. None-
theless, Luso-Africans continued to distinguish themselves from other Africans in Luanda by their affiliation to Christianity, access to education, and
adoption of European architecture and dress. The discrimination toward local
women did not stop foreign men from marrying them, however. In the 1850s,
Valdez remarked that "in consequence of the paucity of white women, the
Portuguese formed alliances with women of color and half-castes, to whom,
and to their children, the offspring of such connections, they manifest great
affection."[102] In spite of the rise of scientific racism in Europe and the enforce-
ment of racial hierarchies in colonial spaces, immigrant men still depended on
local wives to survive and establish trade networks in an unknown environment. In fact, some poor immigrant men of Portuguese and Brazilian origin
were only able to prosper economically in Angola through the wealth and
prestige of their Luso-African wives.

Women who enjoyed economic security continued to be attractive partners
for foreign men after the era of the slave trade, especially orphans and widows.
Dona Tereza de Jesus Pereira Bastos was the *filha natural* (born from parents
who were not married in the Catholic Church) of José António Pereira Bastos
and an unknown woman, probably locally born. Her father died sometime
before 1846, when Dona Tereza was still a child, leaving significant property,
including slaves, land, and urban real estate.[103] His death had probably been
unexpected, giving him no time to make a will. Early in 1846, Dona Tereza,
then ten or eleven years old and living under the protection of a guardian, married a certain Félix de Almeida. This union greatly astonished Luanda authorities, as the bride was an orphaned underage girl.[104] The case appeared in the
local gazette, the *Boletim Oficial de Angola*, as authorities suspected that Almeida
and the girl's guardian were trying to take advantage of her inheritance.[105]

Early in 1848, Dona Tereza, now of legal age, initiated a judicial battle to be recognized as Bastos's heir.[106] On 25 November 1848, a judge in Luanda finally granted Dona Tereza the right to her father's inheritance.[107] Félix de Almeida, however, did not live long enough to benefit from his wife's inheritance. Even before the judge made his decision, in September 1848, she had entered her second marriage, this time with the Portuguese Albino José Soares da Costa Magalhães.[108] Her second husband had arrived in Luanda in the mid-1840s and established himself as a shopkeeper.[109] Dona Tereza, who must then have been around fourteen years old, was already a well-off woman.

Magalhães's career in Angola progressed rapidly after his marriage to Dona Tereza. In 1855 the former shopkeeper and his wife founded the plantation Protótipo in the district of Cazengo, dedicated to the cultivation of coffee. The Protótipo became the largest and most productive coffee plantation in Angola and established Magalhães as one of its wealthiest men.[110] During the 1860s, he acquired several properties, including two islands, three *arimos*, a ship, and a *sobrado*.[111] In 1864, he was one of the founders and associates of the Associação Agrícola de Luanda (Luanda Agricultural Society) alongside former slavers such as Francisco António Flores, Manuel Rodrigues Carmelino, José Bernardo da Silva, Joaquim Guedes de Carvalho Menezes, João Osmundo Toulson, and Isaac Zacary.[112] The society aimed to develop commercial agriculture in the colony. Magalhães's prestige was further enhanced by the title of Comendador da Ordem de Cristo (Knight of the Order of Christ), granted to men for their distinguished service to Portugal.[113] It is unlikely that his ascent would have happened without the financial support and cultural knowledge of his wife. After his marriage to Dona Tereza, the former shopkeeper became known as Barão do Café (Coffee Baron). Following Magalhães's death, Dona Tereza managed the couple's estate until their three children reached adulthood.[114]

The Portuguese António Félix Machado had arrived in Luanda in the 1840s, becoming a tavernkeeper.[115] Like Magalhães, he also chose an orphaned Luso-African as his wife. At the time of Machado's arrival in Angola, Dona Ana Joaquina do Amaral was already a landowner and successful trader, supplying maize to the Terreiro.[116] The couple lived together for several years in a common-law union. During the 1850s, Machado prospered rapidly, entering the list of the main merchants based in Luanda.[117] He was also part of the group of traders who illegally exported captives after 1836.[118] Although some tavernkeepers exported a few captives at a time, it is unlikely that Machado would have acquired the capital to enter the slave trade and become a prominent merchant solely through his activity as a tavernkeeper. He probably built his career with the financial support and commercial networks of his Luso-African wife. In 1859 the couple decided to make their union official. By then, three children had been born from their relationship: Pedro, Isabel, and a newborn child still unbaptized.[119] Before their marriage took place, Dona Ana Joaquina do Amaral called a notary to her house to have her own register of dowry written up. In the document, she specified that she herself was a merchant "trading with her capital and in her own name." In the absence of her parents, she then endowed herself with the capital of her business, evaluated at 10,000 *réis* in credit, and two houses in Luanda, which she declared she had acquired with her own resources.[120] The self-endowment guaranteed Dona Ana Joaquina separate ownership of the assets she brought to the marriage, as well as those she had acquired herself during the period of her common-law union with Machado.

By the mid-nineteenth century, women merchants in Luanda were able to achieve wealth outside their relationships with foreign men, presumably affording them greater independence. Dona Ana Joaquina and Machado officialized their union through a marriage contract, and, as was her wish, husband and wife were to co-own only the assets they acquired together from that date onward. As a Luso-African, Dona Ana Joaquina was no doubt aware of the benefits conferred upon her by Portuguese law. She signed her own register of dowry and the marriage contract, indicating that she had access to some sort of formal education. Her literacy and wealth certainly brought her advantages in this colonial society. Her choices evidence that she was well aware of the risks involved in marrying a man with no attachment to the land.

Living with the Enslaved

THE WITHDRAWAL OF BRAZIL from the slave traffic in 1850 resulted in the decline in shipments from Angola. The merchant community of Luanda intensified the use of slave labor locally, retaining enslaved Africans who previously would have been exported across the Atlantic Ocean. The final chapter of this book examines the local use of slave labor and the interactions between slaveholders and the enslaved in the era of legitimate commerce. Luanda merchants employed slave labor in the production and transport of alternative goods for the export market at the same time that they invested in the specialization of enslaved Africans to meet the demands of a city in expansion.

A New Alexandria Built with Slave Labor

Foreigners who passed by or settled in the Angolan capital by the mid-nineteenth century noticed the urban development then taking place in the city. Lopes de Lima stated enthusiastically in the mid-1840s that Luanda, "the capital of both kingdoms [Angola and Benguela], is certainly deserving of this position as the most majestic, opulent, and beautiful of the European towns that have been founded in the African continent." The town, he suggested, could become a new Alexandria, if only communication with the eastern part of the continent could be opened through the interior.[1] Early in the 1850s, Carlos José Caldeira noted that Luanda had public lighting in its streets and was well policed, with wide squares and streets, elegant carriages and horses, and many shops where all sorts of goods could be found.[2] Shopkeepers supplied Europeans and the Luso-African population with imports, including food and items of apparel. In 1851 Francisco da Silva Teles offered in his store "perfume of superior quality, suspenders, gloves, fur, and cotton among other products."[3] Residents could also enjoy fine pastries at the shop of João Carlos Lemos dos Santos and at the Confeitaria Esperança, which opened its doors in September 1851.[4]

These foreign observers, however, failed to point out that the main port and administrative center of Angola would not have been able to function without the labor of enslaved Africans. During the 1960s and 1970s, a romantic view of an egalitarian Africa contributed to the scholarly denial of stratification and exploitation within indigenous societies. Also, the comparison with the chattel slavery system in the Americas further perpetuated the notion that African domestic slavery was relatively benign.[5] Since then scholarly discourse has demonstrated that Africans generated, traded, and used slaves as labor and as symbols of prestige. During the era of the slave trade, merchants not only exported slaves but also made use of slave labor locally. The enslaved performed all kinds of work in the city: they carried water, washed the linens of the elite, tended the land in the *arimos* and gardens, and were the main labor force in the *oficinas* (craft workshops). During the era of legitimate commerce, they tended the land in plantations and brought tropical commodities from inland areas to the coast.

With the 1850 law that prohibited the importation of captives to Brazil, the number of slaves exported from Angola dropped drastically—from 260,399 between 1846 and 1850 to only 36,740 between 1851 and 1855. Consequently, with the precipitous drop in demand, the price of captives collapsed all along the coast and in the interior. While in the mid-1840s, the price of a slave had been about 40,000 *réis* in *fazendas*, in the 1850s it dropped to 20,000 *réis*.[6] The collapse of slave prices had been previously experienced in other areas of the West African coast, if only temporarily.[7] Meanwhile, the growth of the overseas trade in legitimate goods increased the demand for labor in Angola, as it did elsewhere in Africa.[8] In this context, enslaved Africans who would have been exported were now retained locally, contributing to an increase in the population of the main ports.

Of the 12,565 people living in Luanda in 1850, some 6,020, or 48 percent, were enslaved. Women represented 63.5 percent of the enslaved population of the city, reflecting their importance in the labor force.[9] The profile of the enslaved population resulted in part from the higher number of men who were exported in the Atlantic market.[10] As well, women were preferred in the African domestic market because of their productive and reproductive capacities.[11] As the population of the capital grew, the need for more housing and food and for the production of basic goods also expanded.[12] Traditionally a slave society, Luanda met part of this demand by incorporating large numbers of slaves into its population.

Among the enslaved, men dominated artisan crafts, which all required training in workshops. Following the model applied in Lisbon, in the Portuguese overseas territories, *mestres* (master tradesmen or craftsmen) conducted the training of apprentices in workshops supervised by municipal officials called *almotacés*. Apprenticeship in a skilled trade was restricted to males and usually took between two and six years to complete, after which the apprentices were submitted to an examination to receive the title of *oficial* (qualified skilled tradesman). Some skilled workers become *mestres*, a title that conferred on them the right to open a workshop and train apprentices.[13] The Câmara Municipal oversaw the processes of training and examination of artisans, conferring titles on approved candidates, issuing licenses, and inspecting workshops.[14]

As was the case in other slave societies, few slaves achieved the office of *mestre* in Luanda.[15] Skilled slaves were more likely to find employment in urban contexts, especially in workshops and public works undertaken by the Portuguese administration. In 1850 the number of master craftsmen heading workshops in Luanda reached 111 (see table 6.1), and many skilled workers at the time were enslaved Africans. Having slaves learning a trade was an investment for slaveholders, who could subsequently hire them out or get a better price for them in case of sale. While an ordinary slave was then worth 20,000 to 40,000 *réis*, the price of a slave proficient in any trade could reach 100,000 *réis* or more.[16] Former slavers did not hesitate now to invest in the training of enslaved men. In 1855 the former slave dealer João Bernardino da Costa Carneiro registered eleven slaves who had received training in artisan workshops: Manuel, a tailor; José, Augustinho, and Lourenço, coopers; Francisco and Joaquim Cadoque, weavers; Domingos, a cobbler; Caalla, a tinsmith; Joaquim, a barber; Albino, a mason; and Manuel Segundo, a carpenter.[17] Augusto Garrido registered eight enslaved artisans: Leão, a caulker; Francisco and André, carpenters; Pedro, Francisco, and Gansa, masons; João, a goldsmith; and Serafim, a barber. Garrido also owned another six slaves who were receiving training in workshops to become caulkers, tailors, barbers, and carpenters.[18] A few among the enslaved artisans did acquire the title of master and were allowed to run workshops and train apprentices. In 1852 the master barber Manuel António, slave of Dona Ana Joaquina dos Santos Silva, operated a workshop in town.[19] These skilled slaves worked on their own accounts, paying a fee to their owners and keeping the remainder of what they earned.[20] Some among them may have lived independently in the many *cubatas* located in the suburbs.[21]

The presence of women in training workshops was uncommon in Portugal. In the metropole, they could only enter female weaving workshop under the supervision of a *mestra* (trade mistress). Widowed wives could take over the workshops of their deceased husbands under the condition that they remained single or married a *mestre* who worked in the same trade.[22] These rules kept poor and enslaved women away from artisan crafts in Lisbon and in Portugal's

Table 6.1. Workshops in Luanda, 1850

Tailors, masters	20	Joiner, master	1
Skilled workers	53	Skilled workers	3
Apprentices	80	Apprentices	6
Barbers, masters	11	Goldsmiths, masters	5
Skilled workers	34	Skilled workers	6
Apprentices	30	Apprentices	10
Carpenters, masters	11	Masons, masters	18
Skilled workers	34	Skilled workers	62
Apprentices	40	Apprentices	105
Shoemakers, masters	15	Painters, masters	8
Skilled workers	22	Skilled worker	1
Apprentices	32	Apprentices	6
Tinsmiths, masters	4	Coppersmiths, masters	11
Skilled workers	10	Skilled workers	18
Apprentices	12	Apprentices	28
Blacksmiths, masters	3	Turners, masters	2
Skilled workers	14	Skilled worker	1
Apprentices	17	Apprentices	2
Farriers, master	1	Watchmakers, master	1

Source: *Boletim Oficial de Angola*, no. 303, 19 July 1851, 1–2.

overseas territories, where they were limited to performing most of the domestic services and to retail trade.

In the Portuguese territories in general, the free inhabitants seem to have had an aversion to manual tasks—activities considered unworthy of them and dishonorable.[23] In Luanda, as in other slave societies, the enslaved were responsible for domestic services, including food preparation, household chores, clothes mending, and laundering. Lopes de Lima noted in his visit to the city that the wealthiest families held impressive quantities of slaves, who "crowded the houses as luxury objects." He observed in particular that it was "common to find ten, twelve, or twenty slaves at a bachelor's house who would find it difficult to employ two or three servants."[24] In contrast to men's domination of artisan crafts, women represented the majority of slaves performing domestic services.[25] These activities did not require training in workshops, let alone examinations, allowing greater numbers of women to enter into them. Tutors who privately educated the daughters of the local elite also trained enslaved women in the arts of washing, starching, ironing, and sewing, among other skills.[26] A large number of enslaved women specialized in these tasks. In 1855 Ana, an enslaved woman who belonged to Dona Joana Maria da Conceição Bastos, was a seamstress and a washerwoman. Dona Joana owned four other women who washed the linens and clothes of the household and likely also offered their services to other inhabitants of the city.[27]

Another major occupation in which women were present was in retail sales. In 1850 the capital of Angola had two hundred *quitandeiras*, a number that did not reflect the total of street vendors, as many women peddled goods without a license.[28] On 20 September 1852, an inspector of the Municipal Council fined Félix José Ferreira Campos 7,500 *réis* because his *quitandeira* Eufrásia was peddling without a license.[29] Similarly, on 22 September 1852, the merchant André da Silva Marques Braga paid a fine of the same amount for sending a slave woman to sell glass beads on the streets without a license.[30] Masters were usually responsible for paying for licenses and providing the items their slaves peddled around the city. These enslaved women enjoyed more mobility than those who were restricted to the household, and it is possible that some among them also engaged in prostitution—freely or being forced into it by unscrupulous masters wishing to increase their income. The presence of enslaved women in taverns that attracted men interested in gambling and alcohol consumption suggests that males may also have been able to find casual sexual partners in these establishments.[31]

Women in other occupations also found opportunities in offering their services to the population. In a city with only two public wells, the work of water-carriers was extremely important. These women carried water to supply their masters' households and, for a fee, the households of others.[32] Washerwomen and seamstresses too could earn some income during the hours when they were not working for their owners. Slaveholders commonly advertised the services of slaves, whether for sale or rent, in the gazettes that circulated in Luanda. In September 1852, Bento Bernardo da Costa announced that he had a wet nurse for rent.[33] Wet nurses had to leave their infant child unattended while they breastfed and cared for other children, which often resulted in the malnutrition of their own offspring. Masters likely encouraged enslaved women's entrepreneurship, as they could pocket a handsome income from the women's work.

Nevertheless, labor was not the only reason why men and women acquired slaves; prestige was another. The Luso-African elite distinguished themselves from other Africans by their ownership of slaves and symbols of prestige such as hammocks and European garments. Only the wealthy owned *mucamas* (chambermaids) and *maxilas* (carriers) and were able to afford the equipment and spare slaves to perform such work. Travelers often described wealthy men and women carried in hammocks and followed by a retinue of slaves on outings through the city. In the 1830s, Frenchman Jean Baptiste Douville noted, "When the wealthiest ladies show themselves outside of their households . . . they are then followed by a multitude of slaves so that, the first time I saw one of those trains I confused it with a procession."[34] A few years later, the Italian Tito Omboni indeed confused such processions with funerals.[35] The journey to the Sunday mass and business meetings was another opportunity to display wealth and reinforce social standing. The merchant Joaquim dos Santos Monteiro, for example, was carried in a hammock to public functions by his *maxilas* João, Francisco, Roberto, and José.[36]

Large-scale commercial agriculture employed slaves on plantations owned by both foreign and Luso-African investors. Wealthy Luanda residents owned *arimos* and plantations in the interior, where slaves tended the land, growing crops for the export market and staples to feed urban dwellers. Dona Ana Joaquina dos Santos Silva owned *arimos* in the districts of Zenza do Golungo, Icolo e Bengo, and Dande, where enslaved workers cultivated maize, cassava, beans, and sugarcane.[37] In his early 1850s visit to Dona Ana Joaquina's sugar mill in the district of Bengo, Valdez was informed by the overseer that she had fourteen hundred slaves on this property alone.[38] She also had slaves in other agricultural properties and in town as well as in her many *feitorias*, probably making her one of the largest slave owners in the colony. Albino José Soares da Costa Magalhães employed four hundred slaves in the cultivation of coffee on his plantation, Protótipo, in the district of Cazengo.[39] An additional number tended the land in his *arimos* and assisted with the daily needs of his family in Luanda.[40] Augusto Garrido similarly employed sizable numbers of slaves in town as well as on farms and *feitorias* throughout Angola.[41]

The Vulnerability of Enslaved Persons

Household slaves were required by their owners to perform various personal services, such as preparing food, taking care of children, and accompanying their masters on public functions throughout the city and on trips to the interior—all positions of trust. That household slaves were part of the everyday lives of their owners did not necessarily mean that they were well treated, however. They suffered as much or perhaps even more punishment as slaves working in the *arimos* and *musseques*, as their owners were able to oversee their work at close quarters.[42] Enslaved women, in particular, were vulnerable to violence within the household. Late in 1841, having found accommodations at the house of the surgeon general in Luanda, the German doctor Gustav Tams reportedly heard sounds of slaves being punished by order of his host's wife, the Spanish-born Dona Catarina:

> I had scarcely been in possession of my new lodgings for an hour, and was occupied in arranging my effects, when my attention was suddenly attracted by the sound of stripes, repeated at regular intervals. I soon perceived that some person was undergoing corporal chastisement in the court-yard, and at once hastened to the lady of the house. . . . To my anxious inquiry, respecting the loud beating which still continued, she replied, smiling, that one of her needle-women was receiving, by her orders, six dozen palmetadas (blows in the palm of the hand), because her stitches were badly made.[43]

After being beaten, Tams reported, seamstresses were sent back to work with their hands "much swollen and lacerated, nay bleeding."[44] The manner in which Dona Catarina treated her slaves resulted in the German physician believing that Europeans rarely treated their slaves with benevolence, unlike locally born masters, who, in his mind, did not use cruelty to achieve obedience. As an example of these differing behaviors, he pointed to the "benignity" of Dona Ana Ubertali, as "none of her numerous slaves had any sign on their backs of being severely punished." He asserted that she preferred to sell disobedient slaves rather than punish them.[45]

Dona Ana Ubertali may well not have punished her slaves with severity, but the threat of resale and the uncertainty that came with it was a particularly punishing type of psychological coercion that slave owners relied upon. The official suppression of the slave trade in 1836 may have diminished the efficacy of the threat of sale abroad as a means of disciplining slaves. In a similar fashion to Tams, in the 1850s the geologist Joachim John Monteiro claimed, "I never knew or heard of slaves being worked or treated in the hard and cruel manner in which they are said to have been in the Southern States of America, or at the present day in Cuba."[46] Records found in the official documentation and in the gazettes circulating in town do not corroborate such statements.

Throughout the late eighteenth and nineteenth centuries, European empires implemented measures aimed at improving the living conditions of the enslaved on both sides of the Atlantic. In the 1780s, for example, the Spanish enacted legal codes that represented an initial step in improving conditions for slaves. In Cuba, local laws supplemented the Spanish legal codes in 1842, granting slaves the right to legal marriage, to manumission, and even to change masters in instances of mistreatment. Enslaved persons, especially those living in urban areas, drew upon this legislation in order to denounce abusive masters and mistresses.[47] In the African context, Somerset's Proclamation and

Ordinance 19, passed by the British in 1823 and 1826, respectively, granted slaves in Cape Town rights to marriage, food, and clothing, at the same time forbidding the separation of families through sale, limiting the number of hours that slaves could be compelled to work, and establishing rules for punishment.[48]

It was only after the early 1850s, in a context of extreme criticism of slavery, that Portugal effectively began to implement measures aimed at protecting enslaved Africans in Angola.[49] On 7 October 1853, the Portuguese administration introduced an ordinance that forbade masters from punishing slaves and required that they instead treat them "humanely" by handing them over to the police for correction.[50] Depending on the fault committed, correction could include public work, imprisonment, or physical punishment.[51] By the middle of the nineteenth century, correction had emerged as an opportunity for the government to draw upon unpaid labor for a variety of endeavors.[52] The "barbarous and incendiary practice" of masters placing their slaves in irons was also banned; the exception was the shackle, which could be used without the chain for recalcitrant slaves. Irons could be used only on slaves laboring in public works or by order of the government. The 1853 ordinance sought to "end once and forever the barbaric and inhumane practice of masters enforcing rigorous and sometimes unfair punishments according to their will on unfortunate slaves." It advised masters instead to treat their slaves with "humanity and tenderness in order to soften the painful state of slavery but without encouraging through impunity their general tendency to laziness and theft, as they are indolent and uncivilized in nature."[53]

Failure of masters to abide by the restrictions in the ordinance could lead to fines: 4,000 *réis* for the first occurrence, 8,000 *réis* for the second, and 20,000 *réis* for the third. Along with the threat of losing their abused slaves to the Department of Public Works as *libertos*, accused masters had to face judicial proceedings. The 1853 ordinance did not question the need for punishment so long as it occurred legally "in a way that does not misrepresent the authority that the master must have over slaves in order to maintain respect and obedience."[54] On the other hand, the new regulation did challenge the authority of masters, since they had to prove that slaves deserved punishment, and if masters had transgressed the law, they could be fined or lose their human property.

Masters learned of this new decree first through the pages of the *Boletim Oficial de Angola*, which published the ordinance on 8 October 1853. Enslaved Africans, in turn, likely learned of it indirectly, both inside and outside the household. Since Luanda was a Luso-African society, a relatively large proportion of its enslaved residents, especially those born in the town, were able to communicate in Portuguese; some were even literate.[55] The latter likely became a source of information for the illiterate. Whatever the flow of information, one thing is certain: enslaved Africans certainly acquired some degree of knowledge regarding extant legislation, as is illustrated by the cases of slaves who challenged in the court their illegal enslavement during the era of the slave trade.[56]

Starting in September 1855, slaves were able to turn to the Junta Protetora de Escravos e Libertos (Board for the Protection of Enslaved and Freed Africans) for help in cases of gross mistreatment. The board was created in 1854, replacing the Junta de Superintêndencia dos Negros Libertos, established in 1845 to supervise the Africans rescued by the Mixed Commission.[57] In extreme cases, the Junta Protetota rescued mistreated slaves from their owners. Added to the 1853 ordinance, which removed physical punishment from the direct control of slave owners, these innovations imposed further limitations on the power that masters could exercise over their slaves in a context of intensified use of slave labor in Angola. Still, some masters, both men and women, continued to abuse the enslaved.

Slaves took advantages of the instruments of protection at hand to denounce the violence that masters inflicted upon them. In August 1858, an enslaved woman brought her master, Francisco José Ribeiro Guimarães, to court for squeezing her fingers with an instrument of punishment called *anjinhos* (little angels).[58] In April 1864, the chief of police, José Lourenço Marques, sent José Elisbão Ferreira to jail for severely hurting an enslaved woman.[59] Few cases of murder ever became known, however, as masters were careful to conceal their crimes. On December 1857, João José do Vale faced the accusation of murdering his slave Ingrácia. Although the crime took place under Vale's roof, he was absolved of guilt due to "lack of evidence."[60] In August 1864, on the other hand, Caetano Manuel da Conceição went to jail for the murder of an enslaved woman who was his property.[61]

Women were equally as able as their fathers, husbands, and sons to discipline and mete out violence to slaves, particularly when the enslaved in question were women and children. In October 1858, Dona Maria Joana Rodrigues de Bastos Barboza, a Spanish woman, was accused of and subsequently incarcerated for murdering one of her slaves.[62] In May 1859, the police arrested Dona Joana Maria da Conceição Bastos on the charge of murdering one of her slaves and burying the body in her *musseque* to conceal the crime. After an autopsy that confirmed the murder, Dona Joana went to prison.[63]

Slaves who survived cruel punishment were able to disclose other wrongdoings their owners had committed that otherwise would have remained unknown. In March 1866, several slaves of a certain Dona Maria Joana accused her of cruelty. At the time, the enslaved Joana, Esperança, and Agostinho were receiving treatment for their wounds in the Santa Casa de Misericórdia hospital. Dona Maria Joana had stabbed the slave Joana in the mouth with a knife, and Esperança was "in a terrible state" because of various punishments by her mistress. Dona Maria Joana also faced the accusation of the murder of Constança, another enslaved woman.[64] A few days later, a *moleca* (young girl, in this case enslaved) arrived in the same hospital with scars on her body from lashes; she disclosed that her mistress had severely punished her and other slaves and accused the woman of killing another *moleca* through repeated punishments.[65] This report did not identify the mistress in question, which suggests that she was an influential woman.

In every case regarding the mistreatment of slaves, the Junta Protetora required that a physician examine their bodies for supporting evidence. Following confirmation of mistreatment, this institution arranged for the *resgate* (rescue) of the slave by advancing the cost for redemption. Such slaves then moved into the legal category of *liberto* and remained under the custody of the Junta Protetora. Their services were allocated to private individuals or the government in return for the price of redemption.[66] The surviving documentation produced by the curators of the Junta Protetora provides glimpses of enslaved men and women who took their grievances to the board. These cases demonstrate that slaves used colonial institutions to leave their owners and improve their existence.

In 1862 the enslaved Maria Joaquina denounced her master, Joaquim Luiz Pinto de Andrade, for her mistreatment. After Maria's accusation was confirmed, the Junta Protetora proposed to pay for her rescue "to prevent litigation." Andrade, in turn, agreed to the value of 100,000 *réis* for Maria's rescue.[67] The price of her rescue evidences that Maria was a highly skilled woman. In 1863 Catarina, an enslaved woman who belonged to Dona Maria Apolônia, similarly filed a complaint against her mistress. According to Catarina, Dona Maria Apolônia had confined her in heavy irons, which she was still wearing, despite their being forbidden. The curator decided for the rescue of Catarina due to the "poor condition" in which she was found.[68] In April 1864, an enslaved woman named Rosa filed a complaint against her mistress, Dona Josefa Carolina Correia Bittencourt, for continual mistreatment. Following an examination of Rosa's body, which confirmed the abuse, the Junta Protetora decided to remove the enslaved woman permanently from her mistress.[69]

While some slaves faced cruel punishment at the hands of their owners, others were abandoned. References to abandoned slaves wandering the streets appeared frequently in the *Boletim Oficial de Angola*. They begged and stole food and were easily recognized by their nudity and thinness. Abandoned slaves included those whom masters viewed as "useless," particularly elders, children, and the injured. In March 1858, the police reported that an abandoned male slave was in the Santa Casa de Misericórdia hospital with a serious injury to his foot.[70] The fact that the slave had a wounded foot certainly precluded him from working, which may explain why his master abandoned him. Slaves found by police wandering on the streets were first sent to the Junta Protetora and, depending on their condition, were forwarded to the hospital. If masters did not reclaim their slaves, they were legally turned into *libertos* and assigned new masters. The abandonment of injured slaves freed masters from the expenses of treatment and, in the case of death, the cost of a Christian burial. In the early 1860s, a modest burial for an unbaptized slave cost 800 *réis*, while the burial of a baptized Catholic slave amounted to 1,000 *réis*. If the burial required a coffin and a shroud, costs could reach 7,500 *réis*.[71] Although masters usually baptized their slaves, the possibility of such an expense may have led slave-holders to evict aging and ailing slaves from their households.

Paths to Freedom

Although slave resistance has received more attention in the Americas, the phenomenon was no less significant in Africa. Since the 1980s, scholars have investigated the formation of *mutolos* or *quilombos* (communities of runaway slaves) and the repression of fugitive slaves in Angola.[72] Meanwhile, stories of Africans who fought their illegal enslavement during the slave trade era have also begun to become known.[73] Irrespective of their sex and age and whether they were working in urban or rural spaces, slaves attempted to escape from their condition whenever they could, a concern affecting both wealthy and modest slaveholders.

Throughout much of the nineteenth century, the Portuguese administration and slave masters showed a preoccupation with the *mutolos* that constantly formed around Luanda. With the addition of significant numbers of enslaved Africans to the Luanda population after 1836, slave flight emerged as a considerable problem. In 1850 the colonial administration organized a military expedition composed of 610 men to destroy communities of fugitive slaves established between the districts of Icolo and Calumbo.[74] The expedition razed numerous *cubatas* found along the trails and recaptured seventy-five runaways, including slaves and *libertos*. In the course of the expedition, two soldiers were killed and fourteen were injured. The recaptured runaways were taken to Luanda, where they labored in public works until their masters reclaimed them. The fact that *libertos* escaped their masters to join fugitive slaves demonstrates that they identified with the enslaved in spite of their supposedly different condition.

Masters commonly sought to recover fugitive slaves, offering compensation to anyone who captured and returned them. Absconded slaves were announced in the local gazette, with physical descriptions provided to facilitate their identification. On 24 May 1851, Joaquim Manuel Escórcio announced the escape of two of his male slaves, the tailor Bernardo, branded with the letters IMW, and Miguel, branded with the letters AMS. Escórcio added that both slaves were *ladinos*, meaning that they were acculturated and able to speak Portuguese. He offered 20,000 *réis* to anyone who captured and delivered them to his wife in Luanda.[75] On 20 December 1851, Major Rudsky similarly advertised that his slave Frederico, a locksmith, had escaped and that he was willing to pay 10,000 *réis* to anyone who returned him.[76] The rewards offered were not particularly attractive, since the price of skilled slaves like Frederico and Bernardo could reach about 100,000 *réis*.[77] That Frederico, Bernardino, and Miguel were artisans or well acculturated to Luanda society clearly did not dampen their desire for freedom.

The Department of Public Works was in charge of recaptured slaves, where they worked while waiting for masters and mistresses to reclaim them. Slave owners had fifteen days to claim slaves brought in and to pay a recovery fee of 20,000 *réis*. Unclaimed slaves became the property of the Royal Treasury, which subsequently sold them at public auction. Some recaptured runaways, especially those involved in *mutolos*, received punishment in the Pelourinho, the public place of whipping.[78] The daily displays of violence allowed the state and masters to remind the enslaved population of their authority and to promote obedience through fear.

Dona Ana Joaquina dos Santos Silva's name appeared periodically in the *Boletim Oficial de Angola* among the owners of fugitive and recaptured slaves. On 31 July 1852, the police recaptured two of her slaves, João Zua and Ngongo, in the district of Zenza do Golungo and returned them to the Department of Public Works in Luanda.[79] Masters sometimes decided not to reclaim their recaptured runaways; payment of 20,000 *réis* to reacquire troublesome slaves who might again attempt to escape was not always worthwhile. They may have chosen instead to purchase a new slave, who at the time cost about the same amount.

Some enslaved Africans were, however, able to achieve manumission through various means. Enslaved men who were engaged in artisan crafts, for instance, were able to earn incomes and, presumably, buy themselves out of slavery.[80] In 1863 Joaquim Antônio Cristóvão Inácio, the slave of Lourença Francisca Joaquina, proposed to pay for his manumission, valued at 100,000 *réis*, with income he earned as a master bricklayer.[81] Since Joaquim was a skilled slave who had reached the category of master in his trade, a rare achievement among the enslaved, the value of his manumission was high compared to the prices of most slaves in the 1860s (about 20,000 *réis* in trade goods). Likewise, enslaved women who were hired out to perform domestic work, such as sewing and washing clothes, or who engaged in retail trade as *quitandeiras* also had better opportunities to purchase their freedom from the proceeds of several years of work than did women restricted to household chores. In August 1859, the forty-year-old *quitandeira* Engrácia, slave of Dona Josefa de Moraes Moreira, purchased her manumission.[82] In September 1866, the *quitandeira* Carolina, slave of João Pereira de Carvalho, also purchased her freedom.[83] In Saint-Louis, Senegal some enslaved women who became petty traders even earned enough to purchase their own slaves.[84]

In addition to purchasing their manumission, slaves could sometimes acquire it as reward for years of dutiful unpaid service. In either situation, masters had to agree to the arrangement, as they were the only ones with authority to give up personal property by issuing letters of manumission. To avoid any possibility of later contestation, masters registered the grants of freedom with a notary. Nevertheless, even when a slave was eager to pay for manumission, masters could refuse the offer. Cases of disagreement over the value of manumission and instances where masters faced judicial proceedings after refusing offers from slaves must have arisen throughout the mid-nineteenth century in Angola, just as they did in Brazil.[85] Letters of manumission provide a number of insights into why proprietors freed slaves in Luanda. Most enslaved Africans who gained their freedom probably did so through purchasing it. On 25 November 1857, for example, Antónia Francisca paid 40,000 *réis* to Dona Maria Rodrigues da Silva for the freedom of herself and her minor son, Pedro.[86] Dona Maria declared that she had accepted the offer because of the good services Antónia had provided over the years. Had her mistress refused, Antónia would have remained the property of Dona Maria and watched her son grow up as an enslaved person.

Some masters granted slaves conditional manumission. Although manumission was granted free of charge, the master expected the slave to meet certain conditions before enjoying his or her freedom. On 30 May 1856, Teodora Pombo manumitted the enslaved boy José Francisco based on the "good services and friendship" she had received from him. Nevertheless, she imposed the condition that he had to assist her until her death.[87] Slaves granted conditional freedom sometimes faced resistance from heirs who reclaimed possession of them following the owner's death.[88] The granting of manumission certainly contributed to promoting a paternalist image of slave owners.[89] At the same time, the possibility of acquiring freedom may have encouraged slaves to work diligently and serve faithfully, avoiding rebellious attitudes or actions and meeting their masters' wishes—including sexual ones.[90]

Masters sometimes granted manumission to enslaved Africans with neither charges nor conditions as a reward for the good services they had provided. On 28 October 1856, Elena Santiago voluntarily conferred freedom upon Rubina

Joaquina for her "good services."[91] Likewise, on 20 February 1857, Fonseca Varela manumitted Porciana Matilde because of "her good services and exemplary behaviour."[92] The "good services" that enslaved women provided often included satisfying the sexual appetites of their masters. Some enslaved women bore children fathered by their masters. On 22 June 1852, the slave Mariza gave birth to Marcelina, whose father was Mariza's master, the Portuguese army sergeant Joaquim António de Moura.[93] Whether the pregnancy resulted from rape or consensual sex is difficult to ascertain. The line between both is certainly blurred, given the imbalance of power that marked the interactions between enslaved and masters. In slave societies, the sexuality of enslaved women was considered an extension of the services they were to provide to masters.[94]

In some cases, becoming the sexual partner of a free man could bring benefits to enslaved woman and their offspring. Although it was not mandatory, sometimes during baptism, masters freed the children they had fathered; also, upon the masters' death, they might free their children's mothers.[95] That was not the case for Marcelina and her mother, however. In spite of acknowledging Marcelina as his daughter, Sergeant Moura did not free his child at the baptismal font. Instead, Marcelina remained enslaved, as did her mother.

When in 1853 the Portuguese administration advised masters to treat captives with "humanity and tenderness," the intention was clear: to reduce excesses without affecting the status quo or abolishing slavery. The cases of gross punishment that appeared in the local gazette highlight the vulnerability of the enslaved at the same time as they show how slaves made use of colonial institutions such as the Junta Protetora to claim their rights. Women slaveholders drew upon as much violence as their male counterparts to discipline and punish their slaves, especially women and children. Violence and flight were part of the interactions between the enslaved and slaveholders. In a few cases, "good services" could lead to manumission while simultaneously contributing to reinforce the power structure of the slave society.

Conclusion

O N 6 APRIL 1859, Dona Ana Joaquina dos Santos Silva left Luanda and headed to Lisbon accompanied by eight slaves in her service aboard the Portuguese vessel *D. Pedro*.[1] The "Queen of Bengo" was traveling to the Portuguese capital to be treated for an illness. She never arrived, dying during the Atlantic crossing, and her body was likely disposed of at sea.[2] Following her death, a long legal dispute took place in Luanda. Dona Ana Joaquina had disinherited her only daughter, Dona Tereza Luíza, and bequeathed her wealth to her grandchildren.[3] Dona Tereza Luíza had first married António José Cabral de Melo Pinto, a Portuguese lawyer who had arrived in Luanda in August 1827 as a *degredado*.[4] After he died, she married Elísio Guedes Coutinho Garrido, the brother of Augusto Guedes Coutinho Garrido. This second marriage, entered into without the consent of Dona Ana Joaquina, is generally given as the main reason why Dona Tereza Luíza was excluded from her mother's last will.[5] As a merchant, Augusto Garrido was in direct competition with Dona Ana.

Today a replica of the imposing palace where Dona Ana Joaquina lived stands in the *baixa* of Luanda. A plaque on its facade reads "Dona Ana Joaquina's Palace." Until 2019, the palace housed the Luanda Provincial Court of Justice. There is no reference to her activities as a slave trader to be found in the building. In the Slavery Museum, founded in Luanda in 1977, the slave trade is, for the most part, presented as a solely European enterprise. The role played by local slave dealers has been washed from public memory.[6]

Over the course of almost four centuries, the slave trade turned Luanda into a premier port, attracting Portuguese and Brazilian merchants in search of quick enrichment. During the era of the transatlantic slave trade, about 2.9 million enslaved Africans were shipped through the port of Luanda, most of them bound for Brazil. But Africans also crossed the Atlantic voluntarily. Luso-African merchants like Dona Ana Joaquina dos Santos Silva sent their children abroad for education, sought medical treatment overseas, and traveled on business between Angola, Brazil, and Portugal. The movement of people, ideas, and commodities connected these three nodes of the Atlantic world.

Foreign merchants established in Luanda took local wives and headed Luso-African families. Their offspring had the ability to navigate both worlds, occupying positions in the colonial militias and administration as well as becoming merchants in Luanda and its hinterland. They spoke Portuguese, professed Christianity, and adopted European fashions and civil laws. At the same time that they were the product of Portuguese colonialism, Luso-Africans were also connected through personal and commercial links to indigenous populations. They spoke Kimbundu, consulted with African healers, and maintained trade networks with African communities inland. The local women who entered into relationships with foreign men were better able to advance their careers in the international trade. Their husbands provided access to imported goods, which the women traded in shops and taverns, and the more successful among them were able to enter the trade in slaves. As Portuguese subjects, they were entitled to inherit property from their foreign fathers and husbands, which also contributed to increase their wealth.

Over the course of the nineteenth century, the merchant community of Luanda was compelled to respond to the transformations affecting the Atlantic world. After years of competition, in the first decade of that century, many British and French withdrew from the African-controlled ports near the mouth of the Congo River, and Portuguese and Brazilian-born traders were better able to control the shipment of captives from West Central Africa. When the suppression of the Portuguese slave trade north of the equator in 1815 resulted in increased demand for captives from Angola, Luanda-based slave traders responded by enlarging their fleet. Demand for slaves to attend the needs of the Portuguese court in Rio de Janeiro and serve the Brazilian agrarian sector also created opportunities for new investors, including women merchants, who invested in the slave trade either independently or as partners of their foreign husbands.

In December 1836, the Portuguese government officially banned the export of captives from all of its overseas territories in Africa, and by the mid-1840s slave exports from Luanda were virtually nonexistent. The presence of British and Portuguese warships patrolling the port of Luanda forced illegal slave traders to move to areas outside Portuguese control. From remote locations in the north and south of the colony, slave dealers continued shipping captives to Brazil and Cuba. The dispersal of shipments to *feitorias* located away from the capital compromised the ability of antislave cruisers to end the trade. The activities of the Court of the Mixed Commission at Luanda were equally compromised by the social and professional connections of officials with local slave traders. The involvement of merchants in the illegal slave trade did not preclude their receiving noble titles and being nominated for administrative positions in Luanda and in the interior. After all, the colonial state depended upon the financial support of the local elites, including slave dealers.

Colonial authorities in Lisbon and Angola anticipated that the trade in tropical commodities such as coffee, ivory, wax, orchil, cotton, and sugar would replace slave exports after abolition. Luanda merchants, however, proved their resilience by investing in both the illegal slave trade and legitimate commerce. As also happened in the West African ports of Lagos, Ouidah, and Saint-Louis, the two trades developed simultaneously in Luanda. Slave traders like Dona Ana Joaquina, José Maria Matozo de Andrade Câmara, Augusto Garrido, and Dona Ana Ubertali invested in commercial agricultural enterprises at the same time that they shipped captives illegally. The economic structures based on credit that had developed during the slave trade era were extended to the new economic activities, with coastal merchants continuing to provide loans to commercial and agrarian sectors and to those in need even after the establishment of the Banco Nacional Ultramarino (Overseas National Bank) in 1865. Ultimately, only those individuals who were able to diversify their investments survived the end of the slave trade.

While the transatlantic slave trade was controlled by large-scale merchants and firms, legitimate commerce gradually created more opportunities for small-scale traders of European and African descent, including women. As scholars such as Jill R. Dias and Isabel Castro Henriques have demonstrated, Africans played an important role in this economic transition.[7] They had experience with growing coffee and cultivating cotton and tobacco for internal consumption and for a small-scale trade well before these items attracted the attention of the colonial administration and private investors. Africans were also the collectors of ivory and wax, the labor force underpinning the *arimos* and plantations, and the transporters of all kinds of goods. Merchants and the colonial administration thus depended on African labor and expertise to develop the new trade. Women especially found more opportunities in legitimate commerce than in slave trading. During the era of legitimate trade, women merchants constantly traveled from coastal enclaves into the *sertões* and between the northern and southern ports "on business." Both women and men owned farms and *feitorias* that traded in legitimate goods and in slaves for the internal and external markets.

Although some women in Luanda were able to become merchants and acquire wealth through their participation in local and international trade, they did so always within a gendered social structure. More importantly, their presence did not disrupt male domination of commerce; men continued to make up a great majority of merchants engaged in the foodstuff trade, in the slave trade, and in legitimate commerce. Men were also rewarded with titles of Portuguese orders and with military and administrative positions.

After the end of the slave trade era, Luso-Africans had their identity as white and Portuguese questioned. The racial discourses gaining power in Lisbon and in colonial spaces now limited the categories of white and Portuguese to those born in Portugal. Although Luso-Africans continued to distinguish themselves from other Africans by their affiliation to the Catholic Church, access to education, and adoption of European ways, their skills as intermediaries gradually became less important. Nevertheless, well-to-do local women continued to attract the attention of immigrant men eager to prosper in an unfamiliar environment, and interracial marriages continued to play an important role in the integration of foreign males in the colony.

The slave trade did not end with the closure of the Brazilian market in 1850. The shipment of captives to Cuba persisted for another decade, and a traffic of forced laborers that developed between Angola and São Tomé e Príncipe caught the interest of Luanda slave traders. Meanwhile, the development of legitimate commerce ironically increased the need for slaves in the domestic market to work in plantations and urban occupations and in the transport of goods from interior to coastal areas. Although the Portuguese abolished slavery in Angola in 1875, forced labor continued well into the twentieth century.

This book extends the scholarship on Luanda before the formal imposition of colonialism in the late nineteenth century by looking at the strategies of its merchants during the transition from slave trading to legitimate commerce. It also explores interactions between foreign and local people through the spheres of marriage, local trade, and slave ownership. In addition to extending our understanding of this transitional period in Atlantic Africa, *Slave Trade and Abolition: Gender, Commerce, and Economic Transition in Luanda* makes a contribution to urban and labor history as well as women's and gender studies.

Glossary

a seus negócios: On business.

adom: A beverage used by the Ga people of the Gold Coast to settle disputes.

afulada, afulado: A black person of lighter complexion.

aguardente (*de cana*): Sugarcane brandy.

almotacé: Municipal inspector.

almoxarife: Superintendent of the Armazéns Nacionais (Military Arsenal).

amasiamento: The relationship between a man and a woman not married within the Catholic Church.

amásia: Concubine.

ameação: Equal division of assets between husband and wife married through a *carta de ametade* (charter of halves).

anjinhos: Literally, "little angels," an iron instrument of punishment used to squeeze the fingers of slaves.

arimo: An agricultural property dedicated to the production of basic staples and domestic animals for subsistence and to supply urban markets, caravans, and slave ships.

armador (pl. *armadores*): Coastal merchants who supplied imported goods on credit.

armazéns nacionais: National commercial warehouses.

arroba: One *arroba* is equivalent to fifteen kilograms.

avulso: A loose document.

Banco Nacional Ultramarino: The Overseas National Bank, established in Luanda in 1865.

banhos: Banns of marriage, a notice read in the parish churches of future spouses.

banzo: An assortment of imported trade goods provided by merchants to itinerant traders.

batuque: Mbundu celebration with music and dances.

bergantin: A two-masted sailing vessel with square rigging on the foremast and fore-and-aft rigging on the mainmast.

braça: A land measurement used throughout the Portuguese Empire during the nineteenth century. A *braça* was equivalent to approximately 184 centimeters.

branco, branca: A white person or someone classified as white due to her or his social rank.

cabinda: Individual originally from Cabinda, an enclave to the north of the colony of Angola.

Câmara Municipal: Municipal Council.

capitão-mor: Commander of a military district also known as *presídio*.

carregador (pl. *carregadores*): Porter.

carta de ametade: The charter of halves, a document signed during a wedding through which husband and wife became co-owners of the couple's estate.

casa terrea: One-story house in Portuguese style.

cassare: Interracial marriage between a white man and an African woman celebrated in the style of the country on the Gold Coast.

chita: A type of textile.

cidade alta: Upper town.

cidade baixa: Lower town.

códice: Codex.

colono livre: Free settler.

Comendador da Ordem de Cristo: Commander of the Order of Christ.

Conselho Ultramarino: Overseas Council created by Don João IV in 1642 to look after the interests of the Portuguese overseas territories. This consultative body, composed of noblemen, oversaw the administration of the colonies.

contrato de casamento: Contract of marriage, an option for couples who wished to marry without coownership of assets. In these cases, assets were owned according to the specific details set forth in the contract signed by both bride and groom.

cubata: A straw-roofed round house largely inhabited by enslaved persons and the poor.

de efeitos próprios: Independent merchants.

degredado, degredada: A convict sentenced by the Inquisition in Lisbon, Coimbra, and Evora, as well as in Brazil, and by the lay judiciary to "pay" for his crimes overseas.

dendem: Palm oil.

deputado: Member of the Cortes, or Portuguese Parliament (after 1822).

dona: Title granted to noble and royal women in the Iberian Peninsula (Spain and Portugal), subsequently adopted in the overseas territories to designate women of high social rank and familiar with Portuguese culture.

dongo: Flat-bottomed boat built in Luanda.

escritura de dote: Register of dowry, conceded to prospective brides before marriage. The dowry provided to the bride represented an advance payment of the portion of the inheritance she would have received as a daughter.

exeque: Measurement typically used for grains in Angola. Each *exeque* was equivalent to 60 kilograms, or about 132 pounds.

Fazenda Real: Royal Treasury.

fazendas: Imported trade goods.

fazendas secas e molhadas: Wet and dry goods.

feira: An official market for the selling and buying of captives in the hinterlands.

feitoria: A commercial warehouse established in the hinterlands and along the coast.

fiador: Guarantor.

filho natural, filha natural (pl. *filhos naturais*): Child born from parents not married within the Catholic Church.

filho legítimo, filha legítima: Child born from parents married within the Catholic Church.

filho do país: A white person born in Angola.

freguesia: A subdivision of a municipality usually based on the ecclesiastical division of the territory.

fuba: Maize meal.

funante: Itinerant trader. See also *pombeiro e feirante*.

galera: Sailing ship galley.

ganga: African healer.

geribita: Sugarcane brandy produced in Brazil.

ginguba: Peanuts.

habilitação de herdeiros: The entitlement of heirs, a document required for anyone to inherit in Portugal and its overseas colonies.

homem de bem: A white man of high social status

infunge, funje: Porridge made from manioc flour, rice, or maize flour.

juiz ordinário: Justice of the peace.

Juízo de Direito: Court of Justice.

Juízo Eclesiástico: Ecclesiastical Board.

Junta de Defuntos e Ausentes: Board for the Deceased and Absentees.

Junta de Justiça: Board of Justice.

Junta Protetora de Escravos e Libertos: Board for the Protection of Enslaved and Freed Africans, created in 1854.

juramento de Indua: Mbundu ceremony used in cases of dispute between litigants. A healer prepared a beverage that was taken by the litigants; the first person to expel it would be considered innocent.

ladino, ladina: An acculturated slave.

lambamento: African marriage ceremony.

lançados: offspring of Portuguese men and African women acting as independent trade intermediaries in the Senegambian region.

libambo: Coffle or line of enslaved Africans fastened or driven along together.

liberto, liberta: An African liberated following 1836 and/or freed after 1854 in the absence of a register of ownership.

língua geral: Common language used by inhabitants.

maxila: The hammock in which an upper-class individual was carried; also the enslaved carrier.

meeiro: A husband and wife who co-owned the assets brought into the marriage and accumulated by the couple thereafter.

mestre, mestra: A master of a particular trade.

milho americano: Maize.

milho-painço: Millet.

milongo: Medicine prepared by African healers.

missanga: Bead.

moleca, moleque: Young girl, young boy.

mucama: A chambermaid or enslaved woman employed in the household.

muculunto: An overseer of an *arimo*.

mulatress (pl. *mulatresses*): Euro-African women on the Gold Coast, usually married to European men and engaged in trade.

musseque: Term designating a country estate until the late nineteenth century; nowadays, a shanty town.

mutolo, quilombo: A community of runaway slaves.

Muxiloanda: A person originally from the Island of Luanda, opposite to the city of Luanda.

nacional (pl. *nacionais*): Local African people.

negociantes comissários: Commission agents who worked on behalf of Brazilian and Portuguese backers and firms.

ngola: Mbundu political title; also state.

nhara: Woman trader from Afro-Portuguese settlements in West Africa. See also *signare* and *senhora*.

oallo: Beer made from millet and sorghum.

oficial (pl. *oficiais*): A skilled worker.

oficina: Craft workshop.

opanda: Mbundu word for adultery; also, the payment made to a husband by a man accused of having an affair with his wife.

Ordenações Filipinas: Legal code used in Portugal and its domains from 1603 until the nineteenth century.

pai incognito: Unknown father.

pardo, parda: Person of mixed European and African background.

peça: Enslaved person in the prime of life.

pelourinho: Public place of punishment in the cities under Portuguese control.

pipa: Cask with capacity of 500 liters used in the Portuguese and Brazilian trade.

pombeiro: An itinerant bush trader who traded in remote areas in the interior on behalf of *sertanejos*.

presa: A vessel captured for involvement in the illegal slave trade.

presídio: Military fortress.

preto, preta: Black person.

preto livre, preta livre: Free black person

quinta: Portuguese word to designate a country estate.

quintal (pl. *quintais*): Yard where captives destined for the Americas awaited shipment in Luanda.

quitanda: Market where fresh and cooked food was sold.

quitandeira: A retail trade vendor who commercialized fresh and dry food, as well as imported goods in the streets or in market stalls.

réis: Currency used in the Portuguese Empire during the nineteenth century.

resgate: Rescue of an enslaved person following payment of a fee.

reviro: Strategy used by *sertanejos* to increase their profit margins, which consisted in the sale of enslaved Africans to another merchant, who paid more per *peça* than the original supplier of the *banzo*.

sertanejo, feirante, aviado: An itinerant trader who purchased captives in *feiras* or official markets on behalf of merchants established on the coast.

sertão (pl. *sertões*): Interior lands.

serviçal (pl. *serviçais*): Servants.

sevícias: Physical abuse committed by spouses.

signare: A title given to African women of property and social standing along the Senegambian coast. See also *senora* and *nhara*.

senora: Portuguese word for lady. The term was adopted in Portuguese settlements in West Africa to identify women of property usually engaged in trade. See also *signare* and *nhara*.

soba: An African ruler.

sobrado: House with upper stories in Portuguese style where wealthy members of colonial society resided.

tagomaos: Portuguese merchants who lived among the indigenous population in the Senegambia adopting African ways.

tanga: Pieces of cloth made with cotton.

terra baldia, terra inculta: Uncultivated lands.

Terreiro Público: Luanda Public Market, created in 1765 by Governor Francisco Inocêncio de Sousa Coutinho.

Trem Real: Royal Arsenal.

Notes

Introduction

1. David Eltis et al., "Voyages: The Trans-Atlantic Slave Trade Database," 2019, https://www.slavevoyages.org. Recent studies have suggested that this number may have been much higher, reaching about two million. See, for example, Daniel B. Domingues da Silva, "The Transatlantic Slave Trade from Angola: A Port-by-Port Estimate of Slaves Embarked, 1701–1867," *International Journal of African Historical Studies* 46, no. 1 (2013): 121–22.

2. See, for example, Robin Law, *Ouidah: The Social History of a West African Slaving Port, 1727–1892* (Athens: Ohio University Press, 2004); and Randy J. Sparks, *Where the Negroes Are Masters: An African Port in the Era of the Slave Trade* (Cambridge, MA: Harvard University Press, 2014).

3. Roquinaldo A. Ferreira, *Cross-Cultural Exchange in the Atlantic World: Angola and Brazil during the Era of the Slave Trade* (New York: Cambridge University Press, 2012), 50; Mariana P. Candido, *An African Slaving Port and the Atlantic World: Benguela and Its Hinterland* (New York: Cambridge University Press, 2013), chap. 3.

4. See, for example, Boubacar Barry, *Senegambia and the Atlantic Slave Trade* (New York: Cambridge University Press, 1988); Robin Law, *The Slave Coast of West Africa, 1550–1750: The Impact of the Atlantic Slave Trade on an African Society* (New York: Oxford University Press, 1991); and Sparks, *Where the Negroes Are Masters.*

5. A. J. H. Latham, *Old Calabar, 1600–1891: The Impact of the International Economy upon a Traditional Society* (Oxford: Clarendon Press, 1973); Law, *Ouidah*; Robin Law, ed., *From Slave Trade to "Legitimate" Commerce: The Commercial Transition in Nineteenth-Century West Africa* (Cambridge: Cambridge University Press, 1995); Kristin Mann, *Slavery and the Birth of an African City: Lagos, 1760–1900* (Bloomington: Indiana University Press, 2007); Philip Havik, *Silences and Soundbytes: The Gendered Dynamics of Trade and Brokerage in the Pre-colonial Guinea Bissau Region* (Münster: Lit Verlag, 2004).

6. David Birmingham, *Trade and Conflict in Angola: The Mbundu and Their Neighbours under the Influence of the Portuguese, 1483–1790* (Oxford: Clarendon Press, 1966); Phyllis Martin, *The External Trade of the Loango Coast 1576–1870: The Effects of Changing Commercial Relations on the Vili Kingdom of Loango* (New York: Oxford University

Press, 1972); Joseph C. Miller, *Way of Death: Merchant Capitalism and the Angolan Slave Trade, 1730–1830* (Madison: University of Wisconsin Press, 1988); José C. Curto, *Enslaving Spirits: The Portuguese-Brazilian Alcohol Trade at Luanda and Its Hinterland, c. 1550–1830* (Leiden: Brill, 2004); Candido, *An African Slaving Port*; Ferreira, *Cross-Cultural Exchange*; Daniel B. Domingues da Silva, *The Atlantic Slave Trade from West Central Africa, 1780–1867* (New York: Cambridge University Press, 2017); Estevam C. Thompson, "Negreiros nos mares do sul: Famílias traficantes nas rotas entre Angola e Brasil em fins do século XVIII" (MA thesis, Universidade de Brasília, 2006); Maria Cristina Wissenbach, "As Feitorias de Urzela e o Tráfico de Escravos: Georg Tams, José Ribeiro dos Santos e os Negócios da África Centro-Ocidental na Década de 1840," *Afro-Ásia* 43 (2011): 43–90; Stacey Sommerdyk, "Trade and the Merchant Community of the Loango Coast in the Eighteenth Century" (PhD diss., University of Hull, 2012); Stacey Sommerdyk, "Rivalry on the Loango Coast: A Re-Examination of the Dutch in the Atlantic Slave Trade," in *Trabalho Forçado Africano: O caminho de ida*, ed. Arlindo Manuel Caldeira (Porto: CEAUP, 2009), 105–18.

7. W. Gervase Clarence-Smith, *Slaves, Peasants, and Capitalists in Southern Angola, 1840–1926* (New York: Cambridge University Press, 1979); Clarence-Smith, *The Third Portuguese Empire, 1825–1975: A Study in Economic Imperialism* (Manchester: Manchester University Press, 1985); Roquinaldo Ferreira, "Dos sertões ao Atlântico: Tráfico ilegal de escravos e comércio lícito em Angola, 1830–1860" (MA thesis, Universidade Federal do Rio de Janeiro, 1996); Aida Freudenthal, *Arimos e fazendas: A transição agrária em Angola, 1850–1880* (Luanda: Chá de Caxinde, 2005); Jill R. Dias, "Criando um novo Brasil (1845–1870)," in *O império africano, 1825–1890*, ed. Valentim Alexandre and Jill R. Dias (Lisbon: Estampa, 1998), 379–468; Isabel Castro Henriques, *Os pilares da diferença: Relações Portugal-África, séculos XV–XX* (Lisbon: Caleidoscópio Edição, 2004).

8. Philip Curtin, *The Atlantic Slave Trade: A Census* (Madison: University of Wisconsin Press, 1969).

9. Paul E. Lovejoy, *Transformations in Slavery: A History of Slavery in Africa*, 3rd ed. (New York: Cambridge University Press, 2012); Miller, *Way of Death*.

10. See, for example, George Brooks, *Eurafricans in Western Africa: Commerce, Social Status, Gender, and Religious Observance from the Sixteenth Century to the Eighteenth Century* (Athens: Ohio University Press, 2003), xx–xxi; Havik, *Silences and Soundbytes*; Ivana Elbl, "Men without Wives: Sexual Arrangements in the Early Portuguese Expansion in West Africa," in *Desire and Discipline: Sex and Sexuality in the Premodern West*, ed. Jacquelline Murray and Konrad Eisenbichler (Toronto: University of Toronto Press, 1996), 61–86; Hilary Jones, *The Métis of Senegal: Urban Life and Politics in French West Africa* (Bloomington: Indiana University Press, 2013); and Pernille Ipsen, *Daughters of the Trade: Atlantic Slavers and Interracial Marriage on the Gold Coast* (Philadelphia: University of Pennsylvania Press, 2015).

11. See, for example, Júlio de Castro Lopo, "Uma rica dona de Luanda," *Portucale*, no. 3 (1948): 129–38; Selma Pantoja, "Gênero e comércio: As traficantes de escravos na região de Angola," *Travessias*, nos. 4–5 (2004): 79–97; and Vanessa S. Oliveira, "Spouses and Commercial Partners: Immigrant Men and Locally Born Women in Luanda 1831–1859," in *African Women in the Atlantic World: Property, Vulnerability and Mobility, 1660–1880*, ed. Mariana C. Candido and Adam Jones (Woodbridge: James Currey, 2019),

217–32. For women cultural brokers in the southern port of Benguela, see Mariana Candido, "Aguida Gonçalves da Silva, une *dona* à Benguela à la fin du XVIIIe siècle," *Brésil(s): Sciences humaines et sociales,* no. 1 (2012): 33–54; Mariana P. Candido, "Concubinage and Slavery in Benguela, ca. 1750–1850," in *Slavery in Africa and the Caribbean: A History of Enslavement and Identity since the 18th Century,* ed. Nadine Hunt and Olatunji Ojo (London: I.B. Tauris, 2012), 66–84; Mariana Candido, "Strategies for Social Mobility: Liaisons between Foreign Men and Slave Women in Benguela, c. 1770–1850," in *Sex, Power and Slavery: The Dynamics of Carnal Relations under Enslavement,* ed. Gwyn Campbell and Elizabeth Elbourne (Athens: Ohio University Press, 2014), 272–88; and José C. Curto, "The Donas of Benguela, 1797: A Preliminary Analysis of a Colonial Female Elite," in *Angola e as Angolanas: Memória, sociedade e cultura,* ed. Edvaldo Bergamo, Selma Pantoja, and Ana Claudia Silva (São Paulo: Intermeios, 2016), 99–120.

12. Roquinaldo Ferreira, "Ilhas crioulas: O significado plural da mestiçagem na África atlântica," *Revista de história* 155, no. 2 (2006): 17–41; Linda M. Heywood, ed., *Central Africans and Cultural Transformations in the American Diaspora* (Cambridge: Cambridge University Press, 2002), 49–106. For the case of the *lançados* and *tangomaos* in Western Africa, see Brooks, *Eurafricans*; and Havik, *Silences and Soundbytes.*

13. Linda M. Heywood, "Portuguese into African: The Eighteenth-Century Central African Background to Atlantic Creole Cultures," in Heywood, *Central Africans,* 91–114; Candido, *An African Slaving Port,* 81, 318.

14. For examples of "Africanization" of foreigners in Angola, see Kalle Kananoja, "Healers, Idolaters, and Good Christians: A Case Study of Creolization and Popular Religion in Mid-Eighteenth Century Angola," *International Journal of African Historical Studies* 43, no. 3 (2010): 443–65; Candido, *An African Slaving Port,* 114–15, 134, 318; James Sweet, *Recreating Africa: Culture, Kinship, and Religion in the African-Portuguese World, 1441–1770* (Chapel Hill: University of North Carolina Press, 2003).

15. Heywood, "Portuguese into African."

16. Candido, *An African Slaving Port,* 11.

17. John K. Thornton, *Africa and Africans in the Making of the Atlantic World, 1400–1680* (New York: Cambridge University Press, 1998).

18. Jones, *The Métis of Senegal,* 32; Havik, *Silences and Soundbytes,* 173–78.

19. Jill R. Dias, "Angola nas vésperas da abolição do tráfico de escravos (1820–1845)," in *O império africano, 1825–1890,* ed. Valentim Alexandre and Jill R. Dias (Lisbon: Estampa, 1998), 375–76; José de Almeida Santos, *Vinte anos decisivos da vida de uma cidade (1845–1864)* (Luanda: Câmara Municipal, 1970), 29, 96, 99–101.

20. João Pedro Marques, "Arsénio Pompílio Pompeu de Carpo: Um percurso negreriro no século XIX," *Análise social* 36, no. 160 (2001): 609–38; Carlos Pacheco, "Arsénio Pompílio Pompeu de Carpo: Uma vida de luta contra as prepotências do poder colonial em Angola," *Revista internacional de estudos africanos,* nos. 16–17 (1992–94): 49–102; Selma Pantoja, "O litoral angolano até as vésperas da independência do Brasil," *Textos de história* 11, nos. 1–2 (2003): 191.

21. Douglas L. Wheeler, "The Portuguese in Angola, 1836–1891: A Study in Expansion and Administration" (PhD diss., Boston University, 1963), 41–42; Ferreira, *Cross-Cultural Exchange,* 39; Candido, *An African Slaving Port,* 9, 51–53.

22. Joseph C. Miller, "The Slave Trade in Congo and Angola," in *The African Diaspora: Interpretative Essays*, ed. Martin L. Kilson and Robert Rotberg (Cambridge, MA: Harvard University Press, 1976), 83.

23. A similar process took place in Bissau where Portuguese officials became traders. Havik, *Silences and Soundbytes*, 272.

24. Donald Moore and Richard Roberts, "Listening for Silences," *History in Africa*, no. 17 (1990): 319–25.

25. Josephine Beoku-Betts, "Western Perceptions of African Women in the 19th and Early 20th Centuries," in *Readings in Gender in Africa*, ed. Andrea Cornwall (Bloomington: Indiana University Press, 2005), 20–25; Oyèrónké Owewùmí, "Colonizing Bodies and Minds: Gender and Colonialism," in *The Invention of Women: Making an African Sense of Western Gender Discourse*, ed. Nupur Chaudhuri (Minneapolis: University of Minnesota Press, 1997), 121–56.

Chapter 1. Luanda and the Transatlantic Slave Trade

1. David Eltis and David Richardson, *Atlas of the Transatlantic Slave Trade* (New Haven, CT: Yale University Press, 2010), 14–15, 89.

2. Eltis and Richardson, *Atlas*, 23, 37.

3. Eltis and Richardson, *Atlas*, 90.

4. David Birmingham, *The Portuguese Conquest of Angola* (London: Oxford University Press, 1965), 6–7.

5. Birmingham, *Portuguese Conquest*, 7.

6. Birmingham, *Portuguese Conquest*, 7.

7. Birmingham, *Portuguese Conquest*, 8–9.

8. David Birmingham, *Trade and Empire in the Atlantic, 1400–1600* (London: Routledge, 2000), 84.

9. Beatrix Heintze, *Angola nos séculos XVI e XVII: Estudos sobre fontes, métodos e história* (Luanda: Kilombelombe, 2007), 245–48.

10. Beatrix Heintze, "Angola nas garras do tráfico de escravos: As guerras angolanas do Ndongo (1611–1630)," *Revista internacional de estudos africanos*, no. 1 (1984): 11–59.

11. Linda M. Heywood, *Njinga of Angola: Africa's Warrior Queen* (Cambridge, MA: Harvard University Press, 2017), 27.

12. Heintze, *Angola*, 252–55.

13. Heintze, *Angola*, 473–504.

14. For the introduction and development of sugarcane production in São Tomé, see Henriques, *Os pilares da diferença*, 181–205. For the early slave trade from Angola to Brazil and Spanish America, see Stuart Schwartz, "'A Commonwealth within Itself': The Early Brazilian Sugar Industry, 1550–1670," *Revista de Indias* 65, no. 233 (2005): 79–116; Linda Newson and Susie Minchin, *From Capture to Sale: The Portuguese Slave Trade to Spanish South America in the Early Seventeenth Century* (Leiden: Brill, 2007); Kara D. Schultz, "'The Kingdom of Angola Is Not Very Far from Here': The South Atlantic Slave Trade Port of Buenos Aires, 1518–1640," *Slavery and Abolition* 36, no. 3 (2015): 424–44.

15. Mariana P. Candido, "Conquest, Occupation, Colonialism and Exclusion: Land Disputes in Angola," in *Property Rights, Land and Territory in the European Overseas Empires*, ed. José Vicente Serrão et al. (Lisbon: CEHC, ISCTE-IUL, 2014), 225.

16. Heywood, *Njinga of Angola*.

17. Johannes Menne Postma, *The Dutch in the Atlantic Slave Trade, 1600–1815* (New York: Cambridge University Press, 1990).

18. Charles R. Boxer, *Salvador de Sá and the Struggle for Brazil and Angola, 1602–1686* (London: University of London / Athlone Press, 1952).

19. Heywood, *Njinga of Angola*, 175.

20. Virgílio Noya Pinto, *O ouro brasileiro e o comércio anglo-português: Uma contribuição aos estudos da economia atlântica no século XVIII*, 2nd ed. (São Paulo: Companhia Editora Nacional, 1979).

21. David Richardson, "The British Empire and the Atlantic Slave Trade, 1660–1807," in *The Eighteenth Century*, vol. 2, ed. P. J. Marshall (Oxford: Oxford University Press, 1998), 451, estimates that a total of 634,000 captives were exported from West Central Africa by the British between 1662 and 1807. See also Birmingham, *Trade and Conflict*, 137–45, 156–58; and Miller, *Way of Death*, 226–27.

22. Candido, *An African Slaving Port*, 158–60, has located Benguela slaves in the Americas before this period, which indicates that transatlantic merchants were trading people in Benguela during the seventeenth and early eighteenth centuries before it was legal to dispatch slave ships without their having to go to Luanda to pay taxes. See also Jill Dias, "A sociedade colonial de Angola e o liberalismo português (c. 1820–1850)," in *O liberalismo na península Ibérica na primeira metade do século XIX: Comunicações ao colóquio organizado pelo Centro de Estudos de História Contemporânea Portuguesa*, vol. 1, ed. Miriam H. Pereira et al. (Lisbon: Sá da Costa Editora, 1982), 269. For the numbers of slaves exported from the port of Benguela between 1730 and 1828, see José C. Curto, "The Legal Portuguese Slave Trade from Benguela, Angola, 1730–1828: A Quantitative Re-appraisal," *África* 16–17, no. 1 (1993–94): 101–16.

23. Candido, *An African Slaving Port*, 6, 151, 162; Mariana P. Candido, "Os agentes não europeus na comunidade mercantil de Benguela, c. 1760–1820," *Saeculum*, no. 29 (2013): 121; Dias, "A sociedade colonial," 267–68.

24. Joseph C. Miller, "Some Aspects of the Commercial Organization of Slaving at Luanda, Angola 1760–1830," in *The Uncommon Market: Essays in the Economic History of the Atlantic Slave Trade*, ed. Henry A. Gemery and Jan S. Hogendorn (New York: Academic Press, 1979), 81.

25. Joseph C. Miller, "The Political Economy of the Angolan Slave Trade in the Eighteenth Century," *Indian Historical Review* 15, nos. 1–2 (1988–89): 162. For transporters of slaves exported from Angola, see Silva, *The Atlantic Slave Trade*, chap. 2; Mariana P. Candido, "Enslaving Frontiers: Slavery, Trade and Identity in Benguela, 1780–1850" (PhD diss., York University, 2006), 106–9.

26. Curto, *Enslaving Spirits*. For more information on the use of *geribita* and other commodities in the acquisition of enslaved Africans, see Roquinaldo Ferreira, "Dinâmica do comércio intra-colonial: Geribitas, panos asiáticos e guerra no tráfico angolano de escravos (século XVIII)," in *O antigo regime nos trópicos: A dinâmica imperial portuguesa, séculos XVI–XVIII*, ed. João Fragoso, Maria de Fátima Gouvêa, and Maria Fernanda Baptista Bicalho (Rio de Janeiro: Nova Fronteira, 2001), 339–78.

27. Luiz Felipe de Alencastro, *O trato dos viventes: Formação do Brasil no Atlântico Sul* (São Paulo: Companhia das Letras, 2000), 290–300; Miller, "Political Economy," 152, 157.

28. On the French slave trade to Saint-Domingue, see Alex Dupuy, "French Merchant Capital and Slavery in Saint-Domingue," *Latin American Perspectives* 12, no. 3 (1985): 77–102.

29. Richardson, "The British Empire," 451–53; Roger Anstey, *The Atlantic Slave Trade and British Abolition, 1760–1810* (Atlantic Highlands, NJ: Humanities Press, 1975); Miller, "Some Aspects," 79; Wheeler, "The Portuguese in Angola," 50–52.

30. Alan K. Manchester, "The Transfer of the Portuguese Court to Rio de Janeiro," in *Conflict and Continuity in Brazilian Society*, ed. Henry H. Keith and S. F. Edwards (Columbia: University of South Carolina Press, 1969), 148–63; Mary C. Karasch, *Slave Life in Rio de Janeiro, 1808–1850* (Princeton, NJ: Princeton University Press, 1987), 3–28.

31. David Eltis, "The British Trans-Atlantic Slave Trade after 1807," *Maritime History* 4, no. 1 (1974): 1–11; Eltis, "The British Contribution to the Nineteenth Century Trans-Atlantic Slave Trade," *Economic History Review* 32, no. 2 (1979): 211–27; Eltis, *Economic Growth and the Ending of the Transatlantic Slave Trade* (New York: Oxford University Press, 1987); Miller, *Way of Death*, 505–8; Miller, "Political Economy," 170.

32. Richardson, "The British Empire," 446.

33. José C. Curto and Raymond R. Gervais, "The Population History of Luanda during the Late Atlantic Slave Trade, 1781–1844," *African Economic History*, no. 29 (2001): 1–59.

34. José C. Curto, "A Quantitative Re-assessment of the Legal Portuguese Slave Trade from Luanda, Angola, 1710–1830," *African Economic History*, no. 20 (1992): 1–25; Miller, "Political Economy," 164; James Lang, *Portuguese Brazil: The King's Plantation* (New York: Academic Press, 1979); Judith A. Carney, "Landscapes of Technology Transfer: Rice Cultivation and African Continuities," *Technology and Culture* 37, no. 1 (1996): 5–35; Carney, "'With Grains in Her Hair': Rice in Colonial Brazil," *Slavery and Abolition* 25, no. 1 (2004): 1–27; Walter Hawthorne, *From Africa to Brazil: Culture, Identity and an Atlantic Slave Trade, 1600–1830* (New York: Cambridge University Press, 2010).

35. Alexandre Vieira Riberio, "O tráfico atlântico de escravos e a praça mercantil de Salvador, c. 1680–1830" (MA thesis, Universidade Federal do Rio de Janeiro, 2005), 58, 61.

36. Portuguese and Brazilian slavers were not alone, as merchants of other nationalities also moved their activities to West Central Africa. Candido, "Os agentes não europeus," 97–124.

37. Not all Africans remained at these ports of disembarkation, as captives were redistributed to several places in the interior of Brazil, including Minas Gerais, Maranhão, São Paulo, and Rio Grande do Sul. João Luís Fragoso and Roberto Guedes Ferreira, "Alegrias e artimanhas de uma fonte seriada, os códices 390, 421, 424, e 425: Despachos de escravos e passaportes da Intendência de Polícia da Corte, 1819–1833," in *História Quantitativa e Serial: Um balanço*, ed. Tarcísio Rodrigues Botelho et al. (Goiânia: ANPUH, 2001), 239–78; Amilcar Martins Filho and Roberto B. Martins, "Slavery in a Non-export Economy: Nineteenth Century Minas Gerais Revisited," *Hispanic American Historical Review* 63, no. 3 (1983): 569–90.

38. Miller, "The Slave Trade," 83.

39. Roquinaldo A. Ferreira, "The Suppression of the Slave Trade and Slave Departures from Angola, 1830s–1860s," in *Extending the Frontiers: Essay on the New Transatlantic*

Slave Trade Database, ed. David Eltis and David Richardson (New Haven, CT: Yale University Press, 2008), 327.

40. Clarence-Smith, *The Third Portuguese Empire*, 49.

41. Carlos Alberto Lopes Cardoso, "Estudo genealógico da família Matozo de Andrade e Câmara," *Ocidente*, no. 403 (1971): 311–22.

42. Curto, *Enslaving Spirits*, 148, 175–76; José C. Curto, "Alcohol under the Context of the Atlantic Slave Trade: The Case of Benguela and Its Hinterland (Angola)," *Cahiers d'études africaines* 51, no. 201 (2011): 51–85; Candido, *An African Slaving Port*, 166; Candido, "Os agentes não europeus," 100–101.

43. Arquivo Nacional da Torre do Tombo (ANTT), feitos findos, Juízo das Justificações Ultramarinas, África, maço. 29, no. 8.

44. Miller, *Way of Death*, 284.

45. Arquivo Histórico Ultramarino, Lisbon (AHU), Secretaria de Estado da Marinha e Ultramar (SEMU), Direcção Geral do Ultramar (DGU), Angola, Correspondência dos Governadores, primeira secção, códice 79, doc. 66, "Informação breve sobre o terreno de que se compõem o reino de Angola," undated. Itinerant traders were also known as *funantes*, *pombeiros*, and *feirantes*. For an analysis of these terms, see Willy Bal, "Portugais pombeiro, commerçant ambulant du sertão," *Annali dell' Instituto Universitario Orientale* 6, no. 2 (1965): 148–57.

46. BML, códice 030, termos de fiança, 1784–87, fols. 27v, 46v, 58v.

47. Birmingham, *Trade and Conflict*, 138.

48. Mariana P. Candido, "Women's Material World in Nineteenth-Century Benguela," in Candido and Jones, *African Women*, 70–88.

49. On the role of *sertanejos*, see Miller, "Some Aspects," 89–95; Miller, *Way of Death*, 175; Ferreira, *Cross-Cultural Exchange*, 31, 53.

50. Miller, *Way of Death*, 191.

51. Jan Vansina, "The Foundation of the Kingdom of Kasanje," *Journal of African History* 4, no. 3 (1963): 355–74; Joseph C. Miller, *Kings and Kinsmen: Early Mbundu States in Angola* (Oxford: Clarendon Press, 1976); Miller, *Way of Death*, 32, 34; José C. Curto, "Jerebita in the Relations between the Colony of Angola and the Kingdom of Kasanje," *Anais de história de além-mar*, no. 14 (2013): 301–26.

52. Ferreira, "Suppression," 316, 321–22.

53. AHU, "Informação breve." On *pombeiros* and *sertanejos*, see Miller, "Some Aspects," 95; Ferreira, *Cross-Cultural Exchange*, 60–63; Isabel Castro Henriques, *Percursos da modernidade em Angola: Dinâmicas comerciais e transformações sociais no século XIX* (Lisbon: Instituto de Investigação Científica e Tropical, 1997), 116–18.

54. Archivo Nacional de Angola (ANA), Luanda, códice 2862, registo de escravos, fols. 34v–37. For the sale of *pombeiro* slaves, see *Boletim Oficial de Angola* (*BOA*), no. 281, 15 February 1851, 4.

55. Mariana P. Candido, "The Transatlantic Slave Trade and the Vulnerability of Free Blacks in Benguela, Angola, 1780–1830," in *Atlantic Biographies: Individuals and Peoples in the Atlantic World*, ed. Jeffrey A. Fortin and Mark Meuwese (Leiden: Brill, 2014), 193–209.

56. AHU, "Informação breve." On trade goods used in Angola, see L. Rebelo de Sousa, *Moedas de Angola* (Luanda: Banco de Angola, 1969).

57. AHU, "Informação breve." See also Miller, *Way of Death*, 276–79; and Ferreira, "Dos sertões do Atlântico," 198.

58. Candido, *An African Slaving Port*, chap. 3.

59. Elias Alexandre da Silva Corrêa, *História de Angola*, 2 vols. (Lisbon: Editorial Ática, 1937), 1:25–26; Ferreira, *Cross-Cultural Exchange*, 37–38, 44; Candido, "Os agentes não europeus," 113. See the case of Francisco Honorato da Costa in Curto, "Jerebita."

60. AHU, SEMU, DGU, Angola, Correspondência dos Governadores, primeira secção, códice 77, documento 17, João Victo da Silva, "Apontamentos do estado actual da conquista d'Angola que me communicou o illustrissimo e excelentissimo senhor Martinho de Mello e Castro," 1791.

61. Birmingham, *Trade and Conflict*, 136; Ferreira, *Cross-Cultural Exchange*, 7, 30, 50.

62. Birmingham, *Trade and Conflict*, 145–46; Ferreira, *Cross-Cultural Exchange*, 33.

63. Ferreira, *Cross-Cultural Exchange*, 50, 63.

64. On the idea of the Atlantic as a unit, see Jacques Godechot, *Histoire de l'Atlantique* (Paris: Bordas, 1947); Michael Kraus, *The Atlantic Civilization: Eighteenth-Century Origins* (Ithaca, NY: Cornell University Press, 1949); Paul Gilroy, *The Black Atlantic: Modernity and Double Consciousness* (Cambridge, MA: Harvard University Press, 1993); Bernard Bailyn, "The Idea of Atlantic History," *Itinerario* 20, no. 1 (1996): 19–44; David Eltis, "Atlantic History in Global Perspective," *Itinerario* 23, no. 2 (1999): 141–61; and Peter A. Coclanis, "Atlantic World or Atlantic/World?," *William and Mary Quarterly* 63, no. 4 (2006): 725–72.

65. Portuguese officials, including governors, regents, judges, and military officers, were legally prohibited from either direct or indirect involvement in the slave trade. Candido, *An African Slaving Port*, 185–86. According to José Carlos Venâncio, in *A economia de Luanda e hinterland no século XVIII* (Lisbon: Estampa, 1996), 49, many soldiers left their military positions to engage in trade or did both simultaneously. For examples of the involvement of military officers in slaving activities, see Candido, "Enslaving Frontiers," 101–2, 106.

66. Francisco Travassos Valdez, *Six Years of a Traveller's Life in Western Africa*, 2 vols. (London: Hurst and Blackett, 1861), 2:104–5.

67. Valdez, *Six Years*, 2:104–5; Venâncio, *A economia*, 37; Silva Corrêa, *História de Angola*, 1:78–79.

68. Curto and Gervais, "Population History."

69. Curto and Gervais, "Population History."

70. J. C. Curto, "The Anatomy of a Demographic Explosion: Luanda, 1844–1850," *International Journal of African Historical Studies* 32 (1999): 381–405. For the gender makeup of enslaved Africans exported across the Atlantic, see Lovejoy, *Transformations in Slavery*; Patrick Manning, *Slavery and African Life: Occidental, Oriental and African Slave Trades* (New York: Cambridge University Press, 1990).

71. Mário António Fernandes de Oliveira, "Para a história do trabalho em Angola: A escravatura luandense do terceiro quartel do século XIX," *Boletim do Instituto do Trabalho, Providência e Ação Social*, no. 2 (1963): 45–60.

72. See the burial records of free black Africans in Bispado de Luanda (BL), Livro de óbitos, Freguesia dos Remédios, 1851–52.

73. Candido, *An African Slaving Port*, 138.

74. Santos, *Vinte anos decisivos*, 10, 17.

75. Selma Pantoja, "Inquisição, degredo, e mestiçagem em Angola no século XVIII," *Revista lusófona de ciência da religião* 3, nos. 5–6 (2004): 119; Maria Eugenia Vieira, "Registro de carta de guia de degredados para Angola, 1714–1757" (licenciate thesis, Universidade de Lisboa, 1966). Only individuals in advanced age, the sick, or the disabled were exempted from military service; see Pacheco, "Arsénio Pompílio Pompeu de Carpo," 61. Although the placement of *degredados* in administrative positions was forbidden, the lack of capable individuals made them acceptable. See Anabela Cunha, "Degredo para Angola na segunda metade do século XIX" (MA thesis, Universidade de Lisboa, 2004), 17. On the presence of *degredados* in Benguela, see Candido, *An African Slaving Port*, 76–85, 92.

76. Gustav Tams, *Visit to the Portuguese Possessions in South-Western Africa*, vol. 1 (London: T. C. Newby, 1845), 196–97; Joachim John Monteiro, *Angola and the River Congo*, 2 vols. (London: Macmillan, 1875), 2:45–46; Selma Pantoja, "Conexões e identidade de gênero no caso Brasil e Angola, sécs. XVII–XIX" (working paper, Universidade de Brasília, 2008), 7–11.

77. Curto, *Enslaving Spirits*, 173–78; Selma Pantoja, "Aberturas e limites da administração pombalina na África: Os autos de devassa sobre o negro Manoel de Salvador," *Estudos Afro-Asiáticos*, no. 29 (1996): 143–60; Ferreira, *Cross-Cultural Exchange*, chap. 4.

78. Silva Corrêa, *História de Angola*, 1:45.

79. Curto and Gervais, "Population History," 56–57.

80. Wheeler, "The Portuguese in Angola," 60–61. Everywhere on the western coast of Africa, a very small number of married men brought European wives with them. Ipsen, *Daughters of the Trade*, 38; Jones, *The Métis of Senegal*, 36–37.

81. Selma Pantoja, "Luanda: Relações sociais e de gênero," in *A dimensão atlântica da África: II reunião internacional de história da África* (São Paulo: CEA-USP/SDG-Marinha/CAPES, 1997), 78. See also Anne McClintock, *Imperial Leather: Race, Gender and Sexuality in the Colonial Conquest* (New York: Routledge, 1995).

82. Jones, *The Métis of Senegal*, 21.

83. Silva Corrêa, *História de Angola*, 1:92. For the use of a similar argument elsewhere on the western coast of Africa, see Brooks, *Eurafricans*, 212.

84. Candido, *An African Slaving Port*, 11.

85. Valdez, *Six Years*, 2:145; Candido, *An African Slaving Port*, 127; Candido, "Os agentes não europeus," 107.

86. ANA, Códice 5613, fol. 43.

87. Cardoso, *Estudo genealógico*.

88. *BOA*, no. 308, 23 August 1851, 4.

89. Luiz da Silva Pereira Oliveira, *Privilégios da nobreza e fidalguia de Portugal* (Lisbon: João Rodrigues Neves, 1806), 172–73; Maria Beatriz Nizza da Silva, *Donas e plebeias na sociedade colonial* (Lisbon: Estampa, 2002).

90. Ira Berlin, "From Creole to African: Atlantic Creoles and the Origins of African-American Society in Mainland North America," *William and Mary Quarterly* 53, no. 2 (1996): 251–88.

91. Heywood, "Portuguese into African"; Ferreira, "Ilhas crioulas"; Kananoja, "Healers"; Candido, *An African Slaving Port*, 114–15, 318.

92. Heywood, "Portuguese into African"; Candido, *An African Slaving Port*, 122–39; Mariana P. Candido, "Engendering West Central African History: The Role of

Urban Women in Benguela in the Nineteenth Century," *History in Africa*, no. 42 (2015): 7–36; Curto, "'As If from a Free Womb': Baptismal Manumissions in the Conceição Parish, Luanda, 1778–1807," *Portuguese Studies Review* 10, no. 1 (2002): 26–57; Curto, "The Donas of Benguela," 99–120. For the "Africanization" of Europeans in other parts of the western coast of Africa, see Elbl, "Men without Wives," 65, Brooks, *Eurafricans*, 50.

93. Heywood, "Portuguese into African," 94. Pernille Ipsen stated a similar argument about the cultural exchanges between Europeans and Africans in Osu on the Gold Coast. Ipsen, *Daughers of the Trade*, 11–12.

94. Silva Corrêa, *História de Angola*, 1:83.

95. The first classes for girls were established in Luanda only in 1845. Jan Vansina, "Portuguese vs Kimbundu: Language Use in the Colony of Angola (1575–c.1845)," *Bulletin des séances de l'Académie des Sciences d'Outre-Mer*, no. 47 (2001–3): 271, 276.

96. José Pinto de Azeredo, *Ensaios sobre algumas enfermidades d'Angola*, vol. 1 (Lisbon: Regia Officina Typografica, 1799), 53.

97. Silva Corrêa, *História de Angola*, 1:87.

98. Kananoja, "Healers." In fact, seeking help from healers and spirit mediums was far from rare among the Luso-African population in Angola. See, for example, Candido, *An African Slaving Port*, 114–15, 123–25; and Ferreira, *Cross-Cultural Exchange*, 5.

99. António Gil, *Considerações sobre alguns pontos mais importantes da moral religiosa e systema de jurisprundência dos pretos do continente da África Occidental portuguesa além do Equador, tendentes a dar alguma idea do character peculiar das suas institu-icções primitivas* (Lisbon: Typografia da Academia, 1854), 6, 10. Religious practices in seventeenth- and eighteenth-century Angola are discussed in Sweet, *Recreating Africa*.

100. Ipsen, *Daughters of the Trade*, 61.

101. Brooks, *Eurafricans*, 50–51.

102. Havik, *Silences and Soundbytes*, 149–62.

103. José de Sousa Amado, *Notícia do estado em que se acha o povo de Angola, destituído de mestres, parochos e egrejas, e considerações a'cerca da necessidade e facilidade de remediar tão grandes males* (Lisbon: C. M. Martins, 1861), 8. For a similar opinion, see *Quarenta e cinco dias em Angola: Apontamentos de viagem* (Porto: Sebastião José Pereira, 1862), 37–41.

Chapter 2. *Donas*, Foreign Merchants, and the Expansion
of the Slave Trade in the South Atlantic

1. Miller, *Way of Death*, 246–50; Candido, "Enslaving Frontiers," 104–5; Candido, "Os agentes não europeus." The cosmopolitan nature of this merchant community was a feature also found in other African port towns such as Saint-Louis, Cacheu, and Bissau, as well as in the Zambezi Valley. Philip J. Havik, "Women and Trade in the Guinea Bissau Region: The Role of African and Luso-African Women in Trade Networks from the Early 16th to the Mid-19th Century," *Studia*, no. 52 (1994): 96; Tobias Green, "Building Creole Identity in the African Atlantic: Boundaries of Race and Religion in Seventeenth-Century Cabo Verde," *History in Africa*, no. 36 (2009): 103–25; Eugênia Rodrigues, "Colonial Society, Women and African Culture in Mozambique," in *From Here to Diversity: Globalization and Intercultural Dialogues*, ed. Clara Sarmento (Newcastle upon Tyne: Cambridge Scholars, 2010), 253–74; Robin Law and Kristin

Mann, "West Africa in the Atlantic Community: The Case of the Slave Coast," *William and Mary Quarterly* 56, no. 2 (1999): 307–34.

2. Candido, "Os agentes não europeus."

3. Brooks, *Eurafricans*; Havik, *Silences and Soundbytes*; Frances E. White, *Sierra Leone's Settler Women Traders: Women on the Afro-European Frontier* (Ann Arbor: University of Michigan Press, 1987); Emily L. Osborn, *Our New Husbands Are Here: Households, Gender and Politics in a West African State from the Slave Trade to Colonial Rule* (Athens: Ohio University Press, 2011); Eugênia Rodrigues, "Portugueses e Africanos nos rios de Sena: Os prazos da coroa nos séculos XVII e XVIII" (PhD diss., Universidade Nova de Lisboa, 2002); Elbl, "Men without Wives."

4. Twelve orphaned girls arrived in Angola in 1593. Throughout the next centuries, Portuguese women arrived only in small numbers. Boxer, *Mary and Misogyny*, 16–17, 23–27; Pantoja, "Luanda," 76; Pantoja, "O litoral angolano," 196.

5. Jones, *Métis of Senegal*, 24.

6. Biblioteca Nacional de Lisboa (BNL), códice 8744, carta de Dom Francisco Inocêncio de Sousa Coutinho para Dom António de Lencastre, 26 November 1772, fol. 303v.

7. Sílvia Maria Fávero Arend, *Amasiar ou casar? A família popular no final do século XIX* (Porto Alegre: Editora da UFRGS, 2001).

8. BL, Registro de batismos Conceição e Remédios, 1812–22, fols. 69v, 118v.

9. Carlos Pacheco, "A origem napolitana de algumas famílias angolanas," *Anais da Universidade de Évora*, no. 5 (1995): 196.

10. Mariana P. Candido, "Women in Angola," in *Oxford Research Encyclopedia of African History*, ed. Thomas Spear (New York: Oxford University Press, 2018), 2.

11. Claire C. Robertson and Martin Klein, "Women's Importance in African Slave Systems," in *Women and Slavery in Africa*, ed. Claire C. Robertson and Martin Klein (Madison: University of Wisconsin Press, 1983), 3–28; Claude Meillassoux, *The Anthropology of Slavery: The Womb of Iron and Gold* (Chicago: University of Chicago Press, 1991).

12. Catherine Coquery-Vidrovitch, *African Women: A Modern History* (Boulder, CO: Westview Press, 1987), 16; Claire C. Robertson, "Slavery and Women, the Family, and the Gender Division of Labour," in *More than Chattel: Black Women and Slavery in the Americas*, ed. David B. Gaspar and Darlene C. Hine (Bloomington: Indiana University Press, 1996); Niara Sudarkasa, "The 'Status of Women' in Indigenous African Societies," in *Women in Africa and the African Diaspora*, ed. Rosalyn Terborg-Penn and Andrea Benton Rushing (Washington, DC: Howard University Press, 1987), 73–87.

13. Gil, *Considerações*, 18.

14. Carlos José Caldeira, *Apontamentos d'uma viagem de Lisbon á China e da China á Lisbon*, 2 vols. (Lisbon: Typograhia de Castro & Irmão, 1853), 2:224.

15. Heywood, *Njinga of Angola*, 16.

16. Gil, *Considerações*, 17–18.

17. Caldeira, *Apontamentos*, 2:221–22.

18. Miller, *Way of Death*, 292.

19. Reading and writing, however, remained the domain of the privileged few among the elite, especially men.

20. Vanessa S. Oliveira, "Slavery and the Forgotten Women Slave Owners of Luanda (1846–1876)," in *Slavery, Memory and Citizenship*, ed. Paul E. Lovejoy and Vanessa S. Oliveira (Trenton, NJ: Africa World Press, 2016), 129–48.

21. Silva Corrêa, *História de Angola*, 1:83, 87.

22. Oliveira, "Spouses and Commercial Partners."

23. Ipsen, *Daughters of the Trade*, 9.

24. For cases of bigamy elsewhere on the African coast, see Arlindo Manuel Caldeira, *Mulheres, sexualidade e casamento em São Tomé e Príncipe, século XV a XVIII* (Lisbon: Edições Cosmos, 1999), 116–17; Ipsen, *Daughters of the Trade*, 64.

25. Coquery-Vidrovitch, *African Women*, 19; Henriques, *Os pilares da diferença*, 353; Ipsen, *Daughters of the Trade*, 8; Brooks, *Eurafricans*, xxi.

26. George Winius and B. W. Diffie, *Foundations of the Portuguese Empire, 1415–1825* (Minneapolis: University of Minnesota Press, 1977), 1:148. For marriage in Angola, see Miller, *Way of Death*, 246–50. For marriage in Brazil, see Donald Ramos, "Marriage and the Family in Colonial Vila Rica," in *Families in the Expansion of Europe, 1500–1800*, ed. Maria Beatriz Nizza da Silva (Brookfield, VT: Ashgate, 1998), 39–64; Rosenilson da Silva Santos, "Casamento e dote: Costumes entrelaçados na sociedade da Vila Nova do Príncipe (1759–1795)," *Veredas da história* 3, no. 2 (2010): 1–14; Maria Beatriz Nizza da Silva, *Cultura e sociedade no Rio de Janeiro, 1808–1821* (São Paulo: Companhia Editora Nacional, 1977), 96–103; Silva, *História da família*; Maria Beatriz Nizza da Silva, *Vida privada e quotidiano no Brasil na época de D. Maria I e D. João VI* (Lisbon: Editorial Estampa, 1999); Maria Beatriz Nizza da Silva, *Sistema de casamento no Brasil colonial* (São Paulo: Editora da Universidade de São Paulo, 1978).

27. Joan Perkin, *Women and Marriage in Nineteenth-Century England* (Chicago: Lyceum Books, 1989), 4–5.

28. Osborn, *Our New Husbands*; Kristin Mann, *Marrying Well: Marriage, Status and Social Change among the Educated Elite in Colonial Lagos* (New York: Cambridge University Press, 1985); Hilary Jones, "From Marriage à la Mode to Weddings at Town Hall: Marriage, Colonialism, and Mixed-Race Society in Nineteenth-Century Senegal," *International Journal of African Historical Studies* 38, no. 1 (2005): 27–48; Carina Ray, *Crossing the Color Line: Race, Sex, and the Contested Politics of Colonialism in Ghana* (Athens: Ohio University Press, 2015).

29. Jan Vansina, "Ambaca Society and the Slave Trade c. 1760–1845," *Journal of African History* 46, no. 1 (2005): 9. For a similar pattern elsewhere on the Atlantic coast of Africa, see Jones, *The Métis of Senegal*, 79–80; and Brooks, *Eurafricans*, 128.

30. Vansina, "Ambaca Society," 9.

31. Inheritance laws regulated the practice throughout the Portuguese empire. See *Ordenações Filipinas*, livro 4, título XCVII, accessed 18 November 2018, http://www1 .ci.uc.pt/ihti/proj/filipinas/ordenacoes.htm.

32. Isabel Cristina dos Guimarães Sanches e Sá and Maria Eugenia Matos Fernandes, "A mulher e a estruturação do patrimônio familiar," in *Atas do colóquio a mulher na sociedade portuguesa: Visão histórica e perspectivas atuais* (Coimbra: Universidade de Coimbra, 1986), 91–115; Santos, "Casamento," 3; Silva, *Cultura e sociedade*, 96–103; Silva, *Vida privada*, 47–61; *Sistema de casamento*, 98–101, 104–10.

33. See, for example, ANA, códice 5613, escritura de casamento, dote e arrais, fol. 24v.

34. Jones, *Métis of Senegal*, 50–51.

35. BL, termos de fiança, 1837–59, marriage petition of Manuel António Jorge de Carvalho e Sousa, fol. 76.

36. Curto, "'As If from a Free Womb,'" 48.

37. BL, registros de batismos, fol. 118.

38. BL, registros de batismos, fol. 238v.

39. Silva Corrêa, *História de Angola*, 1:88–90.

40. For similar misinterpretations of African marriage practices in other ports in western Africa, see Ipsen, *Daughters of the Trade*, 6; Jones, *The Métis of Senegal*, 75; and Beoku-Betts, "Western Perceptions," 22.

41. According to the jurist António Gil, the cost of bridewealth in the 1840s amounted to about 50,000 *réis*, which was roughly the price of a young captive. Gil, *Considerações*, 18. The value was relatively inexpensive for a European, but it could be a significant sum for common Mbundu men. See also Caldeira, *Apontamentos*, 2:224. For bridewealth elsewhere in western Africa, see Ipsen, *Daughters of the Trade*, 14, 30; Jones, *The Métis of Senegal*, 35; Brooks, *Eurafricans*, 220; and Havik, *Silences and Soundbytes*, 285–86.

42. Silva Corrêa, *História de Angola*, 1:88–90. Later observers tended to disagree on the number of days the bride remained secluded, suggesting anywhere from eight to forty days. See, for example, José Joaquim Lopes de Lima, *Ensaios sobre a statistica das possessões portuguezas*, 3 vols (Lisbon: Imprensa Nacional 1846), 3:197. Caldeira, in *Apontamentos*, 2:224–25, noted that in the mid-nineteenth century, the husband communicated the result by sending a bottle of *aguardante* to the bride's parents. A full bottle indicated that the woman was a virgin, while a half-empty bottle meant that she was not.

43. Gil, *Considerações*, 18–20. See also Ferreira, *Cross-Cultural Exchange*, 197–201.

44. Ipsen, *Daughters of the Trade*, 33–35. For marriage practices elsewhere on the western coast of Africa, see Brooks, *Eurafricans*, 220; James F. Searing, *West African Slavery and Atlantic Commerce: The Senegal River Valley, 1700–1860* (Cambridge: Cambridge University Press, 1993), 65–84; and Jones, "From Marriage à la Mode."

45. On immigrant traders who entered local marriages with daughters of African rulers, see Linda M. Heywood, *Contested Power in Angola, 1840s to the Present* (Rochester, NY: University of Rochester Press, 2000), 19; Candido, "Concubinage," 71; Candido, *An African Slaving Port*, 134; and Henriques, *Percursos da modernidade*, 417.

46. Ipsen, *Daughters of the Trade*, 60.

47. Ray, *Crossing the Color Line*, 69.

48. Jones, *The Métis of Senegal*, 19; Brooks, *Eurafricans*, 220; Ray, *Crossing the Color Line*, 29.

49. Curto, "'As If from a Free Womb,'" 47–48; Candido, "Engendering," 15–16.

50. Ordenações Filipinas, livro 4, títulos 45, 46, 48, 91, 96.

51. Ramos, "Marriage," 223.

52. Ipsen, *Daughters of the Trade*, 10; Brooks, *Eurafricans*, 128.

53. Brooks, *Eurafricans*, 127; Ipsen, *Daughters of the Trade*, 14; Havik, *Silences and Soundbytes*, 172–73; Ray, *Crossing the Color Line*, 33.

54. *Quarenta e cinco dias*, 56.

55. See, for example, *Boletim Oficial de Angola* (*BOA*), no. 351, 19 June 1852, 3.

56. Vanessa S. Oliveira, "The Gendered Dimension of Trade: Female Traders in Nineteenth Century Luanda," *Portuguese Studies Review* 23, no. 2 (2015): 111–12; Candido, "Concubinage."

57. John K. Thornton, "Elite Women in the Kingdom of Kongo: Historical Perspectives on Women's Political Power," *Journal of African History* 47, no. 3 (2006): 437–60; Thornton, *The Kingdom of Kongo: Civil War and Transition, 1641–1718* (Madison: University of Wisconsin Press, 1983). For references on the royal women of the Kongo and their Christian names, see "Carta de um Cônego da Sé do Congo ao Padre Manuel Rodrigues, s.j.," in *Monumenta missionária africana*, vol. 7, *África ocidental (1622–1630)*, ed. António Brásio (Lisbon: Agência Geral do Ultramar, 1956), 291–97; Fillippo Pigafetta and Duarte Lopes, *Relação do reino do Congo e das terras circunvizinhas* (Lisbon: Alfa, 1989), 68; Graziano Saccardo, *Congo e Angola con la storia dell'antica missione dei Cappuccini* (Venice: Curia Provinciale dei Cappuccini, 1983), 3:11–14; Francisco Leite de Faria, "Uma relação de Rui de Pina sobre o Congo escrita em 1492," *Studia*, no. 19 (1996): 259.

58. Giovanni António Cavazzi da Montecuccolo, *Descrição histórica dos três reinos Congo, Matamba, e Angola*, 2 vols. (Lisbon, 1965); António de Oliveira Cadornega, *História geral das guerras angolanas*, vol. 2 (1680; repr., Lisbon: Agência Geral do Ultramar, 1972); Joseph C. Miller, "Nzinga of Matamba in a New Perspective," *Journal of African History* 16, no. 2 (1975): 201–16; John K. Thornton, "Legitimacy and Political Power: Queen Njinga, 1624–1663," *Journal of African History* 32, no. 1 (1991): 25–40.

59. José C. Curto, "A restituição de 10.000 súbditos ndongo 'roubados' na Angola de meados do século XVII: Uma análise preliminar," in *Escravatura e transformações culturais: África–Brasil–Caraíbas*, ed. Isabel Castro Henriques (Lisbon: Vulgata, 2002), 185–208.

60. Biblioteca Municipal de Luanda (BML), códice 037, receita da ciza, fol. 169. For his activities as a manioc flour supplier, see, for example, BML, códice 055, registo de entradas, vol. 1, fols. 244–45.

61. BML, códice 037, receita da ciza, fl. 207.

62. BML, códice 037, receita da ciza, fols. 241, 244, 250, 258, 263.

63. Filipe Martins Barbosa Mascarenhas, *Memórias de Icolo e Bengo: Figuras e famílias* (Luanda: Arte Viva, 2008), 156–57; Douglas L. Wheeler, "Angolan Women of Means: D. Ana Joaquina dos Santos e Silva, Mid-Nineteenth Century Luso-African Merchant-Capitalist of Luanda," *Santa Bárbara Portuguese Studies*, no. 3 (1996): 284; Carlos Alberto Lopes Cardoso, "Ana Joaquina dos Santos Silva, industrial angolana da segunda metade do século XIX," *Boletim cultural da Câmara Municipal de Luanda*, no. 32 (1972): 5. According to Carlos Pacheco, *José da Silva Maia Ferreira: O homem e sua época* (Luanda: União dos Escritores Angolanos, 1990), 208, Joaquim de Santa Ana Nobre dos Santos was a *pardo* (of mixed European and African origin).

64. According to Cardoso, in "Ana Joaquina dos Santos Silva," 9, she had two daughters with her first husband. Cardoso did not, however, offer any source evidencing that possibility.

65. BL, registro de batismos, fol. 74v.

66. See, for example, BML, códice 041, registo de entradas e saídas de feijão, fol. 23v; BML, códice 034, registos diversos incompleto, fol. 3.

67. Pacheco, *José da Silva Maia Ferreira*, 181.

68. Curto, "'As If from a Free Womb'"; Candido, "Engendering."

69. BML, códice 037, receita da ciza, fol. 78.

70. Joseph C. Miller, "Slave Prices in the Portuguese Southern Atlantic, 1600–1830," in *Africans in Bondage: Studies in Slavery and the Slave Trade*, ed. Paul E. Lovejoy (Madison: University of Wisconsin Press, 1986), 43–77.

71. BML, códice 055, registo de entradas, vol. 1, fols. 181–82.

72. BML, códice 037, receita da ciza, fols. 76v, 115, 124v.

73. ANA, Luanda, Avulsos, códice 147, termo de fiança, fols. 217, 219–20; AHU, SEMU, DGU, Angola, Correspondência dos Governadores, segunda secção, códice 6, mappa de navios entrados e sahidos, 16 October 1843; *BOA*, no. 101, 14 August 1847, 4; *BOA*, no. 102, 21 August 1847, 4; *BOA*, no. 124, 22 January 1848, 4; BML, códice 037, receita da ciza, fols. 76v, 115, 124v.

74. Eltis ct al., "Voyages," Voyage ID 47030.

75. Eltis et al., "Voyages," Voyage ID 46265.

76. Cardoso, "Ana Joaquina dos Santos Silva," 9.

77. The individuals elected to represent Angola in the Portuguese Parliament were Fernando da Fonseca Mesquita e Sola, with 214 votes, and Joaquim António de Carvalho e Menezes, who obtained 201 votes. Pacheco, *José da Silva Maia Ferreira*, 37–39.

78. BL, termos de fiança, marriage petition of António Alves da Costa Júnior, fols. 35v–36.

79. Pacheco, *José da Silva Maia Ferreira*, 72, references a letter written by Dona Ana Joaquina to the former governor of Angola, Barão de Santa Comba-Dão, when he left for Portugal in 1834.

80. Tito Omboni, *Viaggi nell'Africa Occidentale: Gia medico di consiglio nel regno d'Angola e sue dipendenze membro della R. Accademia Peloritana di Messina* (Milan: Civelli, 1846), 110–11.

81. Valdez, *Six Years*, 2:273.

82. See, for example, BML, códice 041, registo de entradas, fol. 35v.

83. See registers under her name in BML, códice 041, registo de entradas.

84. Eltis et al., "Voyages," Voyage ID 49000.

85. BML, códice 037, receita da ciza, fol. 45v.

86. Eltis et al., "Voyages," Voyage IDs 22, 1183, 7144, 7177, 7258, 49085.

87. See, for example, BML, códice 041, registo de entradas, fol. 94v.

88. BML, códice 037, receita da ciza, fols. 45v, 60v, 88v.

89. Eltis et al., "Voyages," Voyage IDs 827, 3335, 49053.

90. Daniel B. D. da Silva, "The Supply of Slaves from Luanda, 1768–1806: Records of Ancelmo da Fonseca Coutinho," *African Economic History*, no. 38 (2010): 62. For the use of partnerships in the shipments of slaves by British subjects, see Richardson, "The British Empire."

91. Beatrix Heintze, *Exploradores alemães em Angola (1611–1954): Apropriações etnográficas entre comércio de escravos, colonialismo e ciência* (Berlin, 2010), 391–94, accessed 10 February 2019, www.frobenius-institut.de; David Birmingham, "Slave City: Luanda through German Eyes," *Portuguese Studies Review* 19, nos. 1–2 (2011): 77–92.

92. Tams, *Visit*, 1:256.

93. Tams, *Visit*, 1:256.

94. *BOA*, no. 145, 8 July 1848, 3.

95. Dias, "Angola nas vésperas," 350; BL, livro de óbitos de escravos, Nossa Senhora de Nazareth, fols. 42, 46v, 51v, 80v, 100; ANA, Luanda, Avulsos, códice 128, pasta 8, mappa da pólvora que obteve licença para sahir do depósito da Fortaleza do Penedo, 3 July 1837.

96. Omboni, *Viaggi nell'Africa Occidentale,* 1:108, 115–16.

97. *BOA,* no. 145, 8 July 1848, 3.

98. Tams, *Visita as Possessões Portuguesas,* 214–15.

99. *BOA,* no. 146, 15 July 1848, 4; *BOA,* no. 149, 5 August 1848, 4; *BOA,* no. 150, 12 August 1848, 1.

100. *BOA,* no. 287, 29 March 1851, 4.

101. Today this street is called Rua Direita, but before 1846 it was called Nazareth Street. Manuel da Costa Lobo Cardoso, *Subsídios para a história de Luanda* (Luanda: Edição do Autor, 1967), 130.

102. Ferreira, *Cross-Cultural Exchange,* 33; Candido, "Concubinage," 72–73.

103. See the case of the free black woman Dona Ana Leonor de Carvalho Fonseca, who, in spite of her social status, was arbitrarily captured and sold in Benguela. Mariana P. Candido, "African Freedom Suits and Portuguese Vassal Status: Legal Mechanisms for Fighting Enslavement in Benguela, Angola, 1800–1830," *Slavery and Abolition* 23, no. 3 (2011): 447–59.

Chapter 3. Feeding the Residents of Luanda and Provisioning Slave Ships

1. Stanley B. Alpern, "The European Introduction of Crops into West Africa in Precolonial Times," *History in Africa,* no. 19 (1992): 13–43.

2. Alfred W. Crosby, *The Columbian Exchange: Biological and Cultural Consequences of 1492* (Westport, CT: Greenwood, 1972), 187–88. For implications of the introduction of American crops in West Central Africa, see Joseph C. Miller, "The Significance of Drought, Disease and Famine in the Agriculturally Marginal Zones of West-Central Africa," *Journal of African History* 23, no. 1 (1982): 29.

3. Jean Luíz Neves Abreu, "José Pinto de Azeredo e as enfermidade de Angola: Saber médico e experiências coloniais nas últimas décadas do século XVIII," *Revista de história,* no. 166 (2012): 163–83.

4. Azeredo, *Ensaios,* 58–60.

5. Silva Corrêa, *História de Angola,* 1:114, 131–34. For shops carrying imported foodstuffs, see *BOA,* no. 231, 2 March 1850, 4; *BOA,* no. 241, 11 May 1850, 6.

6. Santos, *Vinte anos decisivos,* 91.

7. Brooks, *Eurafricans,* 134.

8. Brooks, *Eurafricans,* 219.

9. Cadornega, *História geral,* 1:176, 599.

10. Cadornega, *História geral,* 2:36–39, 45–46. According to Cardoso, *Subsídios,* 187, land in the suburb of Bem-Bem was donated to residents of Luanda as early as 1625.

11. Santos, *Vinte anos decisivos,* 26, 39, 93; Valdez, *Six Years,* 2:121.

12. Valdez, *Six Years,* 2:281; Venâncio, *A economia;* Freudenthal, *Arimos e fazendas;* Roquinaldo A. Ferreira, "Agricultural Enterprise and Unfree Labor in Nineteenth-Century Angola," in *Commercial Agriculture, the Slave Trade and Slavery in Africa,* ed. Robin Law, Suzanne Schwartz, Silke Strickrod, and Robin Law (Woodbridge: James

Currey, 2013), 225–43; Tracy Lopes, "The 'Mine of Wealth at the Doors of Luanda': Agricultural Production and Gender in the Bengo," in *O colonialismo português: Novos rumos da historiografia dos PALOP*, ed. Ana Cristina Roque and Maria Manuel Torrão (Porto: Ediçõs Húmus, 2013), 177–205.

13. Silva Corrêa, *História de Angola*, 1:118.

14. AHU, "Informação breve."

15. Henriques, *Os pilares da diferença*, 299–318.

16. Miller, "The Significance"; Jill R. Dias, "Famine and Disease in the History of Angola, c. 1830–1930," *Journal of African History* 22, no. 3 (1981): 349–78.

17. Candido, *An African Slaving Port*, 77.

18. Silva Corrêa, *História de Angola*, 1:113–14; Valdez, *Six Years*, 2:281; Lopes de Lima, *Ensaios*, 3:44. On provisions from Brazil, see Miller, *Way of Death*, 395; Nielson Bezerra, "Mosaicos da escravidão: Identidades africanas e conexões atlânticas no recôncavo da Guanabara (1780–1840)" (PhD diss., Universidade Federal Fluminense, 2010); Bezerra, "Escravidão, farinha e tráfico atlântico: Um novo olhar sobre as relações entre Rio de Janeiro e Benguela" (unpublished paper, Programa Nacional de Apoio a Pesquisa, Fundação Biblioteca Nacional do Rio de Janeiro, 2010).

19. Miller, "The Significance," 57; BML, códice 041, registo de entradas, fols. 68v–69, 77v–78, 81v–82, 98v–99.

20. BNL, códice 8744, carta de Dom Francisco Inocêncio de Sousa Coutinho para Dom António de Lencastre, 26 November 1772, fol. 303v.

21. BML, códice 025, regimento pelo qual se hão de governar os officiaes do Terreyro Público desta cidade, undated, fols. 13–15v; Venâncio, *A economia*, 65, suggests that this measure also was intended to reduce the expenses of the government with respect to provisions for military personnel, who were paid in manioc flour.

22. Venâncio, *A economia*, 41, 80.

23. Lopes, "The 'Mine of Wealth,'" 187.

24. Silva Corrêa, *História de Angola*, 1:112–13.

25. *BOA*, no. 290, 19 April 1851, 3.

26. BML, códice 031, registo de entradas, fol. 16v.

27. BML, códice 025, regimento, fol. 14v.

28. BML, códice 042–043, termo de correção, fol. 10.

29. BML, códice 042–043, termo de correção, fol. 10v.

30. BML, códice 042–043, termo de correção, fol. 10.

31. BML, códice 042–043, termo de correção, fol. 20.

32. Vanessa S. Oliveira, "Trabalho escravo e ocupações urbanas em Luanda na segunda metade do século XIX," in *Em torno de Angola: Narrativas, identidades e as conexões atlânticas*, ed. Selma Pantoja and Estevam C. Thompson (São Paulo: Intermeios, 2014), 265–67.

33. AHU, SEMU, DGU, Angola, Correspondência dos Governadores, Segunda Secção, códices 1105–10, doc. 1107, Apontamentos sobre a administração central das colônias portuguesas e especialmente sobre o governo e administração de Angola por João de Roboredo, 1851, fols. 16–16v.

34. BML, códice 042–043, termo de correção, fol. 2v.

35. Alpern, "The European Introduction," 27.

36. Miller, *Way of Death*, 323.

37. Small quantities of dried fish were also used as a source of protein for slaves in the barracoons and ships. Miller, *Way of Death*, 393, 413–14.

38. BML, códice 041, registo de entradas, fols. 6v–7.

39. Eltis et al., "Voyages," Voyage ID 7413.

40. BML, códice 025, regimento, fol. 13v.

41. BML, códice 041, registo de entradas, fols. 68v–69, 77v–78.

42. BML, códice 041, registo de entradas, fols. 12v–13.

43. BML, códice 041, registo de entradas, fols. 8v–9, 44v–45, 84v–85.

44. Venâncio, *A economia*, 49; Candido, *An African Slaving Port*, 185–86.

45. Ferreira, *Cross-Cultural Exchange*, 44; Candido, "Os agentes não europeus," 113; Mariana P. Candido, *Fronteras de esclavización: Esclavitud, comercio e identidad en Benguela, 1780–1850* (Mexico City: El Colegio de México, 2011), 128–30.

46. BML, códice 041, registo de entradas, fols. 56v–57.

47. BML, códice 041, registo de entradas, fols. 23v–24, 27v–28.

48. BML, códice 041, registo de entradas, fols. 110v–11.

49. BML, códice 041, registo de entradas, fols. 22v–23.

50. Cardoso, *Subsídios*, 122; Selma Pantoja, "Parentesco, comércio e gênero na confluência de dois universos culturais," in *Identidades, memórias e histórias em terras africanas*, ed. Selma Pantoja (Brasília: LGE; Luanda: Nzila, 2006), 87.

51. BML, códice 041, registo de entradas, fols. 44v, 62v, 64v, 66v.

52. BML, códice 041, registo de entradas, fols. 15v–16.

53. BML, códice 041, registo de entradas, fols. 69v–70.

54. On the nomination of Vasconcelos as governor of Benguela, see AHU, SEMU, DGU, Angola, Correspondência dos Governadores, Primeira Secção, Cx. 83, doc. 41, Nomeação de Alexandre José Botelho de Vasconcelos a governador de Benguela.

55. BML, códice 031, registo pelo qual se hão de governar os officiaes do Terreyro Público desta cidade, undated,, fols. 16v–17, 73v–74.

56. BML, códice 041, registo de entradas, fols. 88v–89.

57. See, for example, BML, códice 041, registo de entradas, fols. 35v–36, 88v–89.

58. BML, códice 041, registo de entradas, fols. 12v–13.

59. BML, códice 041, registo de entradas, fol. 25v.

60. BML, códice 041, registo de entradas, fols. 25v–26.

61. Crosby, *The Columbian Exchange*, 173–74, 196; Miller, *Way of Death*, 20–21.

62. Miller, "The Significance," 29; Candido, *An African Slaving Port*, 77.

63. Birmingham, *Trade and Empire*, 86.

64. Miller, "The Significance," 29; Venâncio, *A economia*, 77. For further information on the introduction of cassava plant in Angola, see Miller, *Way of Death*, 20–22; Robert Harms, "Fish and Cassava: The Changing Equation," *African Economic History*, no. 7 (1979): 113–16; Jan Vansina, "Histoire du manioc em Africa central avant 1850," *Paideuma*, no. 43 (1997): 255–79; and Henriques, *Percursos da modernidade*, 291.

65. Miller, "The Significance," 29.

66. Silva Corrêa, *História de Angola*, 1:115.

67. BML, códice 055, registo de entradas, vol. 1, fols. 85v–86.

68. BML, códice 055, registo de entradas, vol. 1, fols. 222v–23.

69. Eltis et al., "Voyages," Voyage IDs 605, 838.

70. Silva Corrêa, *História de Angola*, 1:115–16. Soldiers received part of their wages in manioc flour. Venâncio, *A economia*, 58. Manioc flour was also produced in the

immediate interior of Benguela but not in enough quantities to supply the population who imported it from Luanda. Candido, *An African Slaving Port*, 85.

71. BML, códice 055, registo de entradas, vol. 1, fols. 57v–58, 75v–76, 185v–86.

72. BML, códice 055, registo de entradas, vol. 1, fols. 107v–8, 170v–71, 212v–13.

73. BML, códice 055, registo de entradas, vol. 1, fols. 152v–53.

74. BML, códice 055, registo de entradas, vol. 1, fols. 124v–25.

75. Eltis et al., "Voyages," Voyage ID 48848.

76. BML, códice 055, registo de entradas, vol. 1, fols. 7v–8.

77. BML, códice 055, registo de entradas, vol. 1, fols. 56v–57, 86v–87, 221v–22, 229v–30.

78. BML, códice 055, registo de entradas, vol. 1, fols. 175v–76.

79. BML, códice 055, registo de entradas, vol. 1, fols. 25v–26, 37v–38, 97v–98, 137v–38, 211v–12, 237v–38.

80. BML, códice 055, registo de entradas, vol. 1, fols. 112v–13.

81. Alpern, "The European Introduction," 24–25.

82. Miller, *Way of Death*, 20.

83. Cadornega, *História geral*, 1:45.

84. Silva Corrêa, *História de Angola*, 1:116–17.

85. See, for example, BML, códice 055, registo de entradas e saídas de milho, vol. 2, 1850–57.

86. BML, códice 034, registos diversos, fol. 3v.

87. BML, códice 034, registos diversos, fols. 2v–3.

88. BML, códice 034, registos diversos, fols. 17v–18, 55v–56.

89. BML, códice 034, registos diversos, fols. 3.

90. BML, códice 034, registos diversos, fols. 1v–2.

91. BML, códice 034, registos diversos, fols. 2v–3.

92. Henriques, *Percursos da modernidade*, 277–82; Freudenthal, *Arimos e fazendas*, 98.

93. Amado, *Notícia do estado*, 8–9.

94. Lopes de Lima, *Ensaios*, 3:201–2.

95. João Carlos Feo Cardoso de Castello Branco e Torres, *Memórias contendo a biographia do vice almirante Luiz da Motta Feo e Torres: A história dos governadores e capitaens generaes de Angola, desde 1575 até 1825, e a descripção geographica e política dos reinos de Angola e de Benguella* (Paris: Fantin, 1825), 352–62.

96. Santos, *Vinte anos decisivos*, 24.

97. Venâncio, *A economia*, 67–68, suggests that the slaughterhouse was created in the first half of the seventeenth century.

98. Silva Corrêa, *História de Angola*, 1:81.

99. Silva Corrêa, *História de Angola*, 1:81.

100. Eltis et al., "Voyages," Voyage IDs 879, 1183, 40595, 47017, 48769, 48763, 48844, and 48862.

101. Eltis et al., "Voyages," Voyage IDs 48844, 48862, and 49210.

102. BML, códice 043, registo de termos de arrobamento do gado que serve no açougue desta cidade, 1819–25, fols. 65v–66.

103. Eltis et al., "Voyages," Voyage ID 40545; BML, códice 043, registo de termos, fol. 6v.

104. Eltis et al., "Voyages," Voyage IDs 47310, 47962, 49740; BML, códice 043, registo de termos, fol. 34.

105. For women engaged in the supply of beef elsewhere on the western coast of Africa, see White, *Sierra Leone's Settler Women Traders*, 35.

106. See, for example, BML, códice 055, registo de entradas, vol. 2, fols. 6v–7, 127v–128.

107. BML, códice 043, registo de termos, fols. 84–86.

108. For Dona Maria Bonina's agricultural properties, see ANA, códice 5644, escritura de compra e venda, fol. 34v.

109. BML, códice 041, registo de entradas, fol. 88v; BML, códice 043, registo de termos, fol. 3.

110. BML, códice 045, alistamento do 6º. bairro—mapas de fogos e habitantes, 1823–32, fol. 2v.

111. ANA, Luanda, Avulsos, códice 2735, auto de juramento da constituição, 20 October 1838.

112. Marques, "Arsénio Pompílio Pompeu de Carpo," 623, 636; Pacheco, "Arsénio Pompílio Pompeu de Carpo," 52; Curto, "Jerebita," 8.

Chapter 4. Selling People Illegally

1. Wheeler, "The Portuguese in Angola," 6.

2. Ferreira, *Cross-Cultural Exchange*, 230; Francisco Leite de Faria, "Echoes of the Atlantic: Benguela (Angola) and Brazilian Independence," in *Biography and the Black Atlantic*, ed. Lisa Lindsay and John Sweet (Philadelphia: University of Pennsylvania Press, 2013), 224–47.

3. Curto, *Enslaving Spirits*, 118–19.

4. Santos, *Vinte anos decisivos*, 14; Wheeler, "The Portuguese in Angola," 74.

5. Wheeler, "The Portuguese in Angola," 76.

6. João Pedro Marques, *Os sons do silêncio: O Portugal de oitocentos e a abolição do tráfico de escravos* (Lisbon: Instituto de Ciências Sociais, 1999), 203–14; Dias, "A sociedade colonial," 275.

7. William L. Mathieson, *Great Britain and the Slave Trade, 1839–1865* (London: Longmans, 1929); Leslie M. Bethell, "Britain, Portugal and the Suppression of the Brazilian Slave Trade: The Origins of Lord Palmerston's Act of 1839," *English Historical Review* 80, no. 317 (1965): 761–84; Mary C. Karasch, "The Brazilian Slavers and the Illegal Slave Trade, 1836–1851" (MA thesis, University of Wisconsin, 1967), 3–4.

8. Santos, *Vinte anos decisivos*, 76; *Almanak statístico da província d'Angola e suas dependências para o anno de 1852* (Luanda: Imprensa do Governo, 1851), xxi; Lopes de Lima, *Ensaios*, 3:133. In fact, agitations began before the prohibition, when rumors of the curtailment of the slave trade spread throughout the colony. Wheeler, "The Portuguese in Angola," 80.

9. Karasch, "The Brazilian Slavers," 3–4; Wheeler, "The Portuguese in Angola," 106.

10. Ferreira, "Suppression," 324; Ferreira, "Dos sertões ao Atlântico," 18, 30.

11. Ferreira, "Suppression," 324.

12. Karasch, "The Brazilian Slavers," 44.

13. Valdez, *Six Years*, 2:113.

14. Samuël Coghe, "The Problem of Freedom in Mid-Nineteenth-Century Atlantic Slave Society: The Liberated Africans of the Anglo-Portuguese Mixed Commission in Luanda (1844–1870)," *Slavery and Abolition* 33, no. 2 (2012): 481.

15. José C. Curto, "Producing 'Liberated' Africans in Mid-Nineteenth Century Angola," in *Liberated Africans and the Abolition of the Slave Trade, 1807–1896*, ed. Richard Anderson and Henry B. Lovejoy (Rochester, NY: University of Rochester Press, 2020), 244.

16. Coghe, "Problem," 480.

17. AHU, SEMU, DGU, Angola, Correspondência dos Governadores, Segunda Secção, códice 8AC, pasta 8, carta do governador de Angola Pedro Alexandrino da Cunha para o ministro dos negócios estrangeiros, 25 October 1845.

18. *BOA*, no. 145, 8 July 1848, 3.

19. *Correspondence with the British Commissioners at Sierra Leone, Havana, Rio de Janeiro, Surinam, Cape of Good Hope, Jamaica, Loanda, and Boa Vista Related to the Slave Trade* (London: William Clowes, 1846), 701.

20. Karasch, "The Brazilian Slavers," 47; Dias, "Angola nas vésperas," 371; Ferreira, "Suppression," 232. Only in 1855 did the Portuguese effectively occupy Ambriz to combat the illegal slavers operating in the area. Karasch, "The Brazilian Slavers," 48; Ferreira, "Dos sertões ao Atlântico," 23.

21. Ferreira, "Dos sertões ao Atlântico," 4–5.

22. Ferreira, "Dos sertões ao Atlântico," 21.

23. Law, *Ouidah*, 158.

24. Ferreira, "Dos sertões ao Atlântico," 8–9.

25. AHU, SEMU, DGU, Angola, Correspondência dos Governadores, Segunda Secção, códice 8AC, carta do governador de Angola Pedro Alexandrino da Cunha, 3 October 1845.

26. Ferreira, "Suppression," 327, Ferreira, "Dos sertões ao Atlântico," and Karasch, "The Brazilian Slavers," all explore the trajectories of several slavers involved in the illegal slave trade.

27. Ferreira, "Dos sertões ao Atlântico," 237.

28. Ferreira, "Dos sertões ao Atlântico," 2.

29. Ferreira, "Dos Sertões ao Atlântico"; Karasch, "The Brazilian Slavers."

30. Dias, "Criando," 386; Pacheco, *José da Silva Maia Ferreira*, 72.

31. *BOA*, no. 332, 7 February 1852, 4.

32. Pacheco, *José da Silva Maia Ferreira*, 72.

33. *Quarenta e cinco dias*, 5–6.

34. Tams, *Visit*, 1:251–52.

35. Gil, *Considerações*, 14. Some authors have reproduced the story as true, although there is no proof that such a tunnel ever existed. Maria Isabel Moreira Bastos Feliciano, "Luanda, quotidiano e escravos no século XIX" (MA thesis, Universidade de Lisboa, 2003), 30.

36. Eltis et al., "Voyages," Voyage ID 900217.

37. Eltis et al., "Voyages," Voyage ID 900218.

38. *British and Foreign State Papers*, 1850–51, 40:539–40, Library of the University of Michigan, http://babel.hathitrust.org/cgi/pt?id=hvd.hj1393;view=1up;seq=9.

39. Eltis et al., "Voyages," Voyage ID 2291.

40. Eltis et al., "Voyages," Voyage ID 2309.

41. Eltis et al., "Voyages," Voyage ID 3923.

42. Eltis et al., "Voyages," Voyage ID 47342.

43. AHU, SEMU, DGU, Angola, Correspondência dos Governadores, Segunda Secção, códice 8B, carta de Pedro Alexandrino da Cunha, 26 March 1845.

44. AHU, SEMU, DGU, Angola, Correspondência dos Governadores, Segunda Secção, códice 8B, carta do governador de Angola Lourenço Germack Possolo, 6 August 1845.

45. In the 1850s, slaves were embarked within two hours, according to Ferreira, "Dos sertões ao Atlântico," 130. The speeding up of embarkation times was a noted feature of the illegal slave trade. See Law, *Ouidah*, 157.

46. The term "Cabindas" designated an individual originally from Cabinda, a slaving port to the north of the colony in the vicinity of Cabo Lombo, while "Muxiloanda" referred to someone originally from the Island of Luanda.

47. *BOA*, no. 85, 24 April 1847, 3–5.

48. *BOA*, no. 75, 13 April 1847, 1.

49. *BOA*, no. 74, 6 February 1847, 1.

50. *BOA*, no. 75, 13 February 1847, 1.

51. *BOA*, no. 368, 16 October 1852, 1.

52. Eltis et al., "Voyages," Voyage ID 4137.

53. ANA, Luanda, Avulsos, códice 147, autos de praça para arrematação da sumaca brasileira Paquete Itagoahy, 8 August 1847.

54. Dias, "Angola nas vésperas," 375–76; Santos, *Vinte anos decisivos*, 29, 96, 99–101. Donations emanating from Luanda's elite also benefited the metropole and Cabo Verde.

55. Wheeler, "Angolan Women," 291.

56. AHU, SEMU, DGU, Angola, Correspondência dos Governadores, Segunda Secção, códice 6, carta do governador de Angola José Xavier Bressane Leite, 16 May 1843.

57. *BOA*, no. 189, 12 May 1849, 1–2.

58. *BOA*, no. 188, 5 May 1849, 2–3.

59. Havik, *Silences and Soundbytes*, 205.

60. AHU, SEMU, DGU, Angola, Correspondência dos Governadores, Segunda Secção, códoce 7A, carta do Governador de Angola Lourenço Germack Possolo, 25 June 1844.

61. AHU, SEMU, DGU, Angola, Correspondência dos Governadores, Segunda Secção, códice 8B, carta do Governador de Angola Lourenço Germack Possolo, 6 April 1845. The Municipal Council was composed of a president, six members, and a secretary. Valdez, *Six Years*, 2:107.

62. Eltis et al., "Voyages," Voyage ID 49795.

63. Cardoso, *Subsídios*, 180; Pacheco, *José da Silva Maia Ferreira*, 115; Pacheco, "Arsénio Pompílio Pompeu de Carpo," 52; Jacopo Corrado, "The Rise of a New Consciousness: Early Euro-African Voices of Dissent in Colonial Angola," *Journal of Portuguese History* 5, no. 2 (2007): 7; Marques, "Arsénio Pompílio Pompeu de Carpo," 623, 636.

64. *Accounts and Papers of the House of Commons and Command*, vol. 47, pt. 1 (1852–53) (Cambridge, MA: Harvard College Library, 1880), 125; *BOA*, no. 282, 22 February 1851, 1. On his appointment, see *British and Foreign State Papers*, 40:439.

65. Clarence-Smith, *The Third Portuguese Empire*, 49.

66. According to Dias, "Angola nas vésperas," 370, traders started closing their businesses in Angola in the 1820s due to the uncertainty regarding the continuity of the slave trade.

67. *BOA*, no. 225, 19 January 1850, 4.

68. Jones, *The Métis of Senegal*, 53–54.

69. *BOA*, no. 247, 22 June 1850, 3.

70. *BOA*, no. 247, 22 June 1850, 4.

71. *BOA*, no. 309, 30 August 1851, 4.

72. *BOA*, no. 338, 20 March 1852, 4; *BOA*, no. 242, 17 April 1852, 4; Caldeira, *Apontamentos*, 2:190–91.

73. *BOA*, no. 353, 3 July 1852, 2–9.

74. *BOA* no. 324, 13 December 1851, 4.

75. *BOA* no. 349, 5 June 1852, 4.

76. Freudenthal, *Arimos e fazendas*, 45.

77. Caldeira, *Apontamentos*, 2:200.

78. *British and Foreign State Papers*, 40:539; Gilberto da Silva Guizelin, "A abolição do tráfico de escravos no Atlântico Sul: Portugal, o Brasil e a questão do contrabando de africanos," *Almanack*, no. 5 (2013): 125.

79. *British and Foreign State Papers*, 40:539–40.

80. *British and Foreign State Papers*, 40:540.

Chapter 5. Meeting the Challenges of the Transition

1. Torres, *Memórias*, 334–36.

2. Silva Corrêa, *História de Angola*, 1:112–14; Torres, *Memórias*, 351.

3. Dias, "Criando," 379; Freudenthal, *Arimos e fazendas*, 39.

4. Santos, *Vinte anos decisivos*, 16; Lovejoy, *Transformations in Slavery*, 230–31.

5. A. G. Hopkins, "Economic Imperialism in West Africa: Lagos, 1880–92," *Economic History Review* 21, no. 2 (1968): 580–600. See also Hopkins, *An Economic History of West Africa* (New York: Longman Group, 1973).

6. See, for example, Ralph A. Austin, "The Abolition of the Overseas Slave Trade: A Distorted Theme in West African History," *Journal of the Historical Society of Nigeria* 5, no. 2 (1970): 257–74; A. J. H. Latham, "Palm Oil Exports from Calabar, 1812–1887," in *Figuring African Trade*, ed. G. Leisegang, H. Pash, and A Jones (Berlin: Dietrich Reimer Verlag, 1986), 265–96; Elisee Soumonni, "The Compatibility of the Slave and Palm Oil Trades in Dahomey, 1818–1858," in *From Slave Trade to "Legitimate" Commerce: The Commercial Transition in Nineteenth-Century West Africa*, ed. Robin Law (Cambridge: Cambridge University Press, 1995), 78–92; Mann, *Slavery*.

7. See, for example, Freudenthal, *Arimos e fazendas*; Henriques, *Percursos da modernidade*; Dias, "Criando"; Clarence-Smith, *The Third Portuguese Empire*.

8. Jones, *Métis of Senegal*, 57, 61; Mann, *Slavery*, 140. Martin Lynn, "The West African Palm Oil Trade in the Nineteenth Century and the 'Crisis of Adaptation,'" in Law, *From Slave Trade*, 57–77, details a similar pattern of continuity in the Niger Delta / Old Calabar region.

9. Freudenthal, *Arimos e fazendas*, 52; Clarence-Smith, *The Third Portuguese Empire*, 69.

10. Henriques, *Percursos da modernidade*, 125–26; Freudenthal, *Arimos e razendas*, 130–10.

11. AHU, SEMU, DGU, Angola, Correspondência dos Governadores, Segunda Secção, códice 8B, carta do Governador de Angola Lourenço Germack Possolo, 28 February 1845. See also José de Almeida Santos, "Perspectivas da agricultura de Angola em meados do século XIX: Pedro Alexandrino da Cunha e o pioneiro do Cazengo," *Anais da Academia Portuguesa de História* 36, no. 2 (1990): 147.

12. AHU, SEMU, DGU, Angola, Correspondência dos Governadores, Segunda Secção, códice 8AC, carta do Governador de Angola Pedro Alexandrino da Cunha, 27 December 1845.

13. Caldeira, *Apontamentos*, 2:202.

14. AHU, SEMU, DGU, Angola, Correspondência dos Governadores, Segunda Secção, códice 8AC, carta do governador de Angola Pedro Alexandrino da Cunha, 25 October 1845.

15. Lopes de Lima, *Ensaios*, 3:xxxix.

16. Freudenthal, *Arimos e fazendas*, 136; Lovejoy, *Transformations in Slavery*, 230–31; *BOA*, no. 272, 14 December 1850, 2; *BOA*, no. 276, 11 January 1851, 2–3.

17. *BOA*, no. 230, 23 February 1850, 3–4.

18. Freudenthal, *Arimos e fazendas*, 127–28.

19. See, for example, *BOA*, no. 95, 3 July 1847, 2–3; *BOA*, no. 291, 26 April 1851, 1–4. By 1866, *A Civilização da África Portuguesa*, a private newspaper, also disseminated information on the cultivation of crops following the Brazilian model. See *A Civilização da África Portuguesa* (*CAP*), no. 2, 13 December 1866, 9.

20. Ferreira, "Agricultural Enterprise," 228; Santos, "Perspectivas," 138.

21. Wheeler, "The Portuguese in Angola," 83.

22. BML, códice 048, actas da Companhia Mineralógica de Angola e Benguela, 1839–40.

23. *BOA*, no. 176, 10 February 1849, 6.

24. Caldeira, *Apontamentos*, 2:212–13, 375.

25. *BOA*, no. 375, 4 December 1852, 2.

26. Caldeira, *Apontamentos*, 2:213.

27. Caldeira, *Apontamentos*, 2:212–13.

28. *BOA*, no. 362, 4 September 1852, 6; *BOA*, no. 365, 18 September 1852, 4.

29. Cardoso, "Estudo genealógico," 316–19.

30. ANA, códice 5614, escritura de arrendamento, fol. 85; ANA, códice 7750, escritura de compra e venda, fol. 31; ANA, códice 5614, escritura de dívida e hipoteca, fol. 45; ANA, códice 5614, escritura de demarcação das fazendas Cabolombo e Bemfica, fol. 89.

31. Cardoso, "Estudo genealógico," 318.

32. See, for example, ANA, códice 3843, escritura de compra e venda, fol. 76; ANA, códice 3843, escritura de venda e sociedade, fol. 107; ANA, códice 3843, escritura de compra e venda, fol. 138.

33. ANA, códice 1301, termos de fiança, fols. 31v–34.

34. Dias, "Criando," 385, 399, 427, 461; Jill Dias, "Crise e conflito," in *O império africano, 1825–1890*, ed. Valentim Alexandre and Jill Dias (Lisbon: Estampa, 1998), 488; Lovejoy, *Transformations in Slavery*, 230.

35. BML, códice 037, receita da ciza, fols. 76, 88, 99, 99v, 121v, 128v.

36. Pacheco, *José da Silva Maia Ferreira*, 73; Freudenthal, *Arimos e fazendas*, 155.

37. António José de Souza set up the first sugar mill in 1826 near the Bengo River. *Almanak statístico*, 11; Lopes de Lima, *Ensaios*, 3:10.

38. *Almanak statístico*, 11; Santos, "Perspectivas," 146.

39. ANA, Luanda, Avulsos, códice 147, termo de fiança, fols. 218–19.

40. Valdez, *Six Years*, 2:277.

41. *BOA*, no. 254, 10 August 1850, 2–4. Brazilians played an important role in the transfer of technology related to the production of sugar in Angola; see Freudenthal, *Arimos e fazendas*, 180, 261.

42. Caldeira, *Apontamentos*, 2:211.

43. Law, *Ouidah*, 212. .

44. Mann, *Slavery*, 228.

45. Dias, "Criando," 391.

46. Monteiro, *Angola*, 2:164; Dias, "Criando," 384–85.

47. AHU, SEMU, DGU, Angola, Correspondência dos Governadores, Segunda Secção, códice 7A, carta do Governador de Angola Lourenço Germack Possolo, 3 April 1844.

48. *Almanak statístico*, 11–12. On the trajectory of João Guilherme Barboza, see Santos, "Perspectivas."

49. *Almanak statístico*, 12.

50. Caldeira, *Apontamentos*, 2:211–12. On the cultivation of coffee in colonial Angola, see David Birmingham, "A Question of Coffee: Black Enterprise in Angola," *Canadian Journal of African Studies* 16, no. 2 (1982): 343–46; Birmingham, "The Coffee Barons of Cazengo," *Journal of African History* 19, no. 4 (1978): 523–38; Lovejoy, *Transformations in Slavery*, 230.

51. ANA, Luanda, Avulsos, códice 144, passaporte para o interior, 25 October 1849.

52. ANA, Luanda, Avulsos, códice 144, passaporte para o interior, 25 November 1849.

53. ANA, Luanda, Avulsos, códice 142, registo de passes, passaportes e licenças de embarcações costeiras, 16 December 1868.

54. See, for example, ANA, Luanda, Avulsos, códice 136, passaportes de embarcações costeiras, 11 October 1861, 31 December 1861.

55. In West Africa, indigenous populations had long used palm oil, gum, and cotton for cooking, medicines, and clothing weaving, respectively. See Jones, *The Métis of Senegal*, 44; Mann, *Slavery*, 118; and Law, *Ouidah*, 203.

56. Silva Corrêa, *História de Angola*, 1:127. The only use Africans made of ivory was perhaps in musical instruments. However, with the growing commercial importance of this commodity in the nineteenth century, African rulers began to accept tribute in ivory. Henriques, *Percursos da modernidade*, 342–43.

57. Silva Corrêa, *História de Angola*, 1:127.

58. Silva Corrêa, *História de Angola*, 1:155–56. According to Lopes de Lima, *Ensaios*, 3:10, 54, cotton grew everywhere in abundance in Angola and was as good as that grown in Brazil. For more on the cultivation of cotton in Angola, see Aida Freudenthal, "A baixa de Cassanje: Algodão e revolta," *Revista internacional de estudos africanos*, nos. 18–22 (1995–99): 245–83.

59. Silva Corrêa, *História de Angola*, 1:137–8; Lopes de Lima, *Ensaios*, 3:12.

60. Henriques, *Percursos da modernidade*, 341, 432–47; Joseph C. Miller, "Cokwe Trade and Conquest," in *Pre-colonial Trade in Central Africa*, ed. Richard Gray and

David Birmingham (London: Oxford University Press, 1970), 175–201. By the 1850s, however, elephants had become scarce, and the Cokwe had to migrate in search of ivory. Dias, "Criando," 402–3. For other Africans engaged in the extraction of wax, see Monteiro, *Angola*, 2:164–66.

61. On the importance of porters for the transportation of tropical commodities elsewhere on the west coast of Africa, see Law, *Ouidah*, 213.

62. Alexandre Alberto da Rocha de Serpa Pinto, *Como eu atravessei a África*, vol. 1 (Lisbon: Edições Europa-América, 1980), 284.

63. Dias, "Criando," 385; Gil, *Considerações*, 24.

64. *Quarenta e cinco dias*, 104–5; Gil, *Considerações*, 25.

65. AHU, SEMU, DGU, Angola, Correspondência dos Governadores, segunda secção, códice 8AC, carta de António Francisco das Necessidades, 6 October 1845, fol. 5v. See also *BOA*, no. 361, 28 August 1852, 1.

66. *BOA*, no. 28, 21 March 1846, 1.

67. Monteiro, *Angola*, 2:54–55.

68. *BOA*, no. 105, 11 September 1847, 1.

69. ANA, Luanda, Avulsos, códice 2772, autos civis de acção commercial, 1856.

70. Henriques, *Percursos da modernidade*, 413–15.

71. Dias, "Criando," 399; Henriques, *Percursos da modernidade*, 126.

72. Marina Santos, *Pioneiros africanos: Caravanas de carregadores na África Centro Ocidental, 1850–1890* (Lisbon: Caminho, 2004); Beatrix Heintze, *A África centro-ocidental no século XIX (c. 1850–1890): Intercâmbio com o mundo exterior—apropriação, exploração e documentação* (Luanda: Kilombelombe, 2013).

73. Valdez, *Six Years*, 2:270.

74. Caldeira, *Apontamentos*, 2:214.

75. AHU, SEMU, DGU, Angola, Correspondência dos Governadores, segunda secção, códice 6, carta do Governador de Angola José Xavier Bressane Leite, 17 May 1843.

76. AHU, SEMU, DGU, Angola, Correspondência dos Governadores, segunda secção, códice 8B, carta do Governador de Angola Lourenço Germack Possolo, 27 February 1845.

77. Dias, "Criando," 455.

78. Henriques, *Percursos da modernidade*, 125–26, 341; Dias, "Criando," 456. A *braça* was equivalent to approximately 184 centimeters. Mário Jorge Barroca, *Medidas-padrão medievais portuguesas* (Porto: Universidade do Porto, 1992), 83.

79. Mann, *Slavery*, 128.

80. Curto, "The Anatomy."

81. For a similar pattern elsewhere on the African coast, see Law, *Ouidah*, 223; Lovejoy, *Transformations in Slavery*, chap. 8; and Kristin Mann, "Owners, Slaves and the Struggles for Labour in the Commercial Transition at Lagos," in Law, *From Slave Trade*, 144–71.

82. Caldeira, *Apontamentos*, 2:213.

83. Dias, "Criando," 385–86.

84. BML, códice 051, relação dos indivíduos foreiros deste município, 1849.

85. BML, códice 052, registo de termos de foros, fols. 159–61v.

86. ANA, códice 3843, escritura de arrendamento, fol. 74v.

87. ANA, códice 3844, escritura de compra e venda, fol. 84v.

88. Dias, "Criando," 404.

89. ANA, códice 3843, escritura de venda e sociedade, fol. 107.

90. ANA, códice 3843, escritura de compra e venda, fol. 138.

91. See, for example, ANA, Luanda, Avulsos, códice 142, registo de passes, passaportes e licenças de embarcações costeiras, 6 October 1869, 18 October 1869, 30 October 1869.

92. Dias, "Criando," 439–40. Whites only immigrated to Angola in significant numbers by the 1870s.

93. On European men's perception of African women, see Beoku-Betts, "Western Perceptions."

94. On the challenges women faced with the introduction of cash crops in the Gambia region, see Assan Sarr, "Women, Land and Power in the Lower Gambia River Region," in Candido and Jones, *African Women*, 38–54. For women farmers in mid-nineteenth-century Angola, see Selma Pantoja, "Donas de 'arimos': Um negócio feminino no abastecimento de gêneros alimentícios em Luanda (séculos XVIII e XIX)," in *Entre Áfricas e Brasís*, ed. Selma Pantoja and Carlos Alberto Reis de Paula (Brasília: Paralelo 15 Editores, 2001), 35–49; Mariana P. Candido, "Women, Family, and Landed Property in Nineteenth-Century Benguela," *African Economic History*, no. 43 (2015): 136–61. In the Guinea-Bissau region, women were the pioneers of cultivation for the export market. Havik, *Silences and Soundbytes*, 299.

95. Miller, *Way of Death*, 292; Curto and Gervais, "The Population History of Luanda," 23.

96. José C. Curto, "Whitening the 'White' Population: An Analysis of the 1850 Censuses of Luanda," in *Em torno de Angola: Narrativas, identidades e as conexões atlânticas*, ed. Pantoja Selma and Estevam C. Thompson (São Paulo: Intermeios, 2014), 225–47.

97. Caldeira and Livingstone included the data on the white population of Luanda as reworked by the *Almanak*. David Livingstone, *Missionary Travels and Researches in South Africa* (New York: Harper & Brothers, 1858), 426; Caldeira, *Apontamentos*, 2:260.

98. Ray, *Crossing the Color Line*, 42–43.

99. Ray, *Crossing the Color Line*, 7–9.

100. Monteiro, *Angola*, 2:48–49.

101. Ipsen, *Daughters of the Trade*, 151–52.

102. Valdez, *Six Years*, 2:171.

103. *BOA*, no. 179, 3 March 1849, 3.

104. The age of consent for girls in the Portuguese empire was twelve. *Constituições primeiras do arcebispado da Bahia*, vol. 1, bk. 67, https://archive.org/details/constitu icoensproocath.

105. *BOA*, no. 52, 5 September 1846, 1.

106. *BOA*, no. 179, 29 January 1848, 4.

107. *BOA*, no. 165, 25 November 1848, 2. The entitlement of heirs (*habilitação de herdeiros*) was required for anyone to inherit in Portugal.

108. BL, termos de fiança, fol. 92.

109. *BOA*, no. 237, 13 April 1850, 3.

110. Freudenthal, *Arimos e fazendas*, 173–75.

111. ANA, códice 3928, escritura de compra e venda, fols. 28, 32v.

112. ANA, códice 3844, escritura e regulamento da Associação Agrícola de Luanda, fol. 19.

113. In a register of property sales from 1869, Magalhães is referred to as Comendador da Ordem de Cristo. ANA, códice 3928, escritura de compra e venda, fol. 32v.

114. Freudenthal, *Arimos e fazendas*, 175. For other plantations managed by women in the hinterland of Luanda, see Oliveira, "The Gendered Dimension," 116–17. Women also managed plantations in the region of Benguela, south of Luanda. See, for example, the case of Dona Teresa Barruncho, in Candido, "Women, Family," 149.

115. BML, códice 042–043, termo de correção, fol. 22.

116. BML, códice 055, registo de entradas, vol. 2, 1850–57, fols. 199–200.

117. *Lista geral dos officiaes e empregados da marinha e ultramar* (Lisbon: Imprensa Nacional, 1850), 128.

118. Ferreira, "Dos sertões ao Atlântico," 97.

119. ANA, códice 5613, escritura de dote e casamento, fol. 60.

120. ANA, códice 5613, escritura de dote e casamento, fol. 60.

Chapter 6. Living with the Enslaved

1. Lopes de Lima, *Ensaios*, 3:7–8.

2. Caldeira, *Apontamentos*, 2:196.

3. *BOA*, no. 283, 1 March 1851, 4.

4. *BOA*, no. 337, 13 March 1852, 4; *BOA*, no. 260, 21 September 1850, 4; *BOA*, no. 311, 13 September 1851, 4.

5. See, for example, Suzanne Miers and Igor Kopytoff's introduction to *Slavery in Africa: Historical and Anthropological Perspectives*, ed. Igor Kopytoff and Suzanne Miers (Madison: University of Wisconsin Press, 1977).

6. Gil, *Considerações*, 20. See also David Livingstone, *Family Letters, 1841–1850*, vol. 1 (London: Chatto & Windus, 1859), 252–53.

7. Paul E. Lovejoy and David Richardson, "The Initial 'Crisis of Adaptation': The Impact of British Abolition on the Atlantic Slave Trade in West Africa, 1808–1820," in *From Slave Trade to "Legitimate" Commerce: The Commercial Transition in Nineteenth-Century West Africa*, ed. Robin Law (Cambridge: Cambridge University Press, 1995), 32–56.

8. Law, *Ouidah*, 223; Mann, "Owners, Slaves," 145–46.

9. Curto, "The Anatomy," 402.

10. John K. Thornton, "The Demographic Effect of the Slave Trade on Western Africa, 1500–1850," in *African Historical Demography*, vol. 2, ed. C. Fyfe and D. McMaster (Edinburgh: Centre of African Studies, 1981), 691–720; Lovejoy, *Transformations in Slavery*, 63–64.

11. Robertson and Klein, "Women's Importance"; Paul E. Lovejoy, "Concubinage and the Status of Women Slaves in Early Colonial Northern Nigeria," *Journal of African History* 29, no. 2 (1988): 245–66.

12. Curto, "The Anatomy," 396.

13. José Newton Coelho Meneses, "Artes fabris e serviços banais: Ofícios mecânicos e câmaras no final do antigo regime, Minas Gerais e Lisboa, 1750–1808." (PhD diss., Universidade Federal Fluminense, 2003).

14. BML, códice 026, carta de exame, fols. 67v–68.

15. Maria Helena Ochi Flexor, "Oficiais mecânicos e a vida quotidiana no Brasil," *Oceanos*, no. 42 (2000): 77–84.

16. Gil, *Considerações*, 20; ANA, Luanda, Avulsos, códice 122, atas da sessão da Junta Protetora dos Escravos e Libertos, fol. 23v.

17. ANA, Luanda, códice 2524, registos de escravos, fols. 47v–52.

18. ANA, Luanda, códice 2524, registos de escravos, fols. 62v–67.

19. BML, códice 042–043, termo de correção, fol. 24v.

20. Mary C. Karasch, "From Porterage to Proprietorship: African Occupations in Rio de Janeiro, 1808–1850," in *Race and Slavery in the Western Hemisphere: Quantitative Studies*, ed. S. L. Engerman and E. D. Genovese (Princeton, NJ: Princeton University Press, 1975), 385.

21. Valdez, *Six Years*, 2:104–5.

22. Meneses, "Artes fabris," 124–26.

23. The Jesuit priest André João Antonil stated that in Brazil, slaves were the "hands and feet of masters." *Cultura e opulência do Brasil por suas drogas e minas* (São Paulo: Companhia Melhoramentos, 1922), 89.

24. Lopes de Lima, *Ensaios*, 3:203.

25. For a similar profile of the enslaved population elsewhere in West Africa, see Robertson, "Slavery and Women"; and Candido, *African Slaving Port*, 113–18.

26. *BOA*, no. 308, 23 August 1851, 4.

27. ANA, Luanda, códice 2467, registos de escravos, fols. 95v–98.

28. *BOA*, no. 303, 19 July 1851, 1–2. Retail sales were also a major occupation for enslaved women in the diaspora. For African women and women of African descent engaged in retail sales in Brazil, see Ana Maria de Mello Magaldi and Luciano Raposo de Almeida Figueiredo, "Quitandas e quitutes: Um estudo sobre rebeldia e transgressão femininas numa sociedade colonial," *Cadernos de pesquisa*, no. 54 (1985): 50–61; Mary Karasch, "Suppliers, Sellers, Servants and Slaves," in *Cities and Society in Colonial Latin America*, ed. Lisa Schell Hoberman and Susan Migden Socolow (Albuquerque: University of New Mexico Press, 1986), 268–72; and Cecília Moreira Soares, "As ganhadeiras: Mulher e resistência negra em Salvador no século XIX," *Afro-Ásia*, no. 17 (1996): 57–72.

29. BML, códice 042, termo de correção, fol. 24v.

30. BML, códice 042, termo de correção, fol. 27.

31. Ferreira, *Cross-Cultural Exchange*, 127–28.

32. J. J. da Cunha Moraes, *Africa Occidental: Algum photographico e descriptivo*, vol. 2 (Lisbon: David Corazzi, 1886), 2:18; Valdez, *Six Years*, 2:119–20.

33. BOA, no. 363, 11 September 1852, 4.

34. Jean Baptiste Douville, *Voyage au Congo et dans l'intérieur de l'Afrique équinoxale . . . 1828, 1829, 1830*, 2 vols. (Paris: J. Renouard, 1832), 1:53.

35. Omboni, *Viaggi Nell'Africa Occidentale*, 1:90.

36. ANA, Luanda, códice 2467, registos de escravos, fols. 230v–32.

37. ANA, Luanda, Avulsos, códice 145, passaporte para o interior, 21 September 1849.

38. Valdez, *Six Years*, 2:277.

39. Freudenthal, *Arimos e fazendas*, 173–75.

40. ANA, Luanda, códice 2467, registos de escravos, fols. 222v–30.

41. ANA, Luanda, códice 2524, registos de escravos, fols. 63v–71.

42. Barbara Bush, *Slave Women in Caribbean Society, 1650–1838* (Bloomington: Indiana University Press, 1990), 42.

43. Tams, *Visit*, 1:253.

44. Tams, *Visit*, 1:254.

45. Tams, *Visit*, 1:257.

46. Monteiro, *Angola*, 2:39. British consul Benjamin Campbell had a similar view regarding slavery in mid-nineteenth-century Lagos. See Mann, *Slavery*, 164–65.

47. Manuel Barcia, "Fighting with the Enemy's Weapons: The Usage of the Colonial Legal Framework by Nineteenth-Century Cuban Slaves," *Atlantic Studies* 3, no. 2 (2006): 159–81.

48. Wayne Dooling, "Slavery and Amelioration in the Graaff-Reinet District, 1823–1830," *South African Historical Journal* 27, no. 1 (1992): 75–94; John Mason, *Social Death and Resurrection: Slavery and Emancipation in South Africa* (Charlottesville: University of Virginia Press, 2003).

49. Luanda abolitionists expressed their opinions in the pages of the newspaper *A Civilização da África Portuguesa*. See, for example, *CAP*, no. 13, 14 March 1867, 51.

50. *BOA*, no. 419, 8 October 1853, 1–2.

51. Monteiro, *Angola*, 2:40.

52. *BOA*, no. 470, 30 September 1854, 4.

53. *BOA*, no. 419, 8 October 1853, 1–2.

54. *BOA*, no. 419, 8 October 1853, 2.

55. Heywood, "Portuguese into African."

56. José C. Curto, "The Story of Nbena, 1817–1820: Unlawful Enslavement and the Concept of 'Original Freedom' in Angola," in *Trans-Atlantic Dimensions of Ethnicity in the African Diaspora*, ed. Paul E. Lovejoy and David V. Trotman (London: Continuum, 2003), 43–64; José C. Curto, "Struggling against Enslavement: The Case of José Manuel in Benguela, 1816–20," *Canadian Journal of African Studies* 39, no. 1 (2005): 96–122; Candido, "African Freedom Suits."

57. Coghe, "The Problem," 480.

58. *BOA*, no. 647, 28 August 1858, 8. For a description of instruments of punishment applied in slave societies, see Maria de Fátima Rodrigues das Neves, *Documentos sobre a escravidão no Brasil* (São Paulo: Contexto, 1996).

59. ANA, Luanda, Avulsos, códice 2825, guia de apreensão, 6 April 1864.

60. *BOA*, no. 639, 26 December 1857, 10.

61. ANA, Luanda, Avulsos, códice 2825, guia de apreensão, 5 August 1864.

62. *BOA*, no. 680, 23 October 1858, 3.

63. *BOA*, no. 711, 14 May 1859, 4.

64. *BOA*, no. 9, 3 March 1866, 41.

65. *BOA*, no. 50, 15 December 1866, 3.

66. ANA, Luanda, Avulsos, códice 122, atas da sessão da Junta Protetora, fol. 19.

67. ANA, Luanda, Avulsos, códice 122, atas da sessão da Junta Protetora, fol. 21v.

68. ANA, Luanda, Avulsos, códice 122, atas da sessão da Junta Protetora, fols. 29–29v.

69. ANA, Luanda, Avulsos, códice 122, atas da sessão da Junta Protetora, fols. 36–40v.

70. *BOA*, no. 650, 13 March 1858, 5.

71. BML, códice 047, edital da Câmara Municipal de Luanda, fols. 57v–58v.

72. William G. Clarence-Smith, "Runaway Slaves and Social Bandits in Southern Angola, 1875–1913," *Slavery and Abolition* 6, no. 3 (1985): 23–33; Aida Freudenthal, "Os Quilombos de Angola no século XIX: A recusa da escravidão," *Estudos Afro-Asiáticos*, no. 32 (1997): 109–34; Beatrix Heintze, "Asiles toujours menacés: Fuites d'esclaves en Angola au XVIIe siècle," in *Esclavages: Histoire d'une diversité de l'océan Indien à l'Atlantique sud*, ed. Katia de Queirós Mattoso (Paris: L'Harmattan, 1997), 101–22; Roquinaldo A. Ferreira, "Escravidão e revolta de escravos em Angola (1830–1860)," *Revista Afro-Ásia*, nos. 21–22 (1999): 9–44; Ferreira, "Slaving and Resistance to Slaving in West Central Africa," in *The Cambridge World History of Slavery*, vol. 3, ed. David Eltis and Stanley L. Engerman (Cambridge: Cambridge University Press, 2011), 111–31; Martin Lienhard, *O mar e o mato: Histórias da escravidão* (Luanda: Kilombelombe, 2005); José C. Curto, "Resistência à escravidão na África: O caso dos escravos fugitivos recapturados cm Angola, 1846–1876," *Afro-Ásia*, no. 33 (2005): 67–86.

73. Curto, "Struggling"; Curto, "Story of Nbena"; Candido, "African Freedom Suits."

74. AHU, SEMU, DGU, Angola, Correspondência dos Governadores, segunda secção, códice 6A, carta do Governador Geral de Angola Adrião Acácio da Silveira Pinto, 15 September 1850.

75. *BOA*, no. 295, 26 May 1851, 4.

76. *BOA*, no. 325, 20 December 1851, 4.

77. ANA, Luanda, Avulsos, códice 122, atas da sessão da Junta Protetora fol. 23v.

78. *BOA*, no. 263, 12 October 1850, 2; *BOA*, no. 265, 26 October 1850, 1.

79. *BOA*, no. 357, 31 July 1852, 3.

80. Candido, *Fronteras*, 219.

81. ANA, Luanda, Avulsos, códice 122, atas da sessão da Junta Protetora fol. 23v.

82. ANA, Luanda, códice 2524, registo de escravos, fols. 20v–21.

83. ANA, Luanda, códice 2467, registo de escravos, fols. 56v–57. In Saint-Louis, some enslaved women who became petty traders even earned enough to purchase their own slaves. Jones, *The Métis of Senegal*, 49.

84. Jones, *The Métis of Senegal*, 49.

85. Keila Gringberg, "Alforria, direito e direitos no Brasil e nos Estados Unidos," *Estudos históricos*, no. 27 (2001): 65.

86. ANA, códice 5613, carta de liberdade, fol. 19.

87. ANA, códice 5613, carta de liberdade, fol. 7.

88. Sidney Chalhoub and Hebe Maria Mattos located cases of slaves who had their freedom contested by their masters' heirs in Brazil. Sidney Chalhoub, *Visões da liberdade: Uma história das últimas décadas da escravidão na corte* (São Paulo: Companhia das Letras, 1990), 111–12; Hebe Maria Mattos, *Das cores do silêncio: Os significados da liberdade no sudeste escravista—Brasil, século XIX* (Rio de Janeiro: Nova Fronteira, 1998).

89. Sheldon Augusto Soares de Carvalho, "As perspectivas de senhores, escravos e libertos em torno do pecúlio e das redes familiars no desagregar da escravidão em Barbacena, 1871–1888" (PhD diss., Universidade Federal Fluminense, 2008), 239.

90. Mario Borges Silva, "Experiências de liberdade: Estratégias de senhores e escravos nos anos finais da escravidão—Jataí, 1871–1888," *Catalão* 13, no. 2 (2013): 340; João José Reis and Eduardo Silva, *Negociação e conflito: A resistência negra no Brasil escravista* (São Paulo: Companhia das Letras, 2009).

91. ANA, códice 5613, carta de liberdade, fol. 7v.

92. ANA, códice 5613, carta de liberdade, fol. 10.

93. BL, livro de batismo da Freguesia dos Remédios, 1852–62, fol. 67v.

94. Bush, *Slave Women*, 11–22; Douglas Hall, ed., *In Miserable Slavery: Thomas Thistlewood in Jamaica, 1750–1786* (Barbados: University of West Indies Press, 1999).

95. Candido, "Concubinage," 73–77; Curto, "'As If from a Free Womb,'" 42–46.

Conclusion

1. *BOA*, no. 706, 9 April 1859, 11.

2. Freudenthal, *Arimos e fazendas*, 305.

3. *BOA*, no. 805, 9 March 1861, 5. For further information on her inheritance, see Cardoso, "Ana Joaquina dos Santos Silva," 11–13.

4. Pacheco, *José da Silva Maia Ferreira*, 100.

5. Cardoso, "Ana Joaquina dos Santos Silva," 9–10.

6. Mariana P. Candido and Marcia Schenck, "Uncomfortable Pasts: Talking about Slavery in Angola," in *African Heritage and Memory of Slavery in Brazil and the South Atlantic World*, edited by Ana Lúcia Araújo (Amherst, NY: Cambria Press, 2015), 213–52.

7. Henriques, *Percursos da modernidade*, 432–47; Dias, "Criando," 402–3.

Bibliography

Unpublished Primary Sources

Arquivo Histórico Ultramarino, Lisbon (AHU), Secretaria de Estado da Marinha e Ultramar (SEMU), Direcção Geral do Ultramar (DGU), Angola
  Correspondência dos Governadores, primeira secção, códices 57, 77, 79, 82, 83
  Correspondência dos Governadores, segunda secção, códices 6, 6A, 6B, 7A, 7B, 8AC, 8B, 1105–10
Arquivo Nacional da Torre do Tombo, Lisbon (ANTT)
  Feitos findos, Juízo das Justificações Ultramarinas, África: maço. 29, no. 8.
Arquivo Nacional de Angola (ANA)
  Avulsos, códices 122, 128, 136, 142, 143, 144, 145, 147, 1192, 1138, 1335, 1736, 2735, 2737, 2772, 2825
  Núcleo geral dos códices 538, 1301, 2467, 2482, 2467, 2482, 2524, 2862, 3070, 3186, 3665, 3843, 3844, 3927, 3928, 5613, 5614, 5644, 7615, 7741, 7750, 8400, 10060
Biblioteca Nacional de Lisboa (BNL)
  Códice 8744
Biblioteca Municipal de Luanda (BML)
  Códices 025, 026, 030, 031, 034, 037, 041, 042, 043, 045, 047, 048, 051, 052, 055 (vols. 1 and 2)
Bispado de Luanda (BL)
  Livro de batismos Conceição (sé velha) 1812–22, e Remédios, 1816–22
  Livro de óbitos, Freguesia dos Remédios, 1851–52
  Livro de óbitos de escravos, Nossa Senhora de Nazareth, 1835–36
  Registros de batismos, 1812–22
  Termos de fiança, 1837–59

Published Primary Sources

A Civilização da África Portuguesa (CAP). 1866–67.
Accounts and Papers of the House of Commons and Command. Vol. 47. Cambridge, MA: Harvard College Library, 1880.
Almanak statístico da província d'Angola e suas dependências para o anno de 1852. Luanda: Imprensa do Governo, 1851.

Amado, José de Sousa. *Notícia do estado em que se acha o povo de Angola, destituído de mestres, parochos e egrejas, e considerações a'cerca da necessidade e facilidade de remediar tão grandes males*. Lisbon: C. M. Martins, 1861.

Azeredo, José Pinto de. *Ensaios sobre algumas enfermidades d'Angola*. Lisbon: Regia Officina Typografica, 1799.

Boletim Oficial de Angola (BOA). 1845–67.

Brásio, António, ed. *Monumenta missionária africana*. 11 vols. Lisbon: Agência Geral do Ultramar, 1956.

British and Foreign State Papers. 1850–51. Vol. 40. Library of the University of Michigan. http://babel.hathitrust.org/cgi/pt?id=hvd.hj1393;view=1up;seq=9.

Cadornega, António de Oliveira. *História geral das guerras angolanas*. 3 vols. 1680; repr., Lisbon: Agência Geral do Ultramar, 1972.

Caldeira, Carlos José. *Apontamentos d'uma viagem de Lisboa á China e da China á Lisbon*. 2 vols. Lisbon: Typograhia de Castro & Irmão, 1853.

Constituições primeiras do arcebispado da Bahia. Vol. 1, bk. 67. https://archive.org/details/constituicoensproocath.

Correspondence with the British Commissioners at Sierra Leone, Havana, Rio de Janeiro, Surinam, Cape of Good Hope, Jamaica, Loanda, and Boa Vista Related to the Slave Trade. London: William Clowes, 1846.

Douville, Jean Baptiste. *Voyage au Congo et dans l'intérieur de l'Afrique équinoxale . . . 1828, 1829, 1830*. 2 vols. Paris: J. Renouard, 1832.

Eltis, David, et al. "Voyages: The Trans-Atlantic Slave Trade Database." 2019. https://www.slavevoyages.org.

Gil, António. *Considerações sobre alguns pontos mais importantes da moral religiosa e systema de jurisprundência dos pretos do continente da África Occidental portuguesa além do Equador, tendentes a dar alguma idea do character peculiar das suas instituicções primitivas*. Lisbon: Typografia da Academia, 1854.

Lista geral dos officiaes e empregados da marinha e ultramar. Lisbon: Imprensa Nacional, 1850.

Livingstone, David. *Family Letters, 1841–1850*. Vol. 1. London: Chatto & Windus, 1859.

———. *Missionary Travels and Researches in South Africa*. London: John Murray, 1857.

Lopes de Lima, José Joaquim. *Ensaios sobre a statistica das possessões portuguezas*. Vol. 3. Lisbon: Imprensa Nacional, 1846.

Montecuccolo, Giovanni Antonio Cavazzi da. *Descrição histórica dos três reinos Congo, Matamba, e Angola*. 2 vols. Lisbon, 1965.

Monteiro, Joachim John. *Angola and the River Congo*. 2 vols. London: Macmillan, 1875.

Moraes, J. J. da Cunha. *Africa Occidental: Algum photographico e descriptive*. Vol. 2. Lisbon: David Corazzi, 1886.

Omboni, Tito. *Viaggi nell'Africa Occidentale: Gia medico di consiglio nel regno d'Angola e sue dipendenze membro della R. Accademia Peloritana di Messina*. Milan: Civelli, 1846.

Ordenações Filipinas. http://www1.ci.uc.pt/ihti/proj/filipinas/ordenacoes.htm.

Pigafetta, Fillippo, and Duarte Lopes. *Relação do reino do Congo e das terras circunvizinhas*. Lisbon: Alfa, 1989.

Quarenta e cinco dias em Angola: Apontamentos de viagem. Porto: Sebastião José Pereira, 1862.

Saccardo, Graziano. *Congo e Angola con la storia dell'antica missione dei Cappuccini.* Venice: Curia Provinciale dei Cappuccini, 1983.

Serpa Pinto, Alexandre Alberto da Rocha de. *Como eu atravessei a África.* 2 vols. Lisbon: Edições Europa-América, 1980.

Silva Corrêa, Elias Alexandre da. *História de Angola.* 2 vols. Lisbon: Editorial Ática, 1937.

Tams, Gustav. *Visit to the Portuguese Possessions in South-Western Africa.* 2 vols. London: T. C. Newby, 1845.

Torres, João Carlos Feo Cardoso de Castello Branco e. *Memórias contendo a biographia do vice almirante Luiz da Motta Feo e Torres: A história dos governadores e capitaens generaes de Angola, desde 1575 até 1825, e a descripção geographica e política dos reinos de Angola e de Benguella.* Paris: Fantin, 1825.

Valdcz, Francisco Travassos. *Six Years of a Traveller's Life in Western Africa.* 2 vols. London: Hurst and Blackett, 1861.

Unpublished Secondary Sources

Bezerra, Nielson. "Escravidão, farinha e tráfico atlântico: Um novo olhar sobre as relações entre Rio de Janeiro e Benguela." Unpublished paper, Programa Nacional de Apoio a Pesquisa, Fundação Biblioteca Nacional do Rio de Janeiro, 2010.

———. "Mosaicos da escravidão: Identidades africanas e conexões atlânticas no recôncavo da Guanabara (1780–1840)." PhD diss., Universidade Federal Fluminense, 2010.

Candido, Mariana P. "Enslaving Frontiers: Slavery, Trade and Identity in Benguela, 1780–1850." PhD diss., York University, 2006.

Carvalho, Sheldon Augusto Soares de. "As perspectivas de senhores, escravos e libertos em torno do pecúlio e das redes familiares no desagregar da escravidão em Barbacena, 1871–1888." PhD diss., Universidade Federal Fluminense, 2008.

Cunha, Anabela. "Degredo para Angola na segunda metade do século XIX." MA thesis, Universidade de Lisboa, 2004.

Feliciano, Maria Isabel Moreira Bastos. "Luanda, quotidiano e escravos no século XIX." MA thesis, Universidade de Lisboa, 2003.

Ferreira, Roquinaldo. "Dos sertões ao Atlântico: Tráfico ilegal de escravos e comércio lícito em Angola, 1830–1860." MA thesis, Universidade Federal do Rio de Janeiro, 1996.

Heywood, Linda M. "Production, Trade and Power: The Political Economy of Central Angola, 1850–1949." PhD diss., Columbia University, 1984.

Karasch, Mary C. "The Brazilian Slavers and the Illegal Slave Trade, 1836–1851." MA thesis, University of Wisconsin, 1967.

Meneses, José Newton Coelho. "Artes fabris e serviços banais: Ofícios mecânicos e câmaras no final do antigo regime, Minas Gerais e Lisboa, 1750–1808." PhD diss., Universidade Federal Fluminense, 2003.

Pantoja, Selma. "Conexões e identidade de gênero no caso Brasil e Angola, sécs. XVII–XIX." Working paper, Universidade de Brasília, 2008.

Ribeiro, Alexandre Vieira. "O tráfico atlântico de escravos e a praça mercantil de Salvador, c. 1680–1830." MA thesis, Universidade Federal do Rio de Janeiro, 2005.

Rodrigues, Eugênia. "Portugueses e Africanos nos rios de Sena: Os prazos da coroa nos séculos XVII e XVIII." PhD diss., Universidade Nova de Lisboa, 2002.

Thompson, Estevam C. "Negreiros nos mares do sul: Famílias traficantes nas rotas entre Angola e Brasil em fins do século XVIII." MA thesis, Universidade de Brasília, 2006.

Vieira, Maria Eugenia. "Registro de carta de guia de degredados para Angola, 1714–1757." Licenciate thesis, Universidade de Lisboa, 1966.

Wheeler, Douglas L. "The Portuguese in Angola, 1836–1891: A Study in Expansion and Administration." PhD diss., Boston University, 1963.

Published Secondary Sources

Abreu, Jean Luíz Neves. "José Pinto de Azeredo e as enfermidade de Angola: Saber médico e experiências coloniais nas últimas décadas do século XVIII." *Revista de história*, no. 166 (2012): 163–83.

Acioli, Gustavo, and Maximiliano M. Menz. "Resgate e mercadorias: Uma análise comparada do tráfico luso-brasileiro de escravos em Angola e na Costa da Mina (século XVIII)." *Afro-Ásia*, no. 37 (2008): 43–73.

Alencastro, Luiz Felipe de. *O trato dos viventes: Formação do Brasil no Atlântico Sul.* São Paulo: Companhia das Letras, 2000.

Almada, José de. *Apontamentos históricos sôbre a escravatura e o trabalho indígena nas colónias portuguesas.* Lisbon: Imprensa Nacional, 1932.

Alpern, Stanley B. "The European Introduction of Crops into West Africa in Precolonial Times." *History in Africa*, no. 19 (1992): 13–43.

Amaral, Ilídio do. *O reino do Congo, os Mbundu (ou Ambundos), o reino dos "Ngola" (ou Angola) e a presença Portuguesa, de finais do século XV a meados do século XVI.* Lisbon: Instituto de Investigação Científica Tropical, 1996.

Anstey, Roger. *The Atlantic Slave Trade and British Abolition, 1760–1810.* Atlantic Highlands, NJ: Humanities Press, 1975.

Antonil, André João. *Cultura e opulência do Brasil por suas drogas e minas.* São Paulo: Companhia Melhoramentos, 1922.

Arend, Sílvia Maria Fávero. *Amasiar ou casar? A família popular no final do século XIX.* Porto Alegre: Editora da UFRGS, 2001.

Austin, Gareth. "Cash Crops and Freedom: Export Agriculture and the Decline of Slavery in Colonial West Africa." *International Review of Social History* 54, no. 1 (2009): 1–37.

Austin, Ralph A. "The Abolition of the Overseas Slave Trade: A Distorted Theme in West African History." *Journal of the Historical Society of Nigeria* 5, no. 2 (1970): 257–74.

Bailyn, Bernard. "The Idea of Atlantic History." *Itinerario* 20, no. 1 (1996): 19–44.

Bal, Willy. "Portugais pombeiro, commerçant ambulant du sertáo." *Annali dell' Instituto Universitario Orientale* 6, no. 2 (1965): 148–57.

Barcia, Manuel. "Fighting with the Enemy's Weapons: The Usage of the Colonial Legal Framework by Nineteenth-Century Cuban Slaves." *Atlantic Studies* 3, no. 2 (2006): 159–81.

Barroca, Mário Jorge. *Medidas-padrão medievais portuguesas.* Porto: Universidade do Porto, 1992.

Barry, Boubacar. *Senegambia and the Atlantic Slave Trade.* New York: Cambridge University Press, 1988.

Beoku-Betts, Josephine. "Western Perceptions of African Women in the 19th and Early 20th Centuries." In *Readings in Gender in Africa*, edited by Andrea Cornwall, 20–25. Bloomington: Indiana University Press, 2005.

Berlin, Ira. "From Creole to African: Atlantic Creoles and the Origins of African-American Society in Mainland North America." *William and Mary Quarterly*, 53, no. 2 (1996): 251–88.

Bethell, Leslie M. "Britain, Portugal and the Suppression of the Brazilian Slave Trade: The Origins of Lord Palmerston's Act of 1839." *English Historical Review* 80, no. 317 (1965): 761–84.

Birmingham, David. "The Coffee Barons of Cazengo." *Journal of African History* 19, no. 4 (1978): 523–38.

———. *The Portuguese Conquest of Angola*. London: Oxford University Press, 1965.

———. "A Question of Coffee: Black Enterprise in Angola." *Canadian Journal of African Studies* 16, no. 2 (1982): 343–46.

———. "Slave City: Luanda through German Eyes." *Portuguese Studies Review*, no. 19 (2011): 77–92.

———. *Trade and Conflict in Angola: The Mbundu and Their Neighbours under the Influence of the Portuguese, 1483–1790*. Oxford: Clarendon Press, 1966.

———. *Trade and Empire in the Atlantic, 1400–1600*. London: Routledge, 2000.

Black, Henry Campbell. *A Law Dictionary*. 2nd ed. Clark, NJ: Lawbook Exchange, 1995.

Boxer, Charles R. *Mary and Misogyny: Women in Iberian Expansion Overseas, 1415–1815; Some Facts, Fancies and Personalities*. London: Duckworth, 1975.

———. *Salvador de Sá and the Struggle for Brazil and Angola, 1602–1686*. London: University of London / Athlone Press, 1952.

Brooks, George. *Eurafricans in Western Africa: Commerce, Social Status, Gender, and Religious Observance from the Sixteenth Century to the Eighteenth Century*. Athens: Ohio University Press, 2003.

———. "A Nhara of the Guinea-Bissau Region: Mãe Aurélia Correia." In *Women and Slavery in Africa*, edited by Claire Robertson and Martin A. Klein, 295–319. Portsmouth, NH: Heinemann, 1997.

———. "The Signares of Saint-Louis and Goree: Women Entrepreneurs in Eighteenth Century Senegal." In *Women in Africa: Studies in Social and Economic Change*, edited by Nancy Hafkin and Edna G. Bay, 19–44. Stanford, CA: Stanford University Press, 1976.

Bush, Barbara. *Slave Women in Caribbean Society, 1650–1838*. Bloomington: Indiana University Press, 1990.

Caldeira, Arlindo Manuel. *Mulheres, sexualidade e casamento em São Tomé e Príncipe, século XV a XVIII*. Lisbon: Edições Cosmos, 1999.

Candido, Mariana P. "Women's Material World in Nineteenth-Century Benguela," in In *African Women in the Atlantic World: Property, Vulnerability and Mobility, 1660–1880*, edited by Mariana C. Candido and Adam Jones, 70–88. Woodbridge: James Currey, 2019.

———. "African Freedom Suits and Portuguese Vassal Status: Legal Mechanisms for Fighting Enslavement in Benguela, Angola, 1800–1830." *Slavery and Abolition* 32, no. 3 (2011): 447–59.

———. *An African Slaving Port and the Atlantic World: Benguela and Its Hinterland*. New York: Cambridge University Press, 2013.

———. "Aguida Gonçalves da Silva, une *dona* à Benguela à la fin du XVIIIe siècle." *Brésil(s): Sciences humaines et sociales*, no. 1 (2012): 33–54.

———. "Concubinage and Slavery in Benguela, ca. 1750–1850." In *Slavery in Africa and the Caribbean: A History of Enslavement and Identity Since the 18th Century*, edited by Nadine Hunt and Olatunji Ojo, 66–84. London: I.B. Tauris, 2012.

———. "Conquest, Occupation, Colonialism and Exclusion: Land Disputes in Angola." In *Property Rights, Land and Territory in the European Overseas Empires*, edited by José Vicente Serrão et al., 223–36. Lisbon: CEHC, ISCTE-IUL, 2014.

———. "Engendering West Central African History: The Role of Urban Women in Benguela in the Nineteenth Century." *History in Africa*, no. 42 (2015): 7–36.

———. *Fronteras de esclavización: Esclavitud, comercio e identidad en Benguela, 1780–1850*. Mexico City: El Colegio de México, 2011.

———. "Merchants and the Business of the Slave Trade in Benguela, c. 1750–1850." *African Economic History*, no. 35 (2008): 1–30.

———. "Negociantes baianos no porto de Benguela: Redes comerciais unindo o Atlântico no setencentos." In *Brasileiros e Portugueses na África (séculos XVI–XIX)*, edited by Roberto Guedes, 67–91. Rio de Janeiro: MAUAD, 2014.

———. "Os agentes não europeus na comunidade mercantil de Benguela, c. 1760–1820." *Saeculum*, no. 29 (2013): 97–124.

———. "Strategies for Social Mobility: Liaisons between Foreign Men and Slave Women in Benguela, c. 1770–1850." In *Sex, Power and Slavery: The Dynamics of Carnal Relations under Enslavement*, edited by Gwyn Campbell and Elizabeth Elbourne, 272–88. Athens: Ohio University Press, 2014.

———. "Trans-Atlantic Links: The Benguela-Bahian Connections, 1700–1850." In *Paths of the Atlantic Slave Trade: Interactions, Identities, and Images*, edited by Ana Lúcia Araújo, 239–72. Amherst, NY: Cambria Press, 2011.

———. "The Transatlantic Slave Trade and the Vulnerability of Free Blacks in Benguela, Angola, 1780–1830." In *Atlantic Biographies: Individuals and Peoples in the Atlantic World*, edited by Jeffrey A. Fortin and Mark Meuwese, 193–209. Leiden: Brill, 2014.

———. "Women, Family, and Landed Property in Nineteenth-Century Benguela." *African Economic History*, no. 43 (2015): 136–61.

———. "Women in Angola." In *Oxford Research Encyclopedia of African History*, edited by Thomas Spear, 2. Oxford: Oxford University Press, 2018.

Candido, Mariana P., and Eugenia Rodrigues. "African Women's Access and Rights to Property in the Portuguese Empire." *African Economic History*, no. 43 (2015): 1–18.

Candido, Mariana P., and Marcia Schenck. "Uncomfortable Pasts: Talking about Slavery in Angola." In *African Heritage and Memory of Slavery in Brazil and the South Atlantic World*, edited by Ana Lúcia Araújo, 213–52. Amherst, NY: Cambria Press, 2015.

Cardoso, Carlos Alberto Lopes. "Ana Joaquina dos Santos Silva, industrial angolana da segunda metade do século XIX." *Boletim cultural da Câmara Municipal de Luanda*, no. 32 (1972): 5–14.

———. "Estudo genealógico da família Matozo de Andrade e Câmara." *Ocidente*, no. 403 (1971): 311–22.

Cardoso, Manuel da Costa Lobo. *Subsídios para a história de Luanda.* Luanda: Edição do Autor, 1967.

Carney, Judith A. "Landscapes of Technology Transfer: Rice Cultivation and African Continuities," *Technology and Culture* 37, no. 1 (1996): 5–35;

———. "'With Grains in Her Hair': Rice in Colonial Brazil." *Slavery and Abolition* 25, no. 1 (2004): 1–27.

Chalhoub, Sidney. *Visões da liberdade: Uma história das últimas décadas da escravidão na corte.* São Paulo: Companhia das Letras, 1990.

Clarence-Smith, W. Gervase. "Runaway Slaves and Social Bandits in Southern Angola, 1875–1913." *Slavery and Abolition* 6, no. 3 (1985): 23–33.

———. *Slaves, Peasants, and Capitalists in Southern Angola, 1840–1926.* New York: Cambridge University Press, 1979.

———. *The Third Portuguese Empire, 1825–1975: A Study in Economic Imperialism.* Manchester: Manchester University Press, 1985.

Coclanis, Peter A. "Atlantic World or Atlantic/World?" *William and Mary Quarterly* 63, no. 4 (2006): 725–42.

Coghe, Samuël. "Apprenticeship and the Negotiation of Freedom: The Liberated Africans of the Anglo-Portuguese Mixed Commission in Luanda (1844–1870)." *Africana Studia*, no. 14 (2010): 255–73.

———. "The Problem of Freedom in Mid-Nineteenth-Century Atlantic Slave Society: The Liberated Africans of the Anglo-Portuguese Mixed Commission in Luanda (1844–1870)." *Slavery and Abolition* 33, no. 2 (2012): 479–500.

Coquery-Vidrovitch, Catherine. *African Women: A Modern History.* Boulder, CO: Westview Press, 1987.

Corrado, Jacopo. "The Rise of a New Consciousness: Early Euro-African Voices of Dissent in Colonial Angola." *Journal of Portuguese History* 5, no. 2 (2007): 1–15.

Crosby, Alfred W. *The Columbian Exchange: Biological and Cultural Consequences of 1492.* Westport, CT: Greenwood, 1972.

Curtin, Philip. *The Atlantic Slave Trade: A Census.* Madison: University of Wisconsin Press, 1969.

Curto, José C. "Alcohol under the Context of the Atlantic Slave Trade: The Case of Benguela and Its Hinterland (Angola)." *Cahiers d'études africaines* 51, no. 201 (2011): 51–85.

———. "The Anatomy of a Demographic Explosion: Luanda, 1844–1850." *International Journal of African Historical Studies*, no. 32 (1999): 381–405.

———. "A restituição de 10.000 súbditos ndongo 'roubados' na Angola de meados do século XVII: Uma análise preliminar." In *Escravatura e transformações culturais: África–Brasil–Caraíbas*, edited by Isabel Castro Henriques, 185–208. Lisbon: Vulgata, 2002.

———. "'As If from a Free Womb': Baptismal Manumissions in the Conceição Parish, Luanda, 1778–1807." *Portuguese Studies Review* 10, no. 1 (2002): 26–57.

———. "The Donas of Benguela, 1797: A Preliminary Analysis of a Colonial Female Elite." In *Angola e as Angolanas: Memória, sociedade e cultura*, edited by Edvaldo Bergamo, Selma Pantoja, and Ana Claudia Silva, 99–120. São Paulo: Intermeios, 2016.

———. *Enslaving Spirits: The Portuguese-Brazilian Alcohol Trade at Luanda and Its Hinterland, c. 1550–1830.* Leiden: Brill, 2004.

————. "Jerebita in the Relations between the Colony of Angola and the Kingdom of Kasanje." *Anais de história de além-mar*, no. 14 (2013): 301–26.

————. "The Legal Portuguese Slave Trade from Benguela, Angola, 1730–1828: A Quantitative Re-appraisal." *África* 16–17, no. 1 (1993–94): 101–16.

————. "Luso-Brazilian Alcohol and the Legal Slave Trade at Benguela and Its Hinterland, c. 1617–1830." In *Négoce blanc en Afrique noire: L'évolution du commerce à longue distance en Afrique noire du 18e au 20e siècles*, edited by Hubert Bonin and Michel Cahen, 351–69. Paris: Publications de la Société Française d'Histoire d'Outre Mer, 2001.

————. "Producing 'Liberated Africans' in Mid-Nineteenth Century Angola." In *Liberated Africans and the Abolition of the Slave Trade, 1807–1896*, edited by Richard Anderson and Henry B. Lovejoy, 238–56. Rochester, NY: University of Rochester Press, 2020.

————. "A Quantitative Re-assessment of the Legal Portuguese Slave Trade from Luanda, Angola, 1710–1830." *African Economic History*, no. 20 (1992): 1–25.

————. "Resistência à escravidão na África: O caso dos escravos fugitivos recapturados em Angola, 1846–1876." *Afro-Ásia*, no. 33 (2005): 67–86.

————. "The Story of Nbena, 1817–1820: Unlawful Enslavement and the Concept of 'Original Freedom' in Angola." In *Trans-Atlantic Dimensions of Ethnicity in the African Diaspora*, edited by Paul E. Lovejoy and David V. Trotman, 43–64. London: Continuum, 2003.

————. "Struggling against Enslavement: The Case of José Manuel in Benguela, 1816–20." *Canadian Journal of African Studies* 39, no. 1 (2005): 96–122.

————. "Whitening the 'White' Population: An Analysis of the 1850 Censuses of Luanda." In *Em torno de Angola: Narrativas, identidades e as conexões atlânticas*, edited by Pantoja Selma and Estevam C. Thompson, 225–47. São Paulo: Intermeios, 2014.

Curto, José C., and Raymond R. Gervais. "The Population History of Luanda during the Late Atlantic Slave Trade, 1781–1844." *African Economic History*, no. 29 (2001): 1–59.

Dias, Jill. "Angola nas vésperas da abolição do tráfico de escravos (1820-1845)," in *O império africano, 1825–1890*, edited by Valentim Alexandre and Jill Dias, 319–78. Lisbon: Estampa, 1998.

————. "A sociedade colonial de Angola e o liberalismo português (c. 1820–1850)." In *O liberalismo na península Ibérica na primeira metade do século XIX: Comunicações ao colóquio organizado pelo Centro de Estudos de História Contemporânea Portuguesa*, vol. 1, edited by Miriam H. Pereira et al., 267–86. Lisbon: Sá da Costa Editora, 1982.

————. "Criando um novo Brasil (1845-1870)," in *O império africano, 1825–1890*, edited by Valentim Alexandre and Jill Dias, 379–471. Lisbon: Estampa, 1998.

————. "Crise e conflito," in *O império africano, 1825–1890*, edited by Valentim Alexandre and Jill Dias, 472–545. Lisbon: Estampa, 1998.

————. "Famine and Disease in the History of Angola, c. 1830–1930." *Journal of African History* 22, no. 3 (1981): 349–78.

Dooling, Wayne. "Slavery and Amelioration in the Graaff-Reinet District, 1823–1830." *South African Historical Journal* 27, no. 1 (1992): 75–94.

Dupuy, Alex. "French Merchant Capital and Slavery in Saint-Domingue." *Latin American Perspectives* 12, no. 3 (1985): 77–102.

Elbl, Ivana. "Men without Wives: Sexual Arrangements in the Early Portuguese Expansion in West Africa." In *Desire and Discipline: Sex and Sexuality in the Premodern West*, edited by Jacquelline Murray and Konrad Eisenbichler, 61–86. Toronto: University of Toronto Press, 1996.

Eltis, David. "African and European Relations in the Last Century of the Transatlantic Slave Trade." In *From Slave Trade to Empire: Europe and the Colonisation of Black Africa, 1780s–1880s*, edited by Olivier Pétré-Grenouilleau, 21–46. London: Routledge, 2004.

———. "Atlantic History in Global Perspective." *Itinerario* 23, no. 2 (1999): 141–61.

———. "The British Contribution to the Nineteenth Century Trans-Atlantic Slave Trade." *Economic History Review* 32, no. 2 (1979): 211–27.

———. "The British Trans-Atlantic Slave Trade after 1807." *Maritime History* 4, no. 1 (1974): 1–11.

———. *Economic Growth and the Ending of the Transatlantic Slave Trade*. New York: Oxford University Press, 1987.

———. "The Nineteenth Century Transatlantic Slave Trade: An Annual Time Series of Imports into the Americas Broken Down by Region." *Hispanic American Historical Review* 67, no. 1 (1987): 109–38.

———. "The Volume and Structure of the Transatlantic Slave Trade: A Reassessment." *William and Mary Quarterly* 58, no. 1 (2001): 17–46.

Eltis, David, Paul E. Lovejoy, and David Richardson. "Slave-Trading Ports: Towards an Atlantic-Wide Perspective." In *Ports of the Slave Trade (Bights of Benin and Biafra)*, edited by Robin Law and Silke Strickrodt, 12–35. Stirling: Centre of Commonwealth Studies, University of Stirling, 1999.

Eltis, David, and David Richardson. *Atlas of the Transatlantic Slave Trade*. New Haven, CT: Yale University Press, 2010.

Erickson, Amy Louise. *Women and Property in Early Modern England*. London: Routledge, 2003.

Faria, Francisco Leite de. "Echoes of the Atlantic: Benguela (Angola) and Brazilian Independence." In *Biography and the Black Atlantic*, edited by Lisa Lindsay and John Sweet, 224–47. Philadelphia: University of Pennsylvania Press, 2013.

———. "Uma relação de Rui de Pina sobre o Congo escrita em 1492." *Studia*, no. 19 (1996): 223–305.

Ferreira, Roquinaldo A. "Agricultural Enterprise and Unfree Labor in Nineteenth-Century Angola." In *Commercial Agriculture, the Slave Trade and Slavery in Africa*, edited by Robin Law, Suzanne Schwartz, and Silke Strickrod, 225–43. Woodbridge: James Currey, 2013.

———. "Atlantic Microhistories: Slaving, Mobility, and Personal Ties in the Black Atlantic World (Angola and Brazil)." In *Cultures of the Lusophone Black Atlantic*, edited by Nancy Naro, Roger Sansi, and David Treece, 99–128. New York: Palgrave Macmillan, 2007.

———. "The Atlantic Networks of the Benguela Slave Trade (1730–1800)." In *Trabalho forçado africano: Experiências coloniais comparadas*, edited by Centro de Estudos Africanos da Universidade do Porto, 66–99. Lisbon: Campo das Letras, 2006.

———. "Biografia, mobilidade e cultura atlântica: A micro-escala do tráfico de escravos em Benguela, século XVIII–XIX." *Tempo* 10, no. 20 (2006): 33–59.

———. "Brasil e Angola no tráfico illegal de escravos." In *Brasil e Angola nas rotas do Atlântico sul,* edited by Selma Pantoja, 143–94. Rio de Janeiro: Bertrand, 1999.

———. *Cross-Cultural Exchange in the Atlantic World: Angola and Brazil during the Era of the Slave Trade.* New York: Cambridge University Press, 2012.

———. "Dinâmica do comércio intra-colonial: Geribitas, panos asiáticos e guerra no tráfico angolano de escravos (século XVIII)." In *O antigo regime nos trópicos: A dinâmica imperial portuguesa, séculos XVI–XVIII,* edited by João Fragoso, Maria de Fátima Gouvêa, and Maria Fernanda Baptista Bicalho, 339–78. Rio de Janeiro: Nova Fronteira, 2001.

———. "Escravidão e revolta de escravos em Angola (1830–1860)." *Revista Afro-Ásia,* nos. 21–22 (1999): 9–44.

———. "Fontes para o estudo da escravidão em Angola: Luanda e Icolo e Bengo no pós-tráfico de escravos." In *Construíndo o passado angolano: As fontes e a sua interpretação; Actas do II Seminário Internacional sobre História de Angola,* edited by Jill R. Dias and Rosa Cruz e Silva, 667–80. Lisbon: Comissão Nacional para as Comemorações dos Descobrimentos Portugueses, 2000.

———. "Ilhas crioulas: O significado plural da mestiçagem na África atlântica." *Revista de história* 155, no. 2 (2006): 17–41.

———. "Slaving and Resistance to Slaving in West Central Africa." In *The Cambridge World History of Slavery,* vol. 3, edited by David Eltis and Stanley L. Engerman, 111–31. Cambridge: Cambridge University Press, 2011.

———. "The Suppression of the Slave Trade and Slave Departures from Angola, 1830s–1860s." In *Extending the Frontiers: Essay on the New Transatlantic Slave Trade Database,* edited by David Eltis and David Richardson, 313–34. New Haven, CT: Yale University Press, 2008.

Filho, Amilcar Martins, and Roberto B. Martins. "Slavery in a Non-export Economy: Nineteenth Century Minas Gerais Revisited." *Hispanic American Historical Review* 63, no. 3 (1983): 569–90.

Flexor, Maria Helena Ochi. "Oficiais mecânicos e a vida quotidiana no Brasil." *Oceanos,* no. 42 (2000): 77–84.

Florentino, Manolo. *Em costas negras: Uma história do tráfico atlântico de escravos entre a África e o Rio de Janeiro.* Rio de Janeiro: Arquivo Nacional, 1995.

Fragoso, João Luís, and Roberto Guedes Ferreira. "Alegrias e artimanhas de uma fonte seriada, os códices 390, 421, 424, e 425: Despachos de escravos e passaportes da Intendência de Polícia da Corte, 1819–1833." In *História quantitativa e serial: Um balanço,* edited by Tarcísio Rodrigues Botelho et al., 239–78. Goiânia: ANPUH, 2001.

Freudenthal, Aida. *Arimos e fazendas: A transição agrária em Angola, 1850–1880.* Luanda: Chá de Caxinde, 2005.

———. "A baixa de Cassanje: Algodão e revolta." *Revista internacional de estudos africanos,* nos. 18–22 (1995–99): 245–83.

———. "Os Quilombos de Angola no século XIX: A recusa da escravidão." *Estudos afro-asiáticos,* no. 32 (1997): 109–34.

Gaspar, David B., and Darlene C. Hine, eds. *More Than Chattel: Black Women and Slavery in the Americas.* Bloomington: Indiana University Press, 1996.

Gilroy, Paul. *The Black Atlantic: Modernity and Double Consciousness.* Cambridge, MA: Harvard University Press, 1993.

Godechot, Jacques. *Histoire de l'Atlantique.* Paris: Bordas, 1947.

Graham, Richard. *Feeding the City: From Street Market to Liberal Reform in Salvador, Brazil, 1780–1860.* Austin: University of Texas Press, 2010.

Green, Tobias, ed. *Brokers of Change: Atlantic Commerce and Cultures in Precolonial Western Africa.* Oxford: Oxford University Press, 2012.

———. "Building Creole Identity in the African Atlantic: Boundaries of Race and Religion in Seventeenth-Century Cabo Verde." *History in Africa*, no. 36 (2009): 103–25.

———. *The Rise of the Trans-Atlantic Slave Trade in Western Africa, 1300–1789.* Cambridge: Cambridge University Press, 2011.

Gringberg, Keila. "Alforria, direito e direitos no Brasil e nos Estados Unidos." *Estudos históricos*, no. 27 (2001): 63–83.

Guizelin, Gilberto da Silva. "A abolição do trafico de escravos no Atlântico Sul: Portugal, o Brasil e a questão do contrabando de africanos." *Almanack*, no. 5 (2013): 123–44.

Hall, Douglas, ed. *In Miserable Slavery: Thomas Thistlewood in Jamaica, 1750–1786.* Barbados: University of West Indies Press, 1999.

Harms, Robert. "Fish and Cassava: The Changing Equation." *African Economic History*, no. 7 (1979): 113–16.

Havik, Philip J. "A dinâmica das relações de gênero e parentesco num contexto comercial: Um balanço comparativo da produção histórica sobre a região da Guiné-Bissau, séculos XVII e XIX." *Afro-Ásia*, no. 27 (2002): 79–120.

———. "From Pariahs to Patriots: Women Slavers in Nineteenth-Century 'Portuguese' Guinea." In *Women and Slavery: Africa and the Western Indian Ocean Islands*, edited by Gwyn Campbell, Suzanne Miers, and Joseph C. Miller, 308–33. Athens: Ohio University Press, 2007.

———. "Gender, Land, and Trade: Women's Agency and Colonial Change in Portuguese Guinea (West Africa)." *African Economic History*, no. 43 (2015): 162–95.

———. *Silences and Soundbytes: The Gendered Dynamics of Trade and Brokerage in the Pre-colonial Guinea Bissau Region.* Münster: Lit Verlag, 2004.

———. "Women and Trade in the Guinea Bissau Region: The Role of African and Luso-African Women in Trade Networks from the Early 16th to the Mid 19th Century." *Studia*, no. 52 (1994): 83–120.

Hawthorne, Walter. *From Africa to Brazil: Culture, Identity and an Atlantic Slave Trade, 1600–1830.* New York: Cambridge University Press, 2010.

Heintze, Beatrix. *A África centro-ocidental no século XIX (c. 1850–1890): Intercâmbio com o mundo exterior—apropriação, exploração e documentação.* Luanda: Kilombelombe, 2013.

———. "Angola nas garras do tráfico de escravos: As guerras angolanas do Ndongo (1611–1630)." *Revista internacional de estudos africanos*, no. 1 (1984): 11–59.

———. *Angola nos séculos XVI e XVII: Estudo sobre fontes, métodos e história.* Luanda: Kilombelombe, 2007.

———. "Angolan Vassal Tributes of the 17th Century." *Revista de história econômica e social*, no. 6 (1980): 57–78.

———. "Asiles toujours menacés: Fuites d'esclaves en Angola au XVIIe siècle." In

Esclavages: Histoire d'une diversité de l'océan Indien à l'Atlantique sud, edited by Katia de Queirós Mattoso, 101–22. Paris: L'Harmattan, 1997.

———. *Exploradores alemães em Angola (1611–1954): Apropriações etnográficas entre comércio de escravos, colonialismo e ciência*. Berlin, 2010. https://www.frobenius -institut.de.

———. "Hidden Transfers: Luso-Africans as European Explorers' Experts in 19th Century West Central Africa." In *The Power of Doubt: Essays in Honor of David Henige*, edited by Paul Landau, 19–40. Madison: University of Wisconsin Press, 2011.

———. "Luso-African Feudalism in Angola?" *Revista portuguesa de história*, no. 18 (1980): 111–31.

Henriques, Isabel Castro. *Os pilares da diferença: Relações Portugal-África, séculos XV– XX*. Lisbon: Caleidoscópio Edição, 2004.

———. *Percursos da modernidade em Angola: Dinâmicas comerciais e transformações sociais no século XIX*. Lisbon: Instituto de Investigação Científica e Tropical, 1997.

Heywood, Linda M. *Contested Power in Angola, 1840s to the Present*. Rochester, NY: University of Rochester Press, 2000.

———. *Njinga of Angola: Africa's Warrior Queen*. Cambridge, MA: Harvard University Press, 2017.

———. "Porters, Trade, and Power: The Politics of Labor in the Central Highlands of Angola, 1850–1914." In *The Workers of African Trade*, edited by Paul E. Lovejoy and Catherine Coquery-Vidrovitch, 243–68. Beverley Hills, CA: Sage, 1985.

———. "Portuguese into African: The Eighteenth-Century Central African Background to Atlantic Creole Cultures." In *Central Africans and Cultural Transformations in the American Diaspora*, edited by Linda M. Heywood, 91–114. Cambridge: Cambridge University Press, 2002.

Heywood, Linda M., ed. *Central Africans and Cultural Transformations in the American Diaspora*. Cambridge: Cambridge University Press, 2002.

Hopkins, A. G. *An Economic History of West Africa*. New York: Longman Group, 1973.

———. "Economic Imperialism in West Africa: Lagos, 1880–92." *Economic History Review*, no. 21 (1968): 580–600.

Ipsen, Pernille. *Daughters of the Trade: Atlantic Slavers and Interracial Marriage on the Gold Coast*. Philadelphia: University of Pennsylvania Press, 2015.

Jones, Hilary. "From Marriage à la Mode to Weddings at Town Hall: Marriage, Colonialism, and Mixed-Race Society in Nineteenth-Century Senegal." *International Journal of African Historical Studies* 38, no. 1 (2005): 27–48.

———. *The Métis of Senegal: Urban Life and Politics in French West Africa*. Bloomington: Indiana University Press, 2013.

Kananoja, Kalle. "Healers, Idolaters, and Good Christians: A Case Study of Creolization and Popular Religion in Mid-Eighteenth Century Angola." *International Journal of African Historical Studies* 43, no. 3 (2010): 443–65.

Karasch, Mary C. "From Porterage to Proprietorship: African Occupations in Rio de Janeiro, 1808–1850." In *Race and Slavery in the Western Hemisphere: Quantitative Studies*, edited by Stanley L. Engerman and Eugene D. Genovese, 369–93. Princeton, NJ: Princeton University Press, 1975.

———. *Slave Life in Rio de Janeiro, 1808–1850*. Princeton, NJ: Princeton University Press, 1987.

————. "Suppliers, Sellers, Servants and Slaves." In *Cities and Society in Colonial Latin America*, edited by Lisa Schell Hoberman and Susan Migden Socolow, 251–83. Albuquerque: University of New Mexico Press, 1986.

Klein, Martin A. "Women and Slavery in Western Sudan." In *Women and Slavery in Africa*, edited by Claire Robertson and Martin A. Klein, 67–92. Portsmouth, NH: Heinemann, 1997.

Kopytoff, Igor, and Suzanne Miers, eds. *Slavery in Africa: Historical and Anthropological Perspectives*. Madison: University of Wisconsin Press, 1977.

Kraus, Michael. *The Atlantic Civilization: Eighteenth-Century Origins*. Ithaca, NY: Cornell University Press, 1949.

Lang, James. *Portuguese Brazil: The King's Plantation*. New York: Academic Press, 1979.

Latham, A. J. H. *Old Calabar, 1600–1891: The Impact of the International Economy upon a Traditional Society*. Oxford: Clarendon Press, 1973.

————. "Palm Oil Exports from Calabar, 1812–1887." In *Figuring African Trade*, edited by G. Leisegang, H. Pash, and A. Jones, 265–96. Berlin: Dietrich Reimer Verlag, 1986.

Law, Robin, ed. *From Slave Trade to "Legitimate" Commerce: The Commercial Transition in Nineteenth-Century West Africa*. Cambridge: Cambridge University Press, 1995.

————. "'Legitimate' Trade and Gender Relations in Yorubaland and Dahomey." In *From Slave Trade to "Legitimate" Commerce: The Commercial Transition in Nineteenth-Century West Africa*, edited by Robin Law, 195–214. New York: Cambridge University Press, 1995.

————. *Ouidah: The Social History of a West African Slaving Port, 1727–1892*. Athens: Ohio University Press, 2005.

————. *The Slave Coast of West Africa, 1550–1750: The Impact of the Atlantic Slave Trade on an African Society*. New York: Oxford University Press, 1991.

Law, Robin, and Kristin Mann. "West Africa in the Atlantic Community: The Case of the Slave Coast." *William and Mary Quarterly* 56, no. 2 (1999): 307–34.

Liberato, Carlos, Mariana P. Candido, Paul E. Lovejoy, and Renée Soulodre-La France. "Laços entre a África e o mundo atlântico durante a era do comércio de africanos escravizados: Uma introdução." In *Laços atlânticos: África e africanos durante a era do comércio transatlântico de escravos*, edited by Carlos Liberato, Mariana P. Candido, Paul E. Lovejoy, and Renée Soulodre-La France, 1–30. Luanda: Ministério da Cultura, Museu Nacional da Escravatura, 2017.

Lienhard, Martin. *O mar e o mato: Histórias da escravidão*. Luanda: Kilombelombe, 2005.

Lopes, Tracy. "The 'Mine of Wealth at the Doors of Luanda': Agricultural Production and Gender in the Bengo." In *O colonialismo português: Novos rumos da historiografia dos PALOP*, edited by Ana Cristina Roque and Maria Manuel Torrão, 177–205. Porto: Edições Húmus, 2013.

Lopo, Júlio de Castro. "Uma rica dona de Luanda." *Portucale*, no. 3 (1948): 129–38.

Lovejoy, Paul E. "Concubinage and the Status of Women Slaves in Early Colonial Northern Nigeria." *Journal of African History* 29, no. 2 (1988): 245–66.

————. "From Slaves to Palm Oil: Afro-European Commercial Relations in the Bight of Biafra, 1741–1841." In *Maritime Empires: British Imperial Maritime Trade in the Nineteenth Century*, edited by David Killingray, Margarette Lincoln, and Nigel Rigby, 13–29. Rochester, NY: Boydell Press, 2004.

————. "The Initial 'Crisis of Adaptation': The Impact of British Abolition on the Atlantic Slave Trade in West Africa, 1808–1820." In *From Slave Trade to "Legitimate" Commerce: The Commercial Transition in Nineteenth-Century West Africa*, edited by Robin Law, 32–56. New York: Cambridge University Press, 1995.

————. *Transformations in Slavery: A History of Slavery in Africa*. 3rd ed. New York: Cambridge University Press, 2012.

Lovejoy, Paul E., and David Richardson. "The Initial 'Crisis of Adaptation': The Impact of British Abolition on the Atlantic Slave Trade in West Africa, 1808–1820." In *From Slave Trade to "Legitimate" Commerce: The Commercial Transition in Nineteenth-Century West Africa*, edited by Robin Law, 32–56. New York: Cambridge University Press, 1995.

Lynn, Martin. *Commerce and Economic Change in West Africa: The Palm Oil Trade in the Nineteenth Century*. Cambridge: Cambridge University Press, 1997.

————. "The West African Palm Oil Trade in the Nineteenth Century and the 'Crisis of Adaptation.'" In *From Slave Trade to "Legitimate" Commerce: The Commercial Transition in Nineteenth-Century West Africa*, edited by Robin Law, 55–77. Cambridge: Cambridge University Press, 1995.

Magaldi, Ana Maria de Mello, and Luciano Raposo de Almeida Figueiredo. "Quitandas e quitutes: Um estudo sobre rebeldia e transgressão femininas numa sociedade colonial." *Cadernos de pesquisa*, no. 54 (1985): 50–61.

Maia, Moacir Rodrigo de Castro. "Tecer redes, proteger relações: Portugueses e africanos na vivência do compadrio (Minas Gerais, 1720–1750)." *Topoi* 11, no. 20 (2010): 36–54.

Manchester, Alan K. "The Transfer of the Portuguese Court to Rio de Janeiro." In *Conflict and Continuity in Brazilian Society*, edited by Henry H. Keith and S. F. Edwards, 148–63. Columbia: University of South Carolina Press, 1969.

Mann, Kristin. *Marrying Well: Marriage, Status and Social Change among the Educated Elite in Colonial Lagos*. New York: Cambridge University Press, 1985.

————. "Owners, Slaves, and the Struggles for Labour in the Commercial Transition at Lagos." In *From Slave Trade to "Legitimate" Commerce: The Commercial Transition in Nineteenth-Century West Africa*, edited by Robin Law, 144–71. Cambridge: Cambridge University Press, 1995.

————. *Slavery and the Birth of an African City: Lagos, 1760–1900*. Bloomington: Indiana University Press, 2007.

————. "Women, Landed Property, and the Accumulation of Wealth in Early Colonial Lagos." *Signs* 16, no. 4 (1991): 682–706.

Manning, Patrick. *Slavery and African Life: Occidental, Oriental and African Slave Trades*. New York: Cambridge University Press, 1990.

Mark, Peter. *"Portuguese" Style and Luso-African Identity: Pre-colonial Senegambia, Sixteenth–Nineteenth Centuries*. Bloomington: Indiana University Press, 2002.

Marques, João Pedro. "Arsénio Pompílio Pompeu de Carpo: Um percurso negreiro no século XIX." *Análise social* 36, no. 160 (2001): 609–38.

————. *Os sons do silêncio: O Portugal de oitocentos e a abolição do tráfico de escravos*. Lisbon: Instituto de Ciências Sociais, 1999.

Martin, Phyllis M. *The External Trade of the Loango Coast 1576–1870: The Effects of Changing Commercial Relations on the Vili Kingdom of Loango*. New York: Oxford University Press, 1972.

Mascarenhas, Filipe Martins Barbosa. *Memórias de Icolo e Bengo: Figuras e famílias.* Luanda: Arte Viva, 2008.

Mason, John. *Social Death and Resurrection: Slavery and Emancipation in South Africa.* Charlottesville: University of Virginia Press, 2003.

Mathieson, William L. *Great Britain and the Slave Trade, 1839–1865.* London: Longmans, 1929.

Mattos, Hebe Maria. *Das cores do silêncio: Os significados da liberdade no sudeste escravista—Brasil, século XIX.* Rio de Janeiro: Nova Fronteira, 1998.

Mauro, Frédéric. *Portugal, o Brasil e o Atlântico.* Lisbon: Estampa, 1997.

McClintock, Anne. *Imperial Leather: Race, Gender and Sexuality in the Colonial Conquest.* New York: Routledge, 1995.

Meillassoux, Claude. *The Anthropology of Slavery: The Womb of Iron and Gold.* Chicago: University of Chicago Press, 1991.

Metcalf, Alia C. "Women and Means: Women and Family Property in Colonial Brazil." In *Families in the Expansion of Europe, 1500–1800,* edited by Maria Beatriz Nizza da Silva, 159–80. Brookfield, CT: Ashgate, 1998.

Miller, Joseph C. "Capitalism and Slaving: The Financial and Commercial Organization of the Angolan Slave Trade, According to the Accounts of Antonio Coelho Guerreiro (1684–1692)." *International Journal of African Historical Studies* 17, no. 1 (1984): 1–56.

———. "Cokwe Trade and Conquest." In *Pre-colonial Trade in Central Africa,* edited by Richard Gray and David Birmingham, 175–201. London: Oxford University Press, 1970.

———. "Credit, Captives, Collateral and Currencies: Debt, Slavery, and the Financing of the Atlantic World." In *Debt and Slavery in the Mediterranean and Atlantic Worlds,* edited by Gwyn Campbell and Alessandro Stanziani, 105–21. London: Pickering & Chatto, 2013.

———. "Imbangala Lineage Slavery (Angola)." In *Slavery in Africa: Historical and Anthropological Perspectives,* edited by Igor Kopytoff and Suzanne Miers, 205–33. Madison: University of Wisconsin Press, 1977.

———. *Kings and Kinsmen: Early Mbundu States in Angola.* Oxford: Clarendon, 1976.

———. "Legal Portuguese Slaving from Angola: Some Preliminary Indications of Volume and Direction." *Revue française d'histoire d'outre mer* 62, nos. 226–27 (1975): 135–76.

———. "The Numbers, Origins, and Destinations of Slaves in the Eighteenth-Century Angolan Slave Trade." *Social Science History* 13, no. 4 (1989): 381–419.

———. "Nzinga of Matamba in a New Perspective." *Journal of African History* 16, no. 2 (1975): 201–16.

———. "The Political Economy of the Angolan Slave Trade in the Eighteenth Century." *Indian Historical Review* 15, nos. 1–2 (1988–89): 152–87.

———. "The Significance of Drought, Disease and Famine in the Agriculturally Marginal Zones of West-Central Africa." *Journal of African History* 23, no. 1 (1982): 17–61.

———. "Slave Prices in the Portuguese Southern Atlantic, 1600–1830." In *Africans in Bondage: Studies in Slavery and the Slave Trade,* edited by Paul E. Lovejoy, 43–77. Madison: University of Wisconsin Press, 1986.

————. "The Slave Trade in Congo and Angola." In *The African Diaspora: Interpretative Essays*, edited by Martin L. Kilson and Robert Rotberg, 75–113. Cambridge, MA: Harvard University Press, 1976.

————. "Some Aspects of the Commercial Organization of Slaving at Luanda, Angola 1760–1830." In *The Uncommon Market: Essays in the Economic History of the Atlantic Slave Trade*, edited by Henry A. Gemery and Jan S. Hogendorn, 77–106. New York: Academic Press, 1979.

————. *Way of Death: Merchant Capitalism and the Angolan Slave Trade, 1730–1830*. Madison: University of Wisconsin Press, 1988.

Moore, Donald, and Richard Roberts. "Listening for Silences." *History in Africa*, no. 17 (1990): 319–25.

Mullin, Michael. "Slave Economic Strategies: Food, Markets and Property." In *From Chattel Slaves to Wage Slaves: The Dynamics of Labor Bargaining in the Americas*, edited by Mary Turner, 68–78. Bloomington: Indiana University Press; London: James Currey, 1995.

Neves, Maria de Fátima Rodrigues das. *Documentos sobre a escravidão no Brasil*. São Paulo: Contexto, 1996.

Newson, Linda, and Susie Minchin. *From Capture to Sale: The Portuguese Slave Trade to Spanish South America in the Early Seventeenth Century*. Leiden: Brill, 2007.

Oliveira, Luiz da Silva Pereira. *Privilégios da nobreza e fidalguia de Portugal*. Lisbon: João Rodrigues Neves, 1806.

Oliveira, Mário António Fernandes de. "Para a história do trabalho em Angola: A escravatura luandense do terceiro quartel do século XIX." *Boletim do Instituto do Trabalho, Providência e Ação Social*, no. 2 (1963): 45–60.

Oliveira, Vanessa S. "The Gendered Dimension of Trade: Female Traders in Nineteenth Century Luanda." *Portuguese Studies Review* 23, no. 2 (2015): 93–121.

————. "Gender, Foodstuff Production and Trade in Late-Eighteenth Century Luanda." *African Economic History*, no. 43 (2015): 57–81.

————. "Mulher e comércio: A participação feminina nas redes comerciais em Luanda (século XIX)." In *Angola e as Angolanas: Memória, sociedade e cultura*, edited by Edvaldo Bergamo, Selma Pantoja, and Ana Claudia Silva, 133–52. São Paulo: Intermeios, 2016.

————. "Notas preliminares sobre punição de escravos em Luanda (século XIX)." In *O colonialismo português: Novos rumos da historiografia dos PALOP*, edited by Ana Cristina Roque and Maria Manuel Torrão, 155–76. Porto: Ediçõs Húmus, 2013.

————. "Slavery and the Forgotten Women Slave Owners of Luanda (1846–1876)." In *Slavery, Memory and Citizenship*, edited by Paul E. Lovejoy and Vanessa S. Oliveira, 129–48. Trenton, NJ: Africa World Press, 2016.

————. "Spouses and Commercial Partners: Immigrant Men and Locally Born Women in Luanda 1831–1859." In *African Women in the Atlantic World: Property, Vulnerability and Mobility, 1660–1880*, edited by Mariana C. Candido and Adam Jones, 217–32. Woodbridge: James Currey, 2019.

————. "Trabalho escravo e ocupações urbanas em Luanda na segunda metade do século XIX." In *Em torno de Angola: Narrativas, identidades e as conexões atlânticas*, edited by Selma Pantoja and Estevam C. Thompson, 249–75. São Paulo: Intermeios, 2014.

Osborn, Emily L. *Our New Husbands Are Here: Households, Gender and Politics in a West African State from the Slave Trade to Colonial Rule.* Athens: Ohio University Press, 2011.

Owewùmí, Oyèrónké. "Colonizing Bodies and Minds: Gender and Colonialism." In *The Invention of Women: Making an African Sense of Western Gender Discourse,* edited by Nupur Chaudhuri, 121–56. Minneapolis: University of Minnesota Press, 1997.

Pacheco, Carlos. "A origem napolitana de algumas famílias angolanas." *Anais da Universidade de Évora,* no. 5 (1995): 181–201.

———. "Arsénio Pompílio Pompeu de Carpo: Uma vida de luta contra as prepotências do poder colonial em Angola." *Revista internacional de estudos africanos,* nos. 16–17 (1992–94): 49–102.

———. *José da Silva Maia Ferreira: O homem e sua época.* Luanda: União dos Escritores Angolanos, 1990.

Pantoja, Selma. "Aberturas e limites da administração pombalina na África: Os autos de devassa sobre o negro Manoel de Salvador." *Estudos afro-asiáticos,* no. 29 (1996).

———. "A dimensão atlântica das quitandeiras." In *Diálogos oceânicos: Minas Gerais e as novas abordagens para uma história do império ultramarino português,* edited by Júnia Ferreira Furtado, 45–67. Belo Horizonte: UFMG, 2001.

———. "As fontes escritas do século XVII e o estudo da representação do feminino em Luanda." In *Construíndo o passado angolano: As fontes e a sua interpretação; Actas do II Seminário Internacional sobre a História de Angola,* edited by Jill R. Dias and Rosa Cruz e Silva, 583–96. Lisbon: Comissão Nacional para as Comemorações dos Descobrimentos Portugueses, 2000.

———. "Donas de 'arimos': Um negócio feminino no abastecimento de gêneros alimentícios em Luanda (séculos XVIII e XIX)." In *Entre Áfricas e Brasís,* edited by Selma Pantoja and Carlos Alberto Reis de Paula, 45–67. Brasília: Paralelo 15 Editores, 2001.

———. "Gênero e comércio: As traficantes de escravos na região de Angola." *Travessias,* nos. 4–5 (2004): 79–97.

———. *Identidades, memórias e histórias em terras africanas.* Brasília/Luanda: LGE/Nzila, 2006.

———. "Imagens e perspectivas culturais: O trabalho feminino nas feiras e mercados luandenses." In *Condição feminina no império colonial português,* vol. 1, edited by Clara Sarmento, 125–39. Porto: Politema, 2008.

———. "Inquisição, degredo, e mestiçagem em Angola no século XVIII." *Revista lusófona de ciência da religião* 3, nos. 5–6 (2004): 117–36.

———. "Luanda: Relações sociais e de gênero." In *A dimensão atlântica da África: II reunião internacional de história da África,* 75–81. São Paulo: CEA-USP/SDG-Marinha/CAPES, 1997.

———. "O litoral angolano até as vésperas da independência do Brasil." *Textos de história* 11, nos. 1–2 (2003): 187–216.

———. "Parentesco, comércio e gênero na confluência de dois universos culturais." In *Identidades, memórias e histórias em terras africanas,* edited by Selma Pantoja, 79–97. Brasília: LGE; Luanda: Nzila, 2006.

———. "Personagens entre mares atlânticos: Visões de Luanda setecentista." *Revista de história comparada* 7, no. 1 (2013): 136–48.

———. "Três leituras e duas cidades: Luanda e Rio de Janeiro nos setecentos." In *Angola e Brasil nas rotas do Atlântico sul*, edited by Selma Pantoja and José Flávio Sombra Saraiva, 99–126. Rio de Janeiro: Bertrand Brasil, 1999.

———. "Women's Work in the Fairs and Markets of Luanda." In *Women in the Portuguese Colonial Empire: The Theatre of Shadows*, edited by Clara Sarmento, 81–94. Newcastle upon Tyne: Cambridge Scholars, 2008.

Perkin, Joan. *Women and Marriage in Nineteenth-Century England*. Chicago: Lyceum Books, 1989.

Pieroni, Geraldo. *Os excluídos do reino*. Brasília: Universidade de Brasília, 2000.

Pinto, Virgílio Noya. *O ouro brasileiro e o comércio anglo-português: Uma contribuição aos estudos da economia atlântica no século XVIII*. 2nd ed. São Paulo: Companhia Editora Nacional, 1979.

Postma, Johannes Menne. *The Dutch in the Atlantic Slave Trade, 1600–1815*. New York: Cambridge University Press, 1990.

Ramos, Donald. "Marriage and the Family in Colonial Vila Rica." In *Families in the Expansion of Europe, 1500–1800*, edited by Maria Beatriz Nizza da Silva, 39–64. Brookfield, CT: Ashgate, 1998.

Ray, Carina. *Crossing the Color Line: Race, Sex, and the Contested Politics of Colonialism in Ghana*. Athens: Ohio University Press, 2015.

Reis, João José, and Eduardo Silva. *Negociação e conflito: A resistência negra no Brasil escravista*. São Paulo: Companhia das Letras, 2009.

Richardson, David. "The British Empire and the Atlantic Slave Trade, 1660–1807." In *The Eighteenth Century*, vol. 2, edited by P. J. Marshall, 440–64. Oxford: Oxford University Press, 1998.

Robertson, Claire C. "Slavery and Women, the Family, and the Gender Division of Labour." In *More Than Chattel: Black Women and Slavery in the Americas*, edited by David B. Gaspar and Darlene C. Hine, 3–40. Bloomington: Indiana University Press, 1996.

Robertson, Claire C., and Martin Klein. "Women's Importance in African Slave Systems." In *Women and Slavery in Africa*, edited by Claire C. Robertson and Martin Klein, 3–28. Madison: University of Wisconsin Press, 1983.

Rockel, Stephen J. *Carriers of Culture: Labor on the Road in Nineteenth-Century East Africa*. Portsmouth, NH: Heinemann, 2006.

Rodrigues, Eugénia. "Ciponda, a senhora que tudo pisa com os pés: Estratégias de poder das donas dos prazos do Zambeze no século XVIII." *Anais de história de além-mar*, no. 1 (2000): 101–31.

———. "Colonial Society, Women and African Culture in Mozambique." In *From Here to Diversity: Globalization and Intercultural Dialogues*, edited by Clara Sarmento, 253–74. Newcastle upon Tyne: Cambridge Scholars, 2010.

———. "Women, Land, and Power in the Zambezi Valley of the Eighteenth Century." *African Economic History*, no. 43 (2015): 19–56.

Sá, Isabel Cristina dos Guimarães Sanches e, and Maria Eugenia Matos Fernandes. "A mulher e a estruturação do patrimônio familiar." In *Atas do colóquio a mulher na sociedade portuguesa: Visão histórica e perspectivas atuais*, 91–115. Coimbra: Universidade de Coimbra, 1986.

Santos, Catarina Madeira. "Luanda: A Colonial City between Africa and the Atlantic, Seventeenth and Eighteenth Centuries." In *Portuguese Colonial Cities in the Early Modern World*, edited by Liam Matthew Brockey, 249–72. Surrey: Ashgate, 2008.

Santos, José de Almeida. *A alma de uma cidade*. Luanda: Câmara Municipal, 1973.

———. "Perspectivas da agricultura de Angola em meados do século XIX: Pedro Alexandrino da Cunha e o pioneiro do Cazengo." *Anais da Academia Portuguesa de História* 36, no. 2 (1990): 134–54.

———. *Vinte anos decisivos da vida de uma cidade (1845–1864)*. Luanda: Câmara Municipal de Luanda, 1970.

Santos, Marina. *Pioneiros africanos: Caravanas de carregadores na África Centro Ocidental, 1850–1890*. Lisbon: Caminho, 2004.

Santos, Rosenilson da Silva. "Casamento e dote: Costumes entrelaçados na sociedade da Vila Nova do Príncipe (1759–1795)." *Veredas da história* 3, no. 2 (2010): 1–14.

Sarr, Assan. "Women, Land and Power in the Lower Gambia River Region." In *African Women in the Atlantic World, 1600–1880: Property, Vulnerability and Mobility*, edited by Mariana P. Candido and Adam Jones, 38–54. Woodbridge: James Curry, 2019.

Schultz, Kara D. "'The Kingdom of Angola Is Not Very Far from Here': The South Atlantic Slave Trade Port of Buenos Aires, 1518–1640." *Slavery and Abolition* 36, no. 3 (2015): 424–44.

Schwartz, Stuart. "'A Commonwealth within Itself': The Early Brazilian Sugar Industry, 1550–1670." *Revista de Indias* 65, no. 233 (2005): 79–116.

Searing, James F. *West African Slavery and Atlantic Commerce: The Senegal River Valley, 1700–1860*. Cambridge: Cambridge University Press, 1993.

Silva, Daniel B. Domingues da. *The Atlantic Slave Trade from West Central Africa, 1780–1867*. New York: Cambridge University Press, 2017.

———. "The Supply of Slaves from Luanda, 1768–1806: Records of Ancelmo da Fonseca Coutinho." *African Economic History*, no. 38 (2010): 53–76.

———. "The Transatlantic Slave Trade from Angola: A Port-by-Port Estimate of Slaves Embarked, 1701–1867." *International Journal of African Historical Studies* 46, no. 1 (2013): 105–22.

Silva, Maria Beatriz Nizza da. *Cultura e sociedade no Rio de Janeiro, 1808–1821*. São Paulo: Companhia Editora Nacional, 1977.

———. *Donas e plebeias na sociedade colonial*. Lisbon: Estampa, 2002.

———. *História da família no Brasil colonial*. 3rd ed. Rio de Janeiro: Nova Fronteira, 1998.

———. *Sistema de casamento no Brasil colonial*. São Paulo: Editora da Universidade de São Paulo, 1978.

———. *Vida privada e quotidiano no Brasil na época de D. Maria I e D. João VI*. Lisbon: Editorial Estampa, 1999.

Silva, Mario Borges. "Experiências de liberdade: Estratégias de senhores e escravos nos anos finais da escravidão—Jataí, 1871–1888." *Catalão* 13, no. 2 (2013): 328–47.

Soares, Cecília Moreira. "As ganhadeiras: Mulher e resistência negra em Salvador no século XIX." *Afro-Ásia*, no. 17 (1996): 57–72.

Soares, Luís Carlos. *O "povo de cam" na capital do Brasil*. Rio de Janeiro: 7 Letras, 2007.

Sommerdyk, Stacey. "Rivalry on the Loango Coast: A Re-Examination of the Dutch in the Atlantic Slave Trade." In *Trabalho Forçado Africano: O caminho de ida*, edited by Arlindo Manuel Caldeira, 105–18. Porto: CEAUP, 2009.

———. "Trade and the Merchant Community of the Loango Coast in the Eighteenth Century." PhD diss, University of Hull, 2012.

Soumonni, Elisee. "The Compatibility of the Slave and Palm Oil Trades in Dahomey, 1818–1858." In *From Slave Trade to "Legitimate" Commerce: The Commercial Transition in Nineteenth-Century West Africa*, edited by Robin Law, 78–92. Cambridge: Cambridge University Press, 1995.

Sousa, L. Rebelo de. *Moedas de Angola*. Luanda: Banco de Angola, 1969.

Sparks, Randy J. *The Two Princes of Calabar: An Eighteenth-Century Atlantic Odyssey.* Cambridge, MA: Harvard University Press, 2004.

———. *Where the Negroes Are Masters: An African Port in the Era of the Slave Trade.* Cambridge, MA: Harvard University Press, 2014.

Sudarkasa, Niara. "The 'Status of Women' in Indigenous African Societies." In *Women in Africa and the African Diaspora*, edited by Rosalyn Terborg-Penn and Andrea Benton Rushing, 73–87. Washington, DC: Howard University Press, 1987.

Sweet, James. *Domingos Alvares, African Healing, and the Intellectual History of the Atlantic World.* Chapel Hill: University of North Carolina Press, 2011.

———. *Recreating Africa: Culture, Kinship, and Religion in the Portuguese World, 1441–1770.* Chapel Hill: University of North Carolina Press, 2003.

Thornton, John K. *Africa and Africans in the Making of the Atlantic World, 1400–1680.* New York: Cambridge University Press, 1998.

———. "The Demographic Effect of the Slave Trade on Western Africa, 1500–1850." In *African Historical Demography*, vol. 2, edited by C. Fyfe and D. McMaster, 691–720. Edinburgh: Centre of African Studies, 1981.

———. "Elite Women in the Kingdom of Kongo: Historical Perspectives on Women's Political Power." *Journal of African History* 47, no. 3 (2006): 437–60.

———. *The Kingdom of Kongo: Civil War and Transition, 1641–1718.* Madison: University of Wisconsin Press, 1983.

———. "Legitimacy and Political Power: Queen Njinga, 1624–1663." *Journal of African History* 32, no. 1 (1991): 25–40.

———. "The Slave Trade in Eighteenth Century Angola: Effects on Demographic Structures." *Canadian Journal of African Studies* 14, no. 3 (1980): 412–27.

Vansina, Jan. "Ambaca Society and the Slave Trade c. 1760–1845." *Journal of African History* 46, no. 1 (2005): 1–27.

———. "The Foundation of the Kingdom of Kasanje." *Journal of African History* 4, no. 3 (1963): 355–74.

———. "Histoire du manioc en Afrique centrale avant 1850." *Paideuma*, no. 43 (1997): 255–79.

———. "Portuguese vs Kimbundu: Language Use in the Colony of Angola (1575–c.1845)." *Bulletin des séances de l'Académie des Sciences d'Outre-Mer*, no. 47 (2001–3): 267–81.

Venâncio, José Carlos. *A economia de Luanda e hinterland no século XVIII.* Lisbon: Estampa, 1996.

————. "Reflexões em torno da política agrária em África e em Angola." In *Em torno de Angola: Narrativas, identidades e as conexões atlânticas,* edited by Selma Pantoja and Estevam C. Thompson, 49–66. São Paulo: Intermeios, 2014.

Wheeler, Douglas L. "Angolan Women of Means: D. Ana Joaquina dos Santos e Silva, Mid-Nineteenth Century Luso-African Merchant-Capitalist of Luanda." *Santa Bárbara Portuguese Studies,* no. 3 (1996): 284–97.

White, E. Frances. *Sierra Leone's Settler Women Traders: Women on the Afro-European Frontier.* Ann Arbor: University of Michigan Press, 1987.

Winius, George, and B. W. Diffie. *Foundations of the Portuguese Empire, 1415–1825.* Vol. 1. Minneapolis: University of Minnesota Press, 1977.

Wissenbach, Maria Cristina. "As Feitorias de Urzela e o Tráfico de Escravos: Georg Tams, José Ribeiro dos Santos e os Negócios da África Centro-Ocidental na Década de 1840." *Afro-Ásia* 43 (2011): 43–90.

Index

Women in Africa and the Diaspora

Holding the World Together: African Women in Changing Perspective
Edited by NWANDO ACHEBE and CLAIRE ROBERTSON

*Engaging Modernity: Muslim Women and the Politics of Agency
in Postcolonial Niger*
OUSSEINA D. ALIDOU

*Muslim Women in Postcolonial Kenya: Leadership, Representation,
and Social Change*
OUSSEINA D. ALIDOU

*Silenced Resistance: Women, Dictatorships, and Genderwashing
in Western Sahara and Equatorial Guinea*
JOANNA ALLAN

I Am Evelyn Amony: Reclaiming My Life from the Lord's Resistance Army
EVELYN AMONY; edited and with an introduction by ERIN BAINES

*Rising Anthills: African and African American Writing on
Female Genital Excision, 1960–2000*
ELISABETH BEKERS

African Women Writing Resistance: An Anthology of Contemporary Voices
Edited by JENNIFER BROWDY DE HERNANDEZ, PAULINE DONGALA,
OMOTAYO JOLAOSHO, and ANNE SERAFIN

Genocide Lives in Us: Women, Memory, and Silence in Rwanda
JENNIE E. BURNET

Tired of Weeping: Mother Love, Child Death, and Poverty in Guinea-Bissau
JÓNÍNA EINARSDÓTTIR

Embodying Honor: Fertility, Foreignness, and Regeneration in Eastern Sudan
AMAL HASSAN FADLALLA

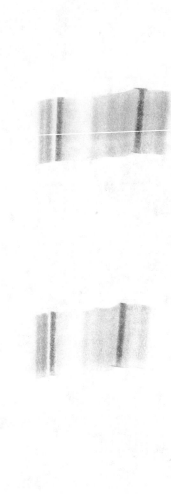

Printed in the USA
CPSIA information can be obtained
at www.ICGtesting.com
CBHW062357240124
3647CB00065B/1390

9 780299 3258